Strategy Dynamics

Strategy Dynamics

The Strategy Faculty,
Henley Management College

edited by Professor Terry Garrison

Henley Management College

This first edition of **Strategy Dynamics** is published 31st July 2001 by the Strategy Faculty at Henley Management College.

Editorial and production services by ELM Publications, Seaton House, Kings Ripton, Huntingdon, PE28 2NJ, (01487 773254, fax 01487 773359), email elm@elm-training.co.uk.

Printed by St Edmundsbury Press, Blenheim Industrial Park, Newmarket Road, Bury St Edmunds, Suffolk, England (01284-701121)

ISBN 1 86181 171 3

British Library Cataloguing-in-Publication Data. A catalogue record for this publication is available from The British Library.

Contents

List of Figures, Tables, Exhibits etc

Preface

Strategy Dynamics is an exciting attempt to achieve a difficult, but worthwhile purpose: to present the informed reader with a kaleidoscope of exciting developmental perspectives in the field of corporate strategy.

Conceived and written by the faculty of one of Europe's leading business schools, this reader in strategy reflects the wide extent of their research and teaching interests and will be found a valuable addition to core textbooks on strategy and its implementation. It is aimed principally at the MBA and DBA student, but will appeal to many practitioners concerned with the changing pattern of strategic thinking.

The book has two focuses. The first is to take familiar concepts and frameworks and re-contextualise them in two contexts: changes in technology and shifts in the pattern of international business. The second is to introduce innovatory thought-forms and insights, explain them and indicate their relevance and importance to strategic analysts and organisation designers.

Whilst the book draws heavily on aspects of strategic theory, it is intended for practitioners. Its aim is to expand the vision of those involved in charting the future strategic directions of organisations, to raise their awareness of new ways of dealing with novel challenges and enrich their understanding. This is done through the abundant use of specific examples and practical illustrations.

The book is divided into four sections, reflecting its twin focuses.

Section 1 consists of three inter-linked chapters which are orientated to the international scene. The first, by Martin Burridge and Terry Garrison, is a structured macro-micro review of the changing global environment, featuring the key drivers for a range of industries and the corresponding critical success factors in them. This introduction is followed by two chapters dealing with international strategy. The first, by Emilio Herbolzheimer, looks at the diverse approaches being pursued by a range of European SMEs in the tense and challenging globalisation context, whilst the second, Janine Stiles, outlines the success criteria involved in creating cross-border joint ventures and business alliances and the manner in which such success is to be achieved.

The three chapters in Section 2 feature core elements of strategic thinking. The values-strategy match chapter, by Scott Lichtenstein, provides a framework for checking on the degree of alignment that exists, or should exist, between them and lays the groundwork for a theme taken up by the subsequent chapter, by Keith MacMillan and Steve Downing, on governance and performance. This examines the way in which the current drive for improved corporate performance is putting the integrity of corporations under stress. A key ingredient in this drive is the extent to which big power-plays in the market-place (mega-mergers etc) are increasingly affecting the way in which business leaders perceive and evaluate risk and vice versa. This is one of the key elements addressed in the chapter, by Terry Garrison, Roger Martin-Fagg and Joseph Tse, entitled Strategy as Gambling.

Section 3 looks at the intriguing subject of the way in which strategic concepts and action orientations themselves are mutating as a result of interplay between theoretical advances and macro changes in the business world. Dominic Swords explores the ways in which contemporary models of strategic thinking – innovation management, for example – have been impacted by modern economic thinking and underlines yet again, if any underlining were needed, the contribution that economic analysis makes to informed decision-making. Jane McKenzie addresses a topic of increasing importance to all managers, and most especially those working in de-layered, knowledge-based organisations in turbulent and uncertain environments: the form, nature and strategic approach of the virtual organisation. This chapter lays bare the scale of the globalisation pressures on firms, the extent to which multiform partnerships will increasingly be forced upon them as a solution to their competitiveness dilemmas and how, increasingly, the virtual organisation will become a dominant format for handling the new complexities.

The final section consists of a discussion on current developments in the world of strategic governance. Issues of corporate performance and reputation are debated in the already-mentioned chapter by Keith MacMillan and Steve Downing, whilst Bernard Taylor and his co-authors reflect on an elaborate Delphi study of the likely future pattern of corporate governance in the UK.

The editorial task of pulling together these four, sometimes diverse, contributions has made the editor and the team of writers only too aware of the wide range of scholarly interests and research orientations of faculty at such a major business school as Henley. Our hope is that, in producing this strategy reader the result is one of kaleidoscope and not cacophony and that MBA students will find *Strategy Dynamics* a powerful adjunct to their studies.

Terry Garrison, Professor of International Business and Faculty Group Leader
Henley Management College
18 June 2001

Chapter 1

THE CHANGING FACE OF INTERNATIONAL BUSINESS: A STRUCTURAL PERSPECTIVE

Martin Burridge and Terry Garrison

Introduction

It is a truism that, since the dawn of civilisation there have been many stages of development through which humankind and its various organisational forms have progressed and that many confusing and complex influences have shaped, and continue to shape, our existence. The study of such contemporary and prospective influences – political, economic, social and technological – is, as we all recognise, a key feature of the strategist's role. This is because the strategist seeks to chart a goal-directed path forward for an organisation in a particular business context at a given time. The more complex and more turbulent the environment faced by the organisation, the more challenging the strategist's task.

For humankind there has never been a more challenging environment than today. The political, economic and technological changes that are being wrought by the combination of what we refer to as globalisation and the New Economy are severely affecting all countries and all business organisations, some positively, some adversely. Some of the mutations taking place in, for example, new technology development in IT or genetics or politico-economic shifts in trade bloc behaviours, amount to such *dislocations* of the past, that it is sometimes difficult to pinpoint the nature of novel cause-effect relationships or to understand the political tensions that are being created by the maelstrom of change. That a new world economic order being shaped at this moment, and that we need to have clearer insights into what this means, is undeniable.

This chapter aims, therefore, to outline and discuss the key structural features of the shifts that that are taking place in the global commercial pattern.

It comprises a macro-environmental overview, of value in itself and as a background to other chapters, which deal more specifically with strategic ramifications.

A Global Economy?

John Dunne's comment that "no man is an island" seems now to be increasingly true of nation states and transnational companies, as well as individuals. Similarities in the food we all eat, the clothes we wear, the IT equipment we use, the cars we drive all bear witness to the fact of the global economy. More and more, we source our requirements, supply our customers and compete globally. It is an essential ingredient of successful management, therefore, that the protagonists in this modern game of industrial and commercial enterprise understand as well as possible the moving context within which their battles for market, technological and financial leadership take place.

Neither the notions behind the management of international trade, nor the concept of competition, have altered unduly: the game is still won by those with the best comparative advantages. All European traders – whether from the Hanseatic League, the Italian city state, the East India Company or today's conglomerates – have played their games of business in an environment of international intrigue and power play. Throughout history, successful entrepreneurs have had to contend with the risk of piracy and the Machiavellian machinations of princes, as well as with the perceived attractiveness of their products and the fragility of their ships. Much remains the same, but much has changed.

The advent of the first industrial revolution, which engulfed Europe during the latter half of the 18th century and subsequently swept across the United States, increasing in pace as it went, transformed the basis of human interaction and the structure of the global economy by creating a Machine Age. When coupled with the fact that western European countries, with a few notable exceptions, were the world's leading colonialists, this revolution bred not only competition among companies for commercial success, but competition among nations for political success. At the time, the theory ran that the trade co-operation between the mother country and the colony was vital to the political integrity of both and constituted *a virtuous circle* of shared prosperity.

It was only after the Second World War that there was a general recognition of the need to curb international trade and industry rivalry in the interests of the greater world good, a recognition accompanied by the gradual de-colonisation and independence of former colonial possessions. Sometimes, this process occurred peacefully, sometimes with considerable tragedy; in some cases, the newly independent country inherited a strong physical and social infrastructure and a capable manufacturing sector; in others, the converse. Thus, the world was divided into the so-called developed, under-developed and developing nations and the previous, century-old trading patterns, between mother country and colonies, were weakened, if not destroyed. The developing countries were those who aspired to a better future and took steps to develop a new industrial base.

Many argue that we are now experiencing the second industrial revolution, the Information Age, and that this will change *everything*. Certainly, the revolution has coupled up breakthrough advances in automated manufacturing, information technology and financial management systems to create a maelstrom of change. It is this that, in its turn, is shaping a new form of one-world competition in which transnational companies, not nations as before, hold the ring. For such corporations to succeed, by making profits and covering their immense R&D costs, they have no choice but to consider trading globally. Crudely speaking, they need to have the opportunity to seek to source in the cheap markets and to sell in the rich.

For this the world's majors need maximum freedom to deploy their resources, a fact which brings an automatic acceptance of *global capitalism* and a strong urge to acquire power of a political, and not just a commercial, form. Once power rested on the pillars of 18th century militarism amongst leading nation states; even up to the end of the 20th century it was possible for states to protect their *crown jewel* industries if they chose to. Now success in the power game is enjoyed by those transnational corporations, some individually more powerful economically than many nation states, which compete best.

Thus, the three fundamental pillars of modern global capitalism appear to be:

- the globalisation of goods and services;
- the ease and speed of round-the-world transfers of capital and technology;
- the prominence of those global corporations or transnational corporations.

To cope with the prospect of a world unsettled, on the one hand, by the rise in the corporate power of the transnationals and, on the other, by the destabilising shifts caused by the so-called New Economy, nation states have tended to band together in trade blocs or other alliances. In so doing, they have attempted to control the forces, like the internet, that simply no longer recognise the boundaries within which nation states have to work. One reason is the loss of political control by states over their own economies. For example, whilst the profit-hungry transnational by definition certainly serves the interests of its customers in any given country, its actions (eg, in *social dumping* or shifting its production out of that country to go to another, cheaper country) may be regarded with hostility by the government of that country. The cases of BMW in Britain in 2000 and Marks & Spencer's in France in 2001 illustrate the challenge faced only too well.

In this way, globalisation, however justifiable to the transnational corporations themselves, is leading to an increasing polarisation, actual or potential, between

- industrialised, industrialising countries and the non-industrial countries, on the basis of a disparity between their relative economic wealth and growth prospects;
- transnationals and the governments whose countries they operate in (host governments) on the basis of possible conflicts of interest. Such difficulties are, in the open global economy, made all the more interesting, of course, by the fact that some governments are now more dependent on major companies than major companies are on governments.

Those nations that are now at the heart of global capitalism can be seen to be increasing their wealth, whilst those outside this wealth-creating circle are effectively "locked out" and are getting relatively poorer. In some cases, they are becoming absolutely poorer, regardless of whether reasons of religion, social and political structure, or predilection locks them out. Leading transnationals, especially those which are technological leaders or major direct investors, are welcomed by all governments, as bringers of jobs and prosperity, but disliked because they cause possible deleterious changes in national culture, the feeling of national autonomy and in economic stability.

But industrialised nation states and their transnational corporations now form the basis of the entire global economy; they are the richest players and use a formula, laissez faire and global capitalism, designed to help them prosper even more. Those economies that have failed to industrialise or are failing to embrace the (some would say dubious) advantages of this formula, face the inexorable consequences of increasing relative poverty and economic apartheid in a divided world. The UN Human Development Report of 1999 stated that:

"Economic globalisation has polarised the world, with the richest fifth of humanity enjoying more than 85 percent of total gross domestic product and the poorest fifth only one percent... Global inequalities in income and living standards

have reached 'grotesque' proportions, and the gap is widening. Thirty years ago, the income ratio of the richest to the poorest countries was 30 to 1. By 1990, the ratio had reached 60 to 1, and now it stands at 74 to 1."

Whilst the old concept of the virtuous circle still holds to some extent in that trade links between the industrialised and the industrialising nation states do remain, the fact is that for people who are *not* playing and winning, the circle can be less than virtuous. To such nations, the economic advantages of globalisation can be negative or zero. Those countries and peoples outside the industrialised and newly industrialising countries benefit neither from the material advantages of increasing economic wealth nor from the social and educational advantages of living in wealth-creating countries. Indeed, the current problem faced by many of the world's poorest countries, that of accumulated debt, proves that the path to industrialisation, the reason for the debt, in the first place, is not easily identifiable, and certainly not quick or easy.

The notion of globalisation is, thus, many-faceted and has by no means a single, universal meaning. Indeed, one of the more populist models, namely that of a world in which all countries enjoy a supply of universal goods and services, is certainly not supported by the facts. The pattern of consumption, or, in economic terms, the product-service market in the developed nations is becoming more standardised, but is certainly not yet identical. And there is a wealth of difference in the consumption pattern of the have and have-not nations.

It is also, relatively speaking, a false concept insofar as the main drivers behind the pattern are concerned. For instance

- the world's leading twelve economies drive the key technologies of biotechnology, electronics, new materials, propulsion and nano-technology;
- world production in major industries like automobiles, electronics, banking and financial services, tourism, shipbuilding, steel, chemicals and pharmaceuticals is controlled by manufacturers based in no more than twenty countries;
- more than 50 percent of world trade is controlled by the United States of America, Japan and the European Union, members of G10.

The evidence suggests strongly that globalisation has not reduced patterns of inequality in some countries that existed in colonial times to the extent that might have been either wished for, or expected. Tariffs and subsidies, kept in place to protect developed countries, are still excluding many developing countries from increasing trade in agriculture and other basic industries in which they have a natural competitive advantage. Indeed, the WTO's 135 member countries have still to agree on free trade in agriculture and other basic industries, a significant omission from the Uruguay Round of trade talks concluded in 1994. Note also that:

- of the world's top 100 transnational corporations less than 50 have more than 50 percent of their assets and employment outside their national economy. Most transnational companies are national corporations are with international operations and
- currently, the richest fifth of the world's population enjoy more than 85 percent of the world's gross domestic product, whilst the poorest fifth have only one percent.

The paradox emerging from these arguments is that globalisation is a global phenomenon, in that it is helping to build a single world market, but that it is not providing equal economic development chances to all. Indeed, as we shall see, it is positively influencing the patterns of production and exchange between a minority of the world's largest and most prosperous economies and benefiting their transnationals. But what it is doing to the rest of the world's economy is open to question.

Shifts in the Global Economy

During the past three decades the dominance of the developed market economies has increased, just as the economic power of the transnational corporations has continued to expand. But there have been many positional changes among these older industrialised countries, particularly in relation to their shares of world manufacturing production and output. In 1963 the United States produced just over 40 percent of the world's manufacturing output, but this had fallen to 24 percent in 1987 and to little over 20 percent in 1998. Japan, a country with half the population of the United States had a gross domestic product in the late 1950s of approximately half that of the United States and only produced five and a half percent of the world's manufacturing output. By 1999, its share of the world's manufacturing output had increased to more than 20 percent, with a GDP of nearly half that of the United States.

During the same period, the European economies performed unevenly, with Britain in particular having a somewhat jaded economic record, until the mid-1990's. In the aftermath of the Second World War, in the early 1960s, the United Kingdom's economy was approximately twice the size of the-then West German economy and three times the size of the French economy, whilst its share of world manufacturing output was approximately six and a half percent. By 1999 the United Kingdom's GDP was only half that of the Republic of Germany, and similar to that of France and Italy. Over the same period, Britain's share of world manufacturing output had fallen to approximately one seventh that of Japan, one third that of the Unified Republic of Germany, and was approximately equal to that of Italy and half that of France.

These apparently stark positional changes between such individual nation states, representing the more mature industrial economies, are not reflected if one takes a more regional view of the global economy. As it has since 1900, the world still revolves around an apparently increasingly concentrated "triad" of economic power, which is based upon the well established elements of the European Union, the North American Free Trade Area and the East and South East Asian trading area. The European Union is responsible for over 40 percent of all world exports; the North American Free Trade Area accounts for some 18 percent; and the East and South East Asia area handles approximately 23 percent.

The share of the non-industrialised nations is falling and, as the increase in merchandise trade stimulates the expansion of all the trade-related services, the non-industrialising countries are locked out of areas of growth; goods and services. Thus we appear to be not so much on the brink of a truly global economy, but a global economy that is highly selective as to who is "in" and who is "out". Only a relatively small number of countries that in the 1960s were regarded as developing countries have experienced substantial economic growth, whilst many of the others have simply fallen by the wayside or, as is the case in many countries in Africa, have sunk into a morass of debt.

Hence, many of the major global shifts in the world's economy over the last 100 years have been concentrated in the old areas of prosperity. The old winners are the new winners. Whilst the relative success of China and India, in particular, seems to on a rising trend, possibly because of the sheer scale effect that both countries exert in South East Asia as well as China's trade linkage with the United States, they are rare amongst the poorer countries. Certainly, they have experienced substantial economic growth and disproportionate injections of foreign capital, whilst other countries are suffering from the *triple whammy* of a growing population, dependence on primary products and a lack of industrialisation.

The compound effect of these three challenges seems to constitute an almost terminal threat for many nation states, as they become more and more locked into a declining cycle of economic inactivity, at the same time as they observe the rising growth of others more favourably endowed. This is typified by falling external incomes resulting from falling world commodity prices, rising birth rates due to low levels of economic growth (or zero) and, therefore, a lack of investment. All leads not to a virtuous circle so much as a cycle of poverty. Countries in this situation are themselves examples of how economic growth can be exceptionally selective and how a lack of industrialisation locks these countries out of the benefits of economic growth.

The three economic areas described below, the trade triad of the NAFTA, EU and Asia pacific, have all benefited from the massive growth in world trade since 1950. This has outstripped world rate of growth of GDP by some three times over the last 50 years and has benefited the industrialised nations, leaving the primary producers and the non-industrialised nations floundering.

The Trade Triad

➢ *The North American Free Trade Area*

The formation of the North American Free Trade Area in 1994 changed the economic map of the North American Continent and created a free trade area of three countries. Furthermore, the GDP per head of Mexico is much smaller than that of the United States of America and Canada, a much larger difference than between any countries in the European Union. The aims of NAFTA were very clearly stated and included the pivotal goal of reducing trade and investment barriers over a decade or so and, therefore, to ensure the free movements of goods and capital between the three countries.

The North American Free Trade Area is perhaps the clearest example of the notion of a group of countries that have entered into an agreement to trade on an equal basis. NAFTA has so far restricted its pursuit of co-operation to the objective of establishing free trade between the three member countries, Canada, the United States of America and Mexico. The formation of such areas is rooted, as we will see, in the classical theoretical model of comparative advantage and the gains to be had from the specialisation. The proceeds from this activity can be exchanged for the products or services of other trading partners in which they are at a relative disadvantage.

The three parties to the agreement had different objectives in entering the NAFTA collaboration. The United States Government saw the consolidation of the free trade area in terms of its long-term commitment to economic and political stability in the region. In addition, it gave American domestic companies access to the relatively cheaper labour of the Mexican economy and the prospect of larger markets. The overall size of NAFTA is comparable to the current GDP and population of the European Union. The Mexican Government were convinced that membership of NAFTA and a close economic relationship with the largest and most advanced single economy in the world would provide them with access to technology, investment, jobs and a consolidation of their economic and social reforms. In Canada, an economy with many similarities of institutions and business attitudes, the Government considered that it was the preferred way to achieve consolidation of the Canada United States Free Trade Agreement.

Political arguments in both America and Canada carried a more brash and divisive tone than those used in Mexico, with politicians such as Ross Perrot arguing that the agreement would mean exporting American jobs and importing unemployment. The agreement has certainly achieved the United States of America's government objectives and promoted liberalisation and economic growth in Mexico. The advantages to Canada are probably less clear, but for the region as a whole it is a fundamental stage in the further development of economic co-operation throughout the Americas, North and South, as the steps towards the creation of the Free Trade Area of the Americas shows.

➢ *The European Union*

As the "European" concept evolved from the post-war Coal and Steel Treaty to the European Union, "The European Union" has become a force in the lives of 273 million people. Europe has expanded to include the European mainland, countries east of Dresden, west of Amsterdam and north of Tallinn. However, the intellectual, economic, legal and political concept has less clear boundaries, with many "ifs" surrounding the concept of precisely what a United Europe will mean in any of those contexts.

Unlike the NAFTA, the origins of the European ideal has a more complex and longer history. Although it evolved from the European Free Trade Area, it has its core in the determination to avoid further conflict on the European mainland; essentially it was born out of two world wars. The First World War engulfed Europe and her peoples, the Second World War embroiled the world in a holocaust and nuclear devastation. It was total, border-less and of such savagery as to demand the end of conflicts within Europe.

Potent ideas have the ability to crystallise changes occurring in the world that gave them birth. Born out of conflict, the European Community is striving to create an identity and purpose relevant to a world of global competition in ideas, politics, goods, services and technology. The evolution of the global economy, the collapse of Eastern European communism and the developing transition of capitalism are the new matrix from which to forge Europe.

The European Union is by far the most advanced and complex attempt to form a collaboration of countries into an economic and political union. Even in its infancy, it always had a wider and more ambitious agenda than simply the free movement of goods and services. Potentially, the European Union is as vital to the future of the European Continent, and possibly the world, as is NAFTA to the future of the North and South American Continents, as a foundation for peace and security. Economically for future prosperity, as the transition of capitalism continues within a global economy against evolving ASEAN models of capitalism. Structurally, to the economic stability of a world of free movement of capital, rapid transfer of technology and the increasing power of regional trade blocs. If all countries are small countries now, a United Europe may be a key to peaceful economic, social, moral and intellectual development of human kind.

As with NAFTA, the European Union is also in transition, its order is certainly not settled and the potential outcomes are shifting rapidly. There are at least three major issues driving the new visions of European Union:

- Firstly, the global market for capital and the power of companies driving for global market position have highlighted the fundamental differences between the European corporate attitudes and free market forces. European companies are no longer able to isolate themselves from the global free market of which Europe is so determined to be a major part.
- Secondly, the Nice constitutional conference on further European expansion had to grapple with the fact that Europe now has a total of 12 aspirant members who are in varying stages of negotiation (preliminary/advanced/detailed) to join the existing 15 members of whom 13 are euro-nations.
- Thirdly, the reality of the global economy and the apparent supremacy of the United States economic models of free market economics and democratic politics seem to be obliging mature economies to follow common economic policy paradigms like balanced budget thinking, New Economy stimulation and popular capitalism. The EU members are no exception.

The first factor is going to have a fundamental influence on the ownership and management of the major corporations of the Union over the next two decades. The aggressive take-over of Mannesmann by Vodaphone in 2000 is almost certainly not the last in what could be a series of consolidations within major industries including automobiles, chemicals, banking and others. Europe's mergers and acquisitions have risen from less than 200 in 1993 to over 1250 in 1999, with the number of hostile acquisitions rising from zero to over ten percent in the same period. The disposal of Rover by the beleaguered BMW automobile company is likely to be simply the first act in a longer running saga, as the direct influence of global (as defined by the advanced industrial countries) corporate economics provides the dominant forces in defining corporate actions.

The second factor is going to take rather longer to exert its impact and the outcome is less certain. The mass resignations of the Commission in 1999 left the EU Council of Ministers in a weakened position, searching for the confidence and vigour it displayed in the 1980's. This has meant that the EU is now grappling with the greatest potential expansion of its existence, when the Commission has to overcome both the legacy of such a massive crisis of confidence as well as the launch of the euro in January 2002. The issues emanating from enlargement of the EU that have yet to be resolved include:

- how much expansion and which countries when?
- which voting arrangements are appropriate in the Council of Ministers and how quickly will qualified majority voting be used for all decisions?
- should flexibility continue to be applied to matters such as defence and monetary union. If so, to what extent?

In spite of the problems generated by the events of 1999, the European Commission is still dominated by its original vision of a Europe united through economics against conflict. The collapse of the Berlin Wall and the subsequent disarray in the former Eastern Bloc countries has, in one sense, re-ignited this flame. At the meeting of the European Council of Ministers in December 1997 in Luxembourg, the heads of state described their achievement glowingly as "the dawn of a new era finally putting an end to the divisions of the past" and "as a pledge of future stability and prosperity" to the European continent.

The dream of European inclusion and integration thus still burns brightly and remains a dominant force within the intellectual core of the political thought of the minds that shape the future actions of the Commission. The problem is not that the European Union has not made dramatic and beneficial progress in achieving its original, primarily political ideals. The key issue is the extent to which those ideals can be translated and implemented within the developing political and economic paradigms of the 21st century. Indeed, more specifically, can the EU members pursue their goal of social justice, as laid down by the social market economy approach espoused in continental Europe, in the context of the demonstrably increasing power of the modern capitalist model, rooted in the US' economic performance in the 1990s?

➢ *The Asia-Pacific Region*

Whilst two of the three major trade blocs in the world economy are driven by the concepts of free trade and the political commitment to pursuing those ideals within the context of regional integration, this is not so of the third. There are no comprehensive arrangements in the Pacific Rim, or East and Southeast Asia except the AFTA agreement, founded as ASEAN by six southeast Asian countries in 1967. Within the past three or four decades there have been many attempts to establish more formal trading agreements between the nations of what was, until 1997, the fastest growing group of economies in the world.

Since 1993 the ASEAN group has held annual summits to set the future direction of the region. What is now the Asian Pacific Economic Co-operation Forum was established at a conference in 1989, chaired by President Clinton, at the instigation of the Australian Government. There are currently 18 member states of the APEC forum and, if one considers that the 15 current members of the EU are a diverse group, then the members of APEC are exceptionally so. They range from China to Taiwan, Japan to New Zealand and include Australia and Indonesia and the three economies of NAFTA. This makes for an eclectic and highly differentiated combination of dynamic economies, that includes the two largest economies and the fastest growing group.

The differences that are evident within the nation states of the EU, where policy matters such as the ERM, unemployment and subsidies to agriculture and other industries have generated heated debate, are indeed small when compared to the diverse agenda of the nations with ASEAN. The reality of the actual level of co-operation between the states within ASEAN is that it is, at least at the beginning of the new century, very limited. Not surprisingly in view of their extreme diversity of size, stage of industrial development, level of exports and integration with the world economy, the members of ASEAN have very different individual agendas.

In brief and selective summary they are as follows:

- **To resist the notion of US hegemony whilst seeking maximum US market access**

The United States of America is determined to signal both its desire influence and be involved in a close economic relationship with this region. President Clinton called the first APEC conference in 1989 and signalled his nation's commitment to the region and its determination not to allow either China or Japan to dominate the region. A central and indeed vital element of the foreign policy of the United States is to straddle the divide between the two major economic regions of the world. Ideally, the United States sees that the expansion of free trade between the regions (with certain provisos of course), is to the long term advantage of the most powerful economic and technological nation in the world. Asia Pacific is resistant to the notion of the United States' tutelage, although it needs the technology, capital and above all consumer demand that the United States has to offer.

- **To deal with the slowness of the Japanese recovery**

Japan, the second largest economy in the world, and a major growth engine for the whole of the Asia pacific region, has suffered a suite of economic setbacks in the last years of last century. Their level of economic growth has declined and, even after the short-term recovery from the dramatic downturn of 1997, economic growth, even by 2001 was still negative. Indeed, at the dawn of the new millennium Japan was still in economic recession and the new (2001) prime minister Junichiro Koizumi was faced with the horrific task of arranging the write-off of $109 billion of unperforming public-private debt. However, aware of the critical importance of its economic and strategic relations with the United States, Japan is highly sensitive to the trade aim of the United States, its major trading partner; Japan runs a massive balance of payments surplus with the United States and Uncle Sam wants this reduced. Furthermore, it is crucial to Japan's economic recovery in the short term and its economic aspirations in the long term that America remains non-protectionist. The most effective way of achieving that goal is to ensure that American politicians of either party can convince the electorate of the need for an open trade agenda.

- **To cope with some facets of anti-westernism**

Malaysia is somewhat unusual in this group in that, early in the APEC conference round, it announced that it did not see any advantage in continuing its membership, that had hardly begun. Furthermore, Malaysia's political elite see many dangers in the "westernisation" of the region and are convinced that it is vital to preserve the Asian cultures. It is important to emphasise that Malaysia has long been unconvinced of the benign influence of the Western nations in the region and the dramatic events of 1997 were placed clearly at the altar of western capitalism in the guise of George Soros. There is remarkable similarity of attitudes between the Malay States and the United Kingdom towards economic union, if for different reasons and at different times.

Australia and New Zealand are probably reluctant and certainly somewhat belated entrants to this region's realpolitik scene. The collapse of the British Empire, and the subsequent re-adjustment of the European region leading to the loss of trade from the United Kingdom, made it imperative that

Australia and New Zealand re-aligned themselves and their economies. The consequences were that two stalwart members of the British Empire re-examined their trade and economic relationships and became part of the Asian region. The fact that Australia initiated the concept of the ASEAN conference is perhaps the most convincing example of the country's commitment to the region and acceptance of its economic future.

China's motivation is dominated by the country's concern to be a major player in the region and not to allow the United States or Japan to dominate the region's economy. The recent rounds of talks between China and the WTO have given a sharper perspective to the their aims and major concerns in the negotiations of admittance to the World Trade Organisation. In principle China is committed to membership of the WTO, but it is the Government's concerns over the massive structural changes to the Chinese economy that will be an inevitable consequence of WTO membership, that have proved to be the impediments to entry. Many of the American demands for liberalisation were resolved in the bilateral talks of 1999, although there was a certain amount of brinkmanship, and both the EU and the United States back China's application for WTO membership. For its part, China seeks to remove the quota sanctions on silk from the US and Europe's quotas on footwear, toys and kitchenware. The United States is still rather more concerned with the liberalisation of China's financial and agricultural sectors and with other issues such as the legal aspects of intellectual capital. It is also concerned with its massive balance of payments deficit with its thrusting partner.

China has accepted that joining the WTO will be economically painful in the short run and the country's leaders are determined to limit the early costs. Their primary concerns are the impact of liberalisation on the banking and financial systems; more than 90 percent of the banks' resources are controlled by the State. However, these are not the only problems that China will face as their State enterprises still employ more than 50 percent of all urban workers and are, in general, inefficient. Nevertheless, the Chinese Government is convinced that, if the country is to continue to benefit from continued foreign direct investment, membership of the WTO is vital.

Key Change Drivers in the International Business Environment

Since the early 1980s, seven fundamental elements have impacted severely both on the context of international business and the manner in which the international economic system works. During the course of the early post-war era, many economists took the view that there was a "virtuous circle of growth" inexorably linking all countries, which would lead to the benefits of economic growth filtering down into even the poorer nation states. It was widely held that the international economic system would bring better economic conditions to all who participated, no matter at what level. However, it was Peter Drucker who wrote (1) about how the links or connections between different levels of economic activity were being broken and how such dis-connections could lead, first, to fundamental changes and then to the massive disparities we see in the wealth and income of different nations.

These fractured links or fundamental changes are as follows:

- **The linkage between the primary producers and the major industrial nations**

This linkage is now extremely tenuous. Commodity prices have been falling in real terms, including, until OPEC took action to curtail supply in 1999, oil. The development of new materials and the increasing productivity of agriculture, to say nothing of the future impact of GM modified food and animals, has reduced the industrialised world's demand for many of the traditional primary products which are marketed and sold by the less developed countries. Because of their lack of foreign earnings, many of the primary producers have been unable to industrialise or improve their agricultural technology. This has excluded them from the benefits of a falling birth rate, usually a consequence of economic growth, the rising population leading to increasingly grinding poverty. However, perhaps more importantly, it has also meant that they have singularly failed to improve their social, economic and, most importantly, educational infrastructure which are the foundations of the modern economy. Whatever the value individual countries place on the nature of modern industrial and commercial society, loving it or loathing it, the fact is that nations locked into merely extractive and/or agrarian activity are tending to isolate themselves from the modern world and its related potential economic benefits.

- **The moving wall of money**

Since the 1970s, the massive impact of the oil crisis upon modern industrial society and, in particular, the huge inflows of capital that resulted from the rises in oil prices, the world's financial system has been living with a "wall of money". There seem to be four major sources of this wall of money, in addition, that is, to the huge inflows of cash from the OPEC countries into the Western banking system, which occurred throughout the 1970s. Firstly, with increasing world trade, companies have been forced to maintain reserves of cash in order to fund the large foreign exchange requirements of their increasing cross-border trade. Secondly, the large financial institutions and investment companies have maintained a high degree of liquidity in order to benefit from the fluctuations in currency movements. Thirdly, following many failed investments in South America and the Pacific Rim in the 1980's and 1990's, many of the large investment institutions have retained cash reserves, as they become more risk averse. Lastly, the savings rate of the developed world is at a very high level as a result of the changing demographic pattern of its population. All other things being equal, the older a rich nation's age profile, the more there is a tendency to save (and invest) rather than spend (and consume). Recognisably, the western world is becoming older and richer.

These factors have all contributed to the large-scale volatility of previously relatively stable currencies and to the increasingly large "wall of money" that now moves around the world following changes in interest rates and resulting in currency fluctuations. When Sterling "fell out" of the ERM in 1992, the inability of the states within the European Union to stem the tide was palpably obvious. The estimated total size of this wall of money is approximately 25 times the value of world trade in goods and services. By contrast, the total value of foreign exchange reserves of the four largest states in the European Union would probably amount to no more than $600 billion dollars.

The wall of money phenomenon has emphasised the impact of changes in interest rates on currency values and transformed many a country's use of interest rates to control its domestic inflation from a tricky operation into a delicate tightrope-walking act. The situation has tended to force governments, particularly those in the Group of Ten, to follow economic policy paths based upon the objectives of stable interest rates, inflation rates and sustainable economic growth. Given that the US $ is the single currency for the North American Free Trade area and that the euro will become the single European currency, policies of this nature are perhaps the most probable avenue to lead to a stabilisation (but not, note, a standardisation) of currency rates.

Such stability is essential to increasing trade and is, moreover, to the advantage of nation states and transnational corporations. Governments have responded to the fact that international market forces have become more powerful in their influence on currency movements than their central banks by, in effect, unifying the power of groups of central banks within trade blocs. In this context "all countries are small countries now". The events of that period seem to bear out the fears of Richard Ley, an economist from the OECD, who pointed out "the potential political backlash of a development where international market forces become more powerful whilst central banks and governments become powerless" (*The European*, 22nd October 1993). According to the empirical evidence, that has not happened but governments have been forced into following extraordinarily similar economic policies. The concerns have led inexorably to a narrowing of the economic policy options open to governments.

"Freedom and the mobility of capital are, on the one hand, the requirements for an optimum allocation of the factors of production because free financial flows, at least in theory, migrate to the 'best host'. However, monetary and economic policy-makers are increasingly concerned about the resulting exchange rate movements, particularly if they think that overshooting of fundamentally unjustified fluctuations is involved." (The European, 22nd October 1993)

- **Trade bloc formation**

As we have seen in the previous section, during the course of the last 30 years, for a number of disparate reasons, various groups of countries have attempted to integrate their economies with respect, particularly, to their trade relations with each other. Differences between the approaches of the European Union, the North American Free Trade area and those of the smaller trade blocs of Africa, the Middle East and South America and the Asia Pacific Economic Conference, are marked and the levels of trade integration vary considerably. The main thrust of all of these trade blocs is, however, an attempt to increase trade between the member states by reducing or eliminating tariffs on goods transferred between them. This has, of course, also led to the drive by the transnational corporations to locate production facilities *within* the individual trade blocs in order to avoid the tariff barriers which exist now more between the trade blocs themselves than between the individual states making up any particular bloc.

- **The increasing integration of the world's business infrastructure**

Another consequence of the relative volatility of exchange rates over the past 15 years and the desire of governments to reduce that volatility and subsequent convergence of economic policies within the G10, has been the increasing integration of the world's banking, financial and technological systems. The Asian crisis of the latter half of the 1990s put their banking and financial systems under question. The somewhat dubious financial activities (involving very high gearing of companies and huge external borrowings on behalf of governments) of large corporations and banks, led to the collapse of many of those currencies. This was a considerable spur to the further integration of the world's financial and banking systems. This integration looks set to continue and will perhaps be yet another force for the divergence between the rich and poor nations of the world.

- **The link between productivity and employment in the major industrial countries of the world**

This link is becoming increasingly tenuous and poses a dilemma for many governments. However, it is important to point out that in almost all of the major industrial countries there is a greater proportion of the population of working age in paid employment than probably at any time since 1900. Furthermore, the demand for qualified and skilled labour, particularly in times of economic growth, still generates concern amongst central bankers when demand generates rising wage levels. Nevertheless, the levels of unemployment within the European Union in particular are higher than they have been for many decades and currently show little sign of reduction. The link between economic growth and unemployment is now less secure as the rising productivity levels generated by new technological processes of production has meant that the additional number of people required to generate an increase in productivity is falling in almost all industries.

Indeed, it seems that this is creating a new "underclass", of people who are effectively reduced to having but a tenuous hold on full citizenship in modern economic society. This may raise questions of the status related to one's occupation or, alternatively, ability to wield economic demand effectively. The welfare state may well have banished (or at least cut down to size) the giants of Want, Disease and Squalor. But if it is going to isolate large groups of people from the very activity which is at the heart of industrial democracy, one questions whether that industrial democracy can sustain itself. The demands of international business are such that the levels of skill and education required to sustain a position within economic activity are increasing and are likely to continue to increase.

- **The structural over-capacity of many industries**

The level of over-capacity of producers in agriculture, automobiles, steel, pharmaceuticals, computing and many other industries is well recorded and currently increasing as transnational corporations build productive capacity within the trade blocs. For example, within NAFTA and the EU the automobile sector has over capacity of some 20 to 25 percent. Transnational corporations are now trading across borders and their influence is increasing so countries can be said to trade with the transnational corporations, rather than with each other. Many of these TNCs are dominant forces in the world economy and of the 100 largest economic units of the world, half are nation states and the other half are transnational corporations.

- **Trans-border oligopolisation**

The final influence that is now re-shaping the international business environment can be described as the emergence of dominant competitors in globally-consolidating industries. Firstly, as producers in many major industries amalgamate, the resultant consolidated industries are characterised by the dominance of a few major corporations worldwide, not just nationally or within individual trading blocs. Examples of such corporations are General Motors, Microsoft, Ford, General Electric, IBM, Siemens and, of course, major international banking corporations like HSBC and Deutsche Bank.

The globalisation of the products produced by these corporations and the increasing competition framed by over-capacity may well continue the drive for further consolidation as profit margins are reduced through over-capacity and a lack of demand. TNCs will clearly seek to exploit to the maximum locational opportunity presented in terms of the size of markets offered by the new trade blocs. The rapid change of new products and the increasing cost of bringing new products to markets require corporations to sell their products in increasing volumes. Their presence in each of the trade blocs therefore becomes a matter of necessity, not necessarily expansion. In addition, locational opportunity has encouraged the development of "clusters" of activity around specific industries, as locations become a magnet for organisations and firms wishing to establish themselves in such industries. These clusters, as described by Michael Porter (2), appear to counter some of the arguments that organisations need to locate themselves in each of the main trading blocs, as these clusters tend to provide levels of innovation, productivity and competitiveness that overcome even the barriers to trade between trading blocs.

Another highly relevant factor is the importance of human intellect and skill, especially in knowledge management industries. This is increasingly creating an international business environment in which companies have to pay more than just lip service to their employees. The phrase "our employees are our greatest asset" that appears with such monotonous regularity in company annual reports, has to be believed and acted upon, not just stated. Even more so, perhaps, the sheer transferability of modern productive processes and technologies (as well as capital) is increasing through the integration of technological and scientific communities as the educational infrastructure of countries becomes closer, with students and teachers moving across borders, particularly within the university world. Perhaps more importantly, attempts by the major trading blocs to increase the transferability of qualifications, whilst still in its infancy, will further accelerate this process. There are several examples of how the skills of individual nations and the infrastructure they developed at an early stage of their economic and industrial development, have been transferred. For example, the area around Bangalore in India is now the world's largest exporter of computer software as well as being the primary location for the processing of much computer-based data.

As corporations struggle for profitability, market share, global reach and growth, they have typically been driven to compete in all of the trade blocs, particularly NAFTA and the EU. However, perhaps more importantly, they are now also being driven to compete in the bigger emerging markets of China, India, the South American states and nations of the Pacific Rim. The level of market growth in Europe and North America is significantly lower than the huge potential of markets in these areas. It is self-evident that all the factors identified above apply to these emerging markets as well as to the more mature markets of the G10. However, there are additional implications for the corporations driven to compete in these emerging markets that will require them to respond to the demands of those markets rather more than they have so far and, as their market empires change, so will they.

Trade freedom dilemmas

The lure of the gains to be had from larger markets and the necessity for multi-national and global corporations to expand their operations to take full advantage of the lure, has generated the countervailing move for countries to "club together", as we have demonstrated. The formation of groups of countries into associations to encourage and legislate for the free movement of goods and services *between* their member nation states has been one of the most important transformations of the world's economy in the past 100 years. It certainly does raise the questions about, firstly, the relative growth of intra-bloc trade as against that of inter-bloc trade, within the GATT and WTO frameworks, and, secondly, whether the rise of the Triad of trade groups/blocs has stifled or encouraged world-wide free trade.

The existence of the Triad of the three trade blocs at the top of the world's economic league table is not, in principle, a necessary obstacle to the development of free trade under the WTO. In one scenario, the Triad could contribute to the level of free trade by controlling themselves and by spreading an open and multilateral system. However, the drive towards regional economic integration, as the movement towards trade blocs is often referred, has been accompanied by a strengthening of the member economies against those outside the systems.

We are, therefore, concerned with the extent to which the principle and practice of free trade have absolute value or suffer from a variety of frictions or limitation. It is a significant matter as the fundamental principle behind the WTO, the political and economic supremacy of the concept of unrestricted trade over any other form of commerce, has long been rooted in classical economic theory.

The desirability of free trading between nations is, of course, anchored in the theory of comparative advantage. This argues that the incomparable economic gains are to be had from specialisation, ie, from one nation state or group of states focussing on only those goods and services that they can produce and export more efficiently than their trading partners and, of course, vice versa. Thus, the trading game and comparative advantage makes the economic activity a non-zero sum game; it is a trade from which everyone can gain advantage.

The sweep of classical economic theory runs from Ricardo's theory of comparative advantage (1817), which capitalised on Adam Smith's earlier work on absolute advantage, to the Heckscher-Ohlin theory of inter-regional and international trade (1993). The first emphasises the primary importance of a *general* competitive edge, the second stresses the vital importance of *a particular* competitive edge, specifically in one or more of the nation's factor endowments, capital, labour etc. Each argues that the benefits that arise to a nation from using its total economic resources in the best possible way (ie, specialisation) and from importing from foreigners that which they cannot produce, satisfactorily outweigh the gains from operating in any other way.

The arguments for trade are obviously more complex than this, but all of the arguments for less-than-free trade accept that the sum of the incomes of the countries involved will be less than if free trade persisted. That is why countries trade. The reasons why they use tariffs and other barriers to free trade are more complex.

The difficulties of the simple comparative advantage case begin when countries include the social cost of allowing declining or stressed industries (such as the industry producing good Y in country B) or firms to die. Even the management of technology change in industry and firm involves social cost. Wherever industry is concentrated, such as in the mining communities in Silesia or the Ruhr, problems are exacerbated. Handling the social costs of change, whether positive (engineering a new beginning) or negative (managing the end-game of an industry), always throws up an entire gamut of political, social and economic issues which governments find very difficult to ignore. Governments, therefore, can and do interfere in such cases, often with the best of intentions, because they have no choice.

However, in an increasingly international trading world involving an increasingly interdependent global community, there are very few examples of individual national governments' being able to support an industry and guarantee its survival whatever their strategic intent. Industries which governments have supported domestically in the past, but which have eventually moved to other more competitive countries, include coal, steel, shipbuilding, automobiles, cotton and wool. Controlling the worldwide movement of capital and industrial ownership is extremely difficult for any nation, if not actually counter-productive.

The difficulties are stark and, placed in such a change management context, often the one thing a government will seek to buy with its support is time for the transition to take place with a minimum of social costs. This is at least part of the reasoning behind support systems such as the Common Agricultural Policy or the European Community's coal and steel policies. In the long run, the terms of trade are difficult to oppose. The trends in the global market place are now stronger than any single economy can overcome individually.

An example of this intervention is the attempt to reduce the social impact of economic change, as industries in one country become economically less efficient relative to the same industry in another country. The EU's Common Agricultural Policy or CAP, is one example of an economic price support system designed to avoid the direct impact of free trade; some supporters would argue that it has an absolute benefit in that it stabilises farm incomes within the EU, whatever the world trade position. It is undeniable that dramatic, and often culturally and socially damaging, impacts could result from free trade, if less efficient farmers are driven off the land because their farms cannot produce agricultural products at the prevailing international (or national) price.

Even the Americans are not averse to government intervention and especially where they see (or claim to see) evidence of uneven playing fields of lack of trade reciprocity. Throughout the 1990s – and specifically in 2001 under President G.W.Bush – the Americans have in their trade negotiations sought to:

- resist any imposition by outsiders of common international technical standards (eg, mobile phone systems);
- attacking the entrenched favouritism in public procurement systems, especially in Europe;
- denounce high technology production subsidies, particularly in European projects such as the Airbus and the Eurofighter.

This has involved them in a variety of high-profile moves to attack trade partners deemed to have taken *unfair* advantage of the US' liberality. For instance, they have energetically tried to:

- chisel away at entry restrictions in markets perceived to be closed to US goods (South Korea and Japan);

- impose trade restrictions, anti-dumping and Super 301, on any trade partner seen as not playing by the rules of the game (eg, over bananas, antibiotic/hormone-fed beef and steel);
- ensure that the US authorities' posture on any cross-border M&A moves by transnationals, which were deemed by the US authorities to be anti-competitive in their effects, was prominently publicised.

The Congress of the United States has repeatedly made itself sensitive to the special pleading of US sectoral interest groups such as steel, semi-conductors, textiles and clothing, to name but a few. In addition, the application of the old GATT (still in the WTO statute book) "escape clause" which can be applied to those domestic producers suffering "serious injury" as a result of trade concessions and unforeseen events is still, as Super 301 shows, an ever-present danger.

Naturally enough, the EU and Asia pacific have sought to counter the US moves by all the power at their disposal, wherever the moves were perceived to damage their interests. The Japanese and the EU have, in particular, been reluctant to open up their markets to US food. The EU, for its part, has not hesitated in condemning anti-freetrade moves by the US whilst trying to maintain its EU-first approach to public procurement.

The fact is, therefore, that "free trade" is currently becoming an increasingly important world commerce phenomenon, but has not yet reached the status of a dominant paradigm. You trade freely, when it is to your advantage to do so; you trade fairly, if you think you might lose; you keep out foreigner's products, if you can, if you think you are going to lose. All this is common sense but made more difficult by the successive GATT round agreements on increasing the scale of global free trade. No wonder there was a backlash by representatives of the world's poor, by US and EU trade unions and by those opposed to global capitalism when the new round of free trade negotiations was launched in Seattle. The ensuing disturbances or riots (depending on your viewpoint) indicated that some opponents regard globalisation simply as Americanisation. They are opposed to new free trade rules because they will be surely be *prescribed by the winners.*

Without question, the stronger economic players are still able to call the economic and *philosophical* shots to a degree. Whether or not trade blocs are actually increasing the tendency or the reality of unfair as against free trade is, however, still a matter of debate. But the probability is that increasing the amount of intra-bloc trade is preferable for all the nations involved, whatever the inter-bloc situation. Unfortunately, the increase in both trade patterns does appear to be exacerbating the problems of those nations locked outside the development of industrialisation and outside the trade blocs. Trade blocs, such as the EU and NAFTA must create a climate of greater trust and freedom and of *inclusiveness*, economically, industrially and technologically, if the goals of the WTO are to be achieved and if the *Seattle syndrome* is to be properly addressed. It is for this reason that discussion of a new economic paradigm is of value.

The New Economic Paradigm?

The "new economic paradigm" that appears to be dominating the ideas of many observers, whether proponents of free trade or Seattle-influenced opponents, is the concept that *a group of economies are, in fact, beyond the fluctuations of the business cycle.* In other words, they will not be exposed in the future to economic swings in which growth is followed by recession or, to what we know more popularly as "boom-bust economics". The notion is, of course, far from value-neutral since it carries a connotation that such a world will possibly be divided into economic winners, near-winners and potential losers.

The concept asserts that the business cycles of the 1960's, 1970's and 1980's lie well and truly in the past and that, in future, growth rates for the economies in question may fluctuate but that growth will be stable and not followed by any recession. Certainly, this has been a major feature of the Western economies in recent years but, more particularly, the US economy is now in the longest sustained growth period in that nation's history. By contrast, economies of the Pacific Rim have certainly not reached this pinnacle of economic nirvana as they suffered from a particularly reversal of fortunes in 1987 and, whilst some countries have begun their recovery, Japan, as we have already noted, remains in recession.

Opinion is divided on the issue of the new economic paradigm as there are strong rationales for believing that the world has, indeed, moved on to a new plane of economic systems stability. But there are equally powerful reasons for thinking that we still live in a world of dislocations where the Old Adam paradigm holds sway.

There are many factors which serve to explain the new paradigm. The nature of the new economic policy systems in place in developed economies and the technological revolution we are living through are critical to the debate. We have selected four factors to illustrate the phenomenon.

- **Economic Management**

The first factor is the assertion that some governments are now more adept than ever before at controlling their economies in a manner that establishes stable and sustainable growth. A key feature in this is the consequences of their *de-politicisation* of the control of monetary policy. This is achieved through the transfer of responsibility for setting interest rates from government to central bank, with the aim of achieving greater economic stability by reducing direct political interference.

There appear to be a number of reasons to accept, *prima facie*, that the increasing responsibility of central banks for monetary policy has, in fact, encouraged governments to place less emphasis on fiscal policy as a stabilising policy instrument. In the past, application of that particular policy instrument often created instability rather than removing it. Currency fluctuations of the early 1990's, when Sterling fell out of the ERM and subsequently lost 19 percent of its exchange rate value in 24 hours, gave a stark lesson to many governments of the impact of the "moving wall of money" on exchange rates and trade. There is empirical evidence to suggest that, since then, many governments have become more conservative in their management of government fiscal policy, sustaining a balanced current account and pursuing remarkably similar economic objectives.

There is one other element that is important in the context of economic management: the reality that a common economic environment now exists in many westernised economies within which governments' are constrained in their options for monetary and fiscal management. Throughout the G10 and, more especially, G7, the economic objectives of governments appear to have a common basis and similar parameters. The common themes of economic policy objectives are:

- sustainable economic growth ie, growth with a low and stable rate of inflation;

- interest rates that are controlled by central banks that are not too high so as to attract increased currency speculation and yet low enough to encourage inward investment;

- a balance of payments that is stable and in balance with major trading partners;

- a public sector borrowing requirement of three percent of GDP or less. Many governments including the United Kingdom have been attempting to run a budgetary surplus, partly with the aim of reducing governmental debt.

These objectives represent the *common ground of economic policy* in the more advanced economies and have served as a key driver in the considerable stability that has been evident in closing years of the millennium. However, the arguments for a long-term or even permanent level of economic stability, zero or even low inflationary growth, or non-cyclical growth are somewhat premature. The fact that economic conditions are different from any period since the mid-19th century is not a necessary, and certainly not a sufficient, condition to prove that we are in a new economic paradigm.

- **The Value of Weightless Assets**

The second factor is the increasing importance of the knowledge-based economy and the impact of "weightless assets", ie, *clicks* as against *bricks*. The main concept behind this is that the main engine of economic growth has changed and that it is now knowledge, often in the form described as "intangible" and "infinitely expansible", which is in the driving seat. It can be highly definable, specific knowledge, such as a financial derivative trade, a genetic code, a music or movie recording, or a piece of software, or it can be less definable, even amorphous – an idea or a concept, for example. The range is so broad that it can even be said to include so-called designer-label goods such as a Fila handbag, a Chanel suit or a pair of designer shoes. The fact is that they all produce numerous opportunities for the increase of growth.

The vitally important aspect of the consumer goods mentioned is that the brand under which they are marketed is distinctly recognisable as a specific part of the perceived value the consumer derives from possession. It is, in fact, the added-value element that takes value beyond the mere functionality of the product and represents an intangible worth in its own right. Similarly, whilst the products themselves (eg, shoes, handbags) may be kept in limited supply, the brand under which they are marketed (eg, Nike) may be available to apply to other products. So far as the Virgin brand is concerned, one sometimes wonders, on the basis of past experience, whether it is limitless.

The fact is that part of this new economic paradigm and the underlying economics is that the marginal cost of expansion for such brands is virtually zero, and those who make it first to market with them may secure the advantages of global status. In addition, media, marketing and advertising are not only crucial to economic growth but are themselves an essential part of the growth of the weightless value that consumers will pay a premium price for.

- **Instant Information**

The third pillar of the new economic paradigm is the availability of information and the ability to store, transform and transport it with an efficiency that is un-paralleled in human history. This has enabled organisations in the public and private sector to control their inventories, to monitor their financial and production processes to minimise the unpleasant surprise and to maximise management control. This should contribute to decreasing the volatility of the production cycle by ensuring a better match between inventory, demand and supply. In addition, the rapid introduction of just-in-time techniques (of which real time information is an essential element) has ensured that companies have reduced the ratio between stocks and demand. In addition, the impact of Japanese production techniques has undoubtedly made the older manufacturing industries more efficient and effective on both sides of the Atlantic. This has led to a better fit between demand and supply in the short run and also a reduction of inflationary pressure as prices as products are comparable in terms of value wherever they are made. The cumulative impact of such changes necessarily dampens oscillations in the performance of mature economies.

- **Advancing Technology**

Not all of the new ideas and concepts that are fuelling the current economic growth of the richest nations on earth are "weightless". Tangible advances in production technology have long been recognised as a factor in economic growth by economists from Shumpeter to Kuznets. (3)

The probability is that the advances that have been achieved in all ranges of technology, especially automation and data-handling, will continue to increase the rate of sustainable growth and even bring about *unsustainable* growth. Sustainable in this context, means ensuring growth without stoking up inflationary pressures in the economy. There are anxieties, for example, about the enormous sums paid by operators for mobile telephony licences in Britain in early 2000.

The Old Adam Paradigm

Proponents of this paradigm argue that, although the breakthrough factors we have considered are real enough, they are not sufficiently powerful as to constitute a shift in the world's economic tectonic plate. Certainly, whether the world economy will become more economically stable remains to be seen, as there are a number of disruptive forces which need to be considered.

- **The Power of Trade Blocs**

It is arguable that it is far too soon to tell whether or not there is a new economic paradigm that will remove the threat of cyclical economic development from the richest nations in the world. Whatever our views as to developed nations are, it is certainly true that nations outside the NAFTA and EU areas are still subject to cyclical economic patterns.

The rise of trade blocs has reduced the power of individual nation states and, in one sense, lowered the height of the walls that nations may want to put round the enterprises and regions within their borders. But it has compensated for this by increasing the political and economic clout of the blocs to which they belong and, therefore, made up for the loss of individual power by the gain of collective power.

For example, the French and German governments are now making moves in the WTO context to seek to corral speculative market forces on a global scale. The US, for its part, is indulging in trading behaviours (over bananas and hormone-fed beef) designed to maximise its self-interest. Both are examples of crude, world-trade power plays in which France and Germany are backed by the EU and America by NAFTA. Safety in numbers is clearly important and nationalistic self-protection lies at the heart of this policy thrust, just as it does in, in fact, in the creation of trade blocs. So, even if the nation state is less important, we are still in a highly competitive world.

- **The Growing Span Of Global Companies And Organisations**

Large multinational corporations have increased their power and presence and their ability to traverse national borders. They increasingly locate themselves where they can gain the maximum economic advantage, regardless of the impact upon the stability of specific national economies. They are driven by the pursuit of global influence, survival and international competition which, as the definition of "foreign" companies become harder to identify, maintains the pressure.

There is increasing openness of markets allowing major companies to locate their production and other assets in the most advantageous locations. The gaps in labour costs, particularly in manufacturing, which continue to exist in the industrialised world, are a major incentive for companies to move assets from one location to another, or between countries. The hourly rates for manufacturing workers in 1998 was $18.24 an hour in the US compared with $27.89 in Germany. Similarly, taxation differences will also be another reason for companies to relocate. This trend will lead to country policies' converging rather than diverging as nations compete for the advantages of jobs and production assets. Governments will also learn that inward investment is not permanent investment, as has been proved by the sale of Rover.

- **The Growing Importance of Speedy Technological Transfer**

The increasingly rapid transfer and importance of technology to the economic development of the world are highly salient as potential de-stabilisers. As the world becomes smaller and the transmission of information, ideas and techniques more and more difficult to protect, the transfer of technology is easier. Not only can companies such as Nissan transfer technology from country to country, but they are able to establish low cost, high productivity centres of manufacture wherever they can acquire a competitive advantage. It is difficult to under-estimate the importance of technology in modern industrial and commercial activity. In manufacturing processes modern production technology provides the opportunity to increase productivity and quality, in the financial and commercial sector the electronic transmission of information and funds has transformed the manner in which banking and service industries operate.

It is not so much the impact on economic cycles that is at issue here as the extent to which constraint-free, country-to-country technology transfer is analogous to the moving "wall of money" phenomenon examined earlier.

- **Geo-political Uncertainties**

The situation in Eastern Europe is one that currently causes considerable geo-political concern amongst the NATO allies and the United Nations. The area is a potential time bomb for the rest of Europe as the CIS states and the rest of the former Russian empire attempt to cross the divide between centralised control of the economy and the market economy. The stakes for the West are high, both in terms of short term security and the eruption of violence in the medium or longer term. Since 1987, the Western economies, including European countries although predominantly the United States, have invested relatively minor amounts (more than $1.5 billion), not including the costs of attempting to contain the violence in Bosnia.

If these economies continue to provide a background of unrest and prevailing violence, the continued reluctance of the western nations to invest in the area will continue. This is likely to result in increasing tensions and probable further military involvement of the Western nations. The potential for disaster for the population is enormous as the strong central controls operated by the former USSR are swept away and the individual nation states struggle for survival. *A fortiori*, we should consider the extent to which Russia specialises in commodity exports like natural gas, on which the EU has a high dependence, and is hoping to hoist its armament sales. A possible Sino-Russian pact would exacerbate matters considerably.

The Middle East is another potential flash-point region. It is a constant source of concern to the Western industrial nations, for primarily economic reasons, as the region is the epicentre of the oil reserves that feed the industrial economies with energy. Political stability in this region is a crucial factor in the future economic growth of all nations and central to the balanced working of westernised economies.

During the past three years the price of Saudi Arabian light crude has climbed above the 1996 high of $22 per barrel, and in mid-2001 stood at $29 having reached over $30 in mid-2000. However, in real terms this price is still below the 1974-89 average, although nearly 150 points above the 1998 low. The fact that OPEC have managed to raise the price of light crude from $9 per barrel to above $30 a barrel is a function of the unusually tight discipline that the cartel has exercised in the past year. This has been possible due to the fact that demand for oil is strong as the world's major industrial economies continue to experience vigorous economic growth. The other crucial factor relates to the power that OPEC wields in relation to the marginal supply of oil to the market. Whilst OPEC now supplies less than 50 percent of the world's total demand, the cartel is still the most flexible supplier and is able to increase or decrease supply faster than any other producers. It is for this reason that it is likely that oil prices will continue to be buoyant and conducive to economic destabilisation.

- **Environmental & Demographic factors**

International concerns over environmental pollution and demographic worries over global population size and make-up in the future are crucial. These concerns are not all inter-related but they do have one thing in common apart from people; the long terms implications for the organisation of societies and the future of their national economies. Of particular significance was the refusal of US President Bush in 2001 to adopt the Kyoto protocol on climate change.

In the developing or less developed nations, often referred to as the Southern nations, the problems caused by population growth and the drive for economic growth are serious ones. The problem is not only that of global warming, involving aspects of growth-driven environmental degradation such as deforestation. This is currently occurring in the world's forests at the rate of some 20 million hectares a year, largely due to the rich northern nations' demand for hardwoods and the poorer southern nations' demand for cultivable land. The drive for growth in the poorer nations is creating environmental pollution, but they are reluctant to acknowledge any cries from the rich northern states to suppress their economic growth in the face of the poverty of their populations.

In the developed nations of the world the rising life expectancy of both males and females, coupled with-the falling birth rates associated with wealthy societies, is creating a rising social security burden that is increasing the level of expenditure on health and social security. It is estimated that by 2010 18 percent of Japan's population will be over 65 years, as against only eleven percent in 1990 and, because of falling birth rates, will be supported by a smaller working population. Therefore, the level of expenditure on social security payments including pensions is estimated to rise from 16 percent in 1994 to over 26 percent in 2010.

Similar patterns are emerging in the European nations with the population pension crunch hitting Europe between 2020 and 2040. At that time the costs of current social security payments will rise at varying rates throughout Europe with those countries, such as Britain and Holland who have large private sector pension funds, being better off. These influences will affect countries such as Spain, France and Italy particularly badly as they tend to fund pensions from the money earned by those in work. A study by the French government predicted that, if pension contributions were not increased to take account of the smaller numbers of workers, contributions would rise from the current 19 percent of payroll to 42 percent of payroll; a potentially devastating blow to the competitiveness of French industry.

The population issue is therefore unlikely to be a problem that only affects the future of the less developed countries. It will certainly alter the relative competitiveness of the industrial nations in the next century. The rich world-poor world divide is a clear force for destabilisation, as the Seattle demonstrations in 1999 showed, and it can only get worse in a world that is digitally-divided.

Conclusion

The balance of arguments we have exposed indicates that it is far too soon to tell whether or not there is a new economic paradigm that will remove the threat of cyclical economic development from the richest nations in the world. However, as this chapter makes plain, the debate is both highly significant and fraught.

There is an undeniably an increasing integration of all countries' economic futures as we become more and more bound to each other through free trade. The rise of trade blocs has certainly reduced the power of individual nation states but, paradoxically, increased their clout *within* their bloc, which now serves in some ways to protect them *against* other, *against* the footloose transnationals and *against* the power of speculative international capital. There is an overwhelming belief in the efficacy of free trade as a developmental mechanism for increasing world prosperity and yet, as the Seattle experience showed, those who see themselves as potential losers are not afraid to make their voices heard. Whatever else, world trade rules are framed by the potential winners.

So, the underlying trends in the global economy are diverse and sometimes confusing. But there is no doubt that technology is forcing us to march – or stagger, as the case may be – along the business trackway into a new Information Age. There can be little doubt that the world of economic policy-making is changing irrevocably.

References

(1) Drucker, Peter, *The Changed World Economy.* Foreign Affairs, 1985, Vol. 64, pp.768-91

(2) Porter, Michael, *The Competitive Advantage of Nations*, Macmillan: London, 1990

(3) Rosenberg, N. *Inside the Black Box: technology & economics,* Cambridge: Cambridge University Press, 1995

Chapter 2

SMEs IN A GLOBAL ENVIRONMENT: MANAGEMENT PERSPECTIVES

Emilio Herbolzheimer

Introduction

The globalisation of the world economy is intensifying. Rates of growth of international trade and foreign investment in the late 1990s, much higher than those of world GDP over the previous two decades, testify to this. Of course, many factors have contributed to this evolution, but the affirmation of US style capitalism, as the *dominant* world-wide economic model after the collapse of communism, has been particularly significant. This has induced a progressive liberalisation of capital markets, deregulation of services, privatisation of state enterprises and transfer of technology. It has also led to an increase of industrial concentration spurred by mergers, acquisitions and alliances.

It is a popular and convincing contention that such concentration is increasingly to the advantage of the large diversified firms with enough resources to straddle world markets and to *dance in a world of giants.* The role of Small and Medium-Sized Enterprises (SMEs) in this future setting is certainly often perceived as being more uncertain than ever before. The aim of this chapter, therefore, is to shed some light on the role of these SME players in the global market from a strategic and managerial perspective. It is also to question preconceptions and to illustrate some of the major challenges SMEs face, if they are to sustain their competitive advantage in future.

The chapter begins with an overview of the literature on the distinctive management practices commonly attributed to SMEs. This sets the groundwork for a further review and analysis of the strategies and practices pursued by SMEs in the process of internationalisation in different business areas. The chapter finally addresses the issue of the lessons to be learned by the newcomers in the international arena and the prospects for the future.

But first we must define what we understand by a small and medium-sized enterprise. Definitions can often be problematic, and certainly are in this case. There is, in fact, no clear, precise and widely-accepted definition. Most commentators use the size of the business as its distinguishing feature, presumably because that it is easier to measure. However, even this is not precise as it varies from sector to sector. For instance, in relation to other businesses in the same sector, a 50-person industrial design firm or travel agency would be large, whilst a 1000-person car manufacturer or telecommunications firm would be small. Similarly, the concept of average size varies from country to country. Thus, in many developing private firms, an employment level above 100 people would be considered large, whereas in the US or Germany, the threshold in the manufacturing sector would be at 500.

In the UK the Department of Trade and Industry (DTI) uses the following definitions:

Micro firm	0 – 9 employees
Small firm	0 – 49 employees (includes micro)
Medium firm	50 – 249 employees
Large firm	Over 250 employees

The number of employees is obviously only one measure, so it needs to be combined with financial data for a more suitable definition. This is the approach adopted by the European Commission, which decided in 1996 to adopt a single definition for its 15 member states in order to overcome the difficulties arising in managing the EC programmes:

Maximum	Medium-sized	Small	Micro-firm
Number of employees	250	50	10
Turnover (million ECU)	40	7	
Balance sheet total (million ECU)	27	5	

The above classification helps us to place the SME in context but it should be noted that, for the purpose of studying strategic policies and management practices, only a small proportion of SMEs is relevant. This is because most SMEs engage in activities centred on providing services or products to a local market with little differentiation or influence on conditions. These are not potential international players. In the UK, for example, 73 percent of all SMEs are micro-firms of one or two people, and, of the rest, the majority are in farming, non-professional services – such as retailing, transport, maintenance and pubs – and in construction. (1)

Management Practices and Features of SMEs

Despite the many differences between types of, and stages of development in, the "smaller" firms, much of the literature points to a number of common managerial aspects. Generally, successful SMEs are associated with clear focus and strong values like independence, flexibility; entrepreneurship and innovation. They have characteristics of closeness to the customer and supplier, working with networks or contractors, personal, rather than system control and taking a longer-term rather than a shorter-term view of the business.

However, we also find in many SMEs informal structures; insufficiently developed administrative and accounting procedures; severe resource shortages; unsystematic, sometimes erratic, decision making processes, compounded by the known problems of family-run businesses, such as nepotism. There is also much evidence of an unwillingness to delegate responsibility to more experienced managers.

The key distinctive management features of SMEs may be grouped as follows:

➢ *The motivations and ambitions of the owner*

Often, outsiders see small businesses as operating at sub-optimal levels of performance. The actual root of failure may be reckoned to lie with the apparently non-rational behaviour and decision-making style of the entrepreneur and/or owner manager who may not obey the "rules" of management theory. Such a criticism can reveal a lack of understanding of the business ambitions of small firm managers.

Life-style	A life-style business is the description often given to a business run by an individual because it not only facilitates, but is also part of, the life-style that individual wants to have. Examples of life-style businesses are frequently to be found in art or craft businesses where the owner lives to practise that craft rather than only practising that craft in order to live.
Comfort zone	A comfort zone business is typically one that provides its owner with sufficient returns for the level of comfort he or she wants in life. Unlike in the case of the life-style business, the basis of the business is less important than the level of benefit it can provide in return from a reasonable amount of effort.
Growth	The "growth" business is the one that approaches closest to what to many is the ideal business, namely one where the owners wish to manage the business to maximise its earning potential, especially for the future.

Table 1: Categorising SME ownership

The values embodied in the business will be those of the owner and are tied up with his/her needs, desires and abilities, a fact which has very distinct strategic implications. The image of a professional manager trying to maximise the business value-added does not always apply. In this context, Bridge *et al.*(2) have grouped the owner into the three categories shown in Table 1, page 37. Hence, the ambition to grow or expand into new foreign markets will be basically determined by the motivational factors and personal aspirations of the owner or manager.

➢ *The entrepreneurial and innovative spirit*

The entrepreneurial spirit and innovative skills of the successful smallish firms are often acclaimed in the management literature. It is apparent that, to compensate for its scarce financial and other physical assets, the smaller firm has to rely on its ability to create and sustain its competitiveness through innovation.

Yet, this perception has not always been shared. In the 1960s and early 1970s a widespread view was that it is the large firms – having the resources and organisational structures to undertake research and development – that were the drivers of innovation. Small firms were considered to be unable to undertake any meaningful research and were basically copiers of, or agents working for, larger firms who told them what to do.

From the mid-1970s to the late 1980s, however, as the oil crisis turned the mood from optimism to a zero growth scenario and as Silicon Valley-type high-tech firms began to demonstrate their enviable innovative abilities, the *small is beautiful* syndrome took shape. The view was that it was the smaller firms that were best placed to take advantage of the possibilities emerging from the technological revolution and the opening-up of international markets. The big firms had become too complacent and sluggish and had much to learn from the small firm which was flexible, closer to the market and highly motivated.

By the late eighties, the complementarity between big and small began to be recognised. The fundamental or basic research requiring ever-increasing budgets was undertaken mainly through government-funded programmes often in public institutions, or by large firms such as Intel, Glaxo-Wellcome or GEC-Alsthom. Most of this occurred under partnership arrangements, in particular strategic alliances and consortia led by large firms. The smaller firms, in turn, were better placed to respond to the market opportunities resulting from the new technological advances and from globalisation by developing the new products and systems. Yet, despite successful achievements in the earlier stages of the innovation process, it was often the case than many SMEs lacked the business acumen and/or the resources to commercialise a project.

Hence, from an innovation perspective SMEs played two roles. One as suppliers of know-how to the larger firms or technology partners in international markets; the other as highly innovative niche players operating in segments that did not bring them into direct competition with the large firm.

A summary of the advantages of small firms as compared to large firms, based on the research of Rothwell and Zegfeld can be found in Table 2, page 40. (3)

➢ *Simple organisational structures and systems*

Since efforts are concentrated not on predicting and controlling the environment but on adapting as quickly as possible to the changing demands of that environment, SMEs tend to have simple organisational structures. Control is exercised by direct supervision that often leads to speedy decision making and shorter reaction times.

Most small business owner-managers have acquired their business knowledge on the job. They will often have been in the job a long time and will, therefore, have a deep experience, but not necessarily a broad one or an objective informed view. The business systems employed, thus, are likely to be of their own devising, based on their experience, and are unlikely to be changed unless experience also suggests it is necessary.

Relationships are often informal, with no precise definition of rights and obligations, duties and responsibilities. Appointments and promotions are often made on the basis of personal contacts rather than on the basis of ability, education and/or technical qualifications.

Thus, the essence of the firm's competitiveness is seldom readily and directly visible. It often has a *tacit* form, with strategic management being practised instinctively. As companies grow they obviously develop more structured organisations and control mechanisms. But, so long as they do not reach a large size demanding highly complex structures, they are likely to remain highly focused.

According to a McKinsey study of medium-sized firms in Germany, for example, successful companies eschew functional or matrix structures in favour of organisations arranged around product groups or business units. Each business unit, in turn, is treated as a profit centre, or where there is no genuine external market, as a cost centre. (4) The organisation's structure and management behaviour will, at any rate, be strongly influenced by the personality of the management team and, particularly, the founder.

Advantages	*Disadvantages*
Long term orientation	Less access to capital markets may curtail growth
Greater independence of action - less (or no) pressure from stock market - less (or no) take-over risk	Confusing organisation - messy structure - no clear division of tasks
Family culture as a source of pride - stability - strong identification/commitment/motivation - continuity in leadership	Nepotism - tolerance of inept family members as managers - inequitable reward systems - greater difficulties in attracting professional management
Greater resilience in hard times - willing to plough back profits	*Spoiled kid* syndrome
Less bureaucratic and impersonal - greater flexibility - quicker decision making	Internecine strife and financial strain - family disputes overflow into business
Knowing the business - early training for family members	Paternalistic/autocratic rule - resistance to change - secrecy - attraction of dependent personalities
	Succession dramas

Table 2: Advantages and Disadvantages of Family Controlled Firms

Source: Adapted from Kets de Vries, p.61

➢ *The eternal problem of resources*

It is almost invariably the case that smallish businesses lack financial resources. Most of them had no access to capital when they started, venture capital being limited, and entrepreneurs had thus to rely on their own or family savings and, usually, to mortgage their homes. Few have the financial reserves to carry them through a lean period and cash flow problems and the need for capital can lead to crisis and possible liquidation for some. Herein lies the problem of capital financing systems like those of the US or UK, which can push the SME into a dangerous dilemma:

"In order to grow they have to resort to capital markets to obtain funding, but the demands of the markets put pressures on companies to increase their profitability and dividend payments, thus discouraging reinvestment for growth. This, in turn, can also make them more vulnerable in the sense that information about their business operations is widely known, and thus run a higher risk of a take-over". (5)

➢ *The family control factor*

But it not just finances which may cause difficulties. SMEs are usually also short of management, both of management time and of management skills. A few people may embrace all aspects of managing the business. This may provide both focus and responsiveness, but it also means that the amount of time that can be spent on a particular problem is very limited and that aspects of management expertise are also likely to be missing. Knowledge of the specialised functions may not be evenly developed and, in some areas, may be severely lacking. (6)

Family businesses come in all sizes and forms.[1] In fact the great majority of firms are family-owned. In most countries publicly-quoted firms are rare and enterprises are either state-owned, not-for-profit, or family-owned. Even in the US, UK and the Netherlands, where stock exchanges are most developed, many of the leading firms are family controlled – such as Mars, Marks and Spencer, C & A or Bechtel and Cargill (US). Still, it is among SMEs where this form of ownership is most prevalent and, therefore, where one can observe in a more dominant form the impact of this form of ownership on management.

Family control can have major managerial advantages, but also disadvantages for a firm. These are summarised in Table 2, page 40, which is taken from a book by Kets de Vries, one of the foremost researchers in this field. Among the various *advantages*, the most important are the possibility of operating with a long-term perspective and the dominance of the family spirit. The values inculcated thereby result in a strong sense of identification and commitment amongst employees and continually reinforce the expertise gained by the family members who have grown up in the business from an early age.

---

[1] Family business does not mean a separate form of legal structure, but instead it refers to any business owned primarily by members of a family in which a family body exercises considerable managerial influence and control of a business. This can happen where, for instance, more than half the voting shares in a business are owned by one family, where a significant proportion of the senior management of the business are drawn from the same family, or where one family group is otherwise in effective control of the business.

This can produce a dependable culture and atmosphere that encourages long-lasting relationships with customers, suppliers and other contacts. Staff are also likely to have a "sense of belonging" and strong commitment to the goals of the organisation. When the owning family are justly proud of the venture, their enthusiasm and commitment can enthuse non-family staff.

This sense of togetherness is a powerful asset in that it focuses the energies of all involved on customers and on the need to serve them. The commitment which results can produce flexibility in terms of working practices, working hours and remuneration. Furthermore, decision making in family firms is centralised, because important decisions are generally the preserve of family members. Centralisation produces quick decisions, and this can be a considerable advantage when reacting to market opportunities in a changing world.

Finally, family firms are normally free from stock market pressure to produce quick results, because they are not quoted on the market and have no institutional shareholders. They can, are a result, often take a longer-term view. They are not forced to vacillate, and can pursue a consistent long-term strategy. This long view is reinforced by the permanent nature of their management teams. Permanent managers allow behavioural norms to emerge and a recognised way of doing things to develop.

Yet, some of the advantages are counterbalanced by some major disadvantages.

Firstly, the pre-eminence of the controlling family, centralised decision making and long-standing management teams can result in static thinking. It can make it less likely that new ideas, which are essential for long-term development, will emerge. They are known for being reluctant to use outside advisers or consultants, preferring the counsel of the family when exploring business matters.

Secondly, managerial difficulties can arise when the family relationships and goals are in conflict with business practice. Incompetent family members may be retained in post as a favour to shore up deteriorating family relationships, and promotion for otherwise eligible non-family managers may be blocked as a result. Business logic and rationale may thus take a back seat in favour of family preference. Even if professional managers are recruited in an attempt to improve the business, such managers may find that they can never achieve the measure of recognition and control that their expertise and contribution merit.

Then, there is the critical issue of succession and the conflict that often emerges between family members, in particular fathers and their children. The father often recognises that he has to let go of the reins and develop his successor, but *his* business is such an important feature of his life that he fears that the "loss" of it will damage his self-image and bring his competence into question. Such behaviour can be resented, and tension can build as a result.

Managing the succession can often be a difficulty in family businesses, especially the transition from one chief executive to another.[2] There is evidence that this is rarely planned in family firms, and that the transition is, as a result, frequently traumatic.

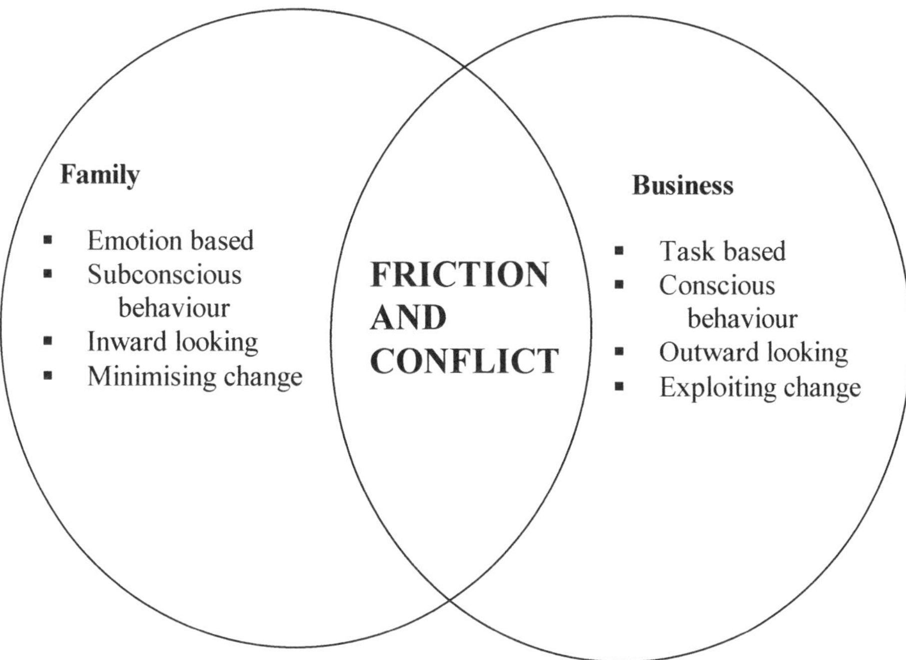

Figure 1: Overlapping systems

[2] Continuity in the family is a common drive. As reflected in a recent UK family business survey, *"Nearly 60 percent of owners said it was their intention to pass the business to the next generation. The older generation may regard bringing in outside shareholders as unpalatable. Venture capital, for example, is seen as a last resort rather than a good business decision at a time when a company is flourishing"*. Selling also proves to be a difficult decision. The "selling enigma" is *"that when you look at why family companies sell or do not sell, the reasons for selling are usually business reasons, whilst the reasons for not selling are emotive."* (7)

Everywhere, studies consistently reveal how few family businesses survive through to the third generation. In a very large survey in the US in the late 1980's, for instance, it was shown that only 30 percent of family businesses reached the second generation, about 20 percent the second generation, and only 13 percent survived the third generation. (8)

The SME in International Markets

While the management traits discussed above may constitute a good basis for competing in domestic markets, the question is how SMEs have fared when they have to compete in international markets. Are SMEs able to operate abroad on the basis of hitherto domestic competitive advantages? Or is it the case that some of the deficiencies and limitations in terms of resources and management styles we have outlined simply become accentuated when operating in different foreign settings?

There is limited understanding of the role of SMEs in international markets. Research has tended to concentrate on the multinationals. This was justified by the fact that, relative to their dominant role in the production of domestic goods and services, they have traditionally been less involved in international trade and investment than the larger firms.

Much of the initial literature on this subject, in fact, seemed to emphasize the difficulties SMEs have in surmounting the barriers of internationalisation. The following quotation of a study on the export performance of Dutch firms in the early 1980's summarises the prevailing view:

"SMEs don't perform well. Too often export is an incidental matter to these firms ...in most cases they do not make well considered plans for export activities. One an hardly speak of marketing policy. Explanations given, are mostly to be considered as rationalisation afterwards. For many enterprises export is a way to get rid of surpluses which cannot be sold on the domestiuc market, or to raise output by increasing sales of already existing products.

Only few SMEs act in terms of specific needs of foreign customers. Those firms.Hardly pay attention to the commercial policy and are satisfied with a limited group of customers, whm they conacted by accident. Very often the first export is trigerred off by a request from abroad. The enterpreneur adopts an attitude of waiting. This picture arises from Dutch, German as well as American surveys". (9)

Most of the problems were attributed to the deficient skill base of SME managers. Jenster and Jarillo stated it in these terms:

"The deficiencies become particularly crucial at the commercial and financial side. The management often has a technical background and only limited

formal commercial training. Because of this skills shortage, these firms tend to downplay the financial controls, whilst spending much efforts on chasing new sales and handling crises. As the internationalisation process evolve, the lack of controls further highlight the underlying systemic problems. With little understanding of working capital requirements and cash flow management, the foreign ventures become larger leading to poor profitability". (10)

While these statements reflect the attitudes and problems encountered in many SMEs, they tend to ignore that a wide range of them have gradually become major international players and have come to represent an increasing share of their national economies' exports and foreign investment. They play a key role in the international value chain. A number of recent studies have shown light into their activities and management practices.

Three main groups can be distinguished from the literature, the *high tech*, the *business services* firms and the industrial *mid-size globalists*. The reasons which have induced them to enter foreign markets are very diverse, a combination of push and pull factors as described in international business strategy theory. (11)

Pull factors, that is, those factors that entice companies away from their domestic markets towards a targeted overseas market may include:

- opportunities to access new, attractive and rapidly-expanding markets;
- an awareness of the possibilities of gaining efficiency by moving some operations abroad or simply seeking economies of scale for their highly specialised offering;
- a chance to exploit superior technology or business know-how;
- a desire to spread the firm's operations over different countries to defend against competitors.

Conversely, *push factors* arise from areas of difficulty in the domestic markets and where a targeted overseas market may offer a solution. Such factors may include:

- the need to follow customers who demand international service from the suppliers;
- a recognition of incipient market saturation in the existing domestic market;
- the fact of increasing costs of domestic supply or production bringing a deterioration in the levels of profitability within the domestic market.

Push factors also include *internal* factors, an element of significance for all small firms. It is clear that the nature of the education and experience of SME managers, especially those who suffer from a relatively limited background and/or under-exposure to foreign business cultures, will tend to affect the likelihood of their adopting an international orientation. Indeed, a new vision in a family-owned business may be the result of a generation change, with the younger manager better trained and motivated to venture into foreign markets. Conversely, the change agent may be a new business partner, especially a financial institution, who *imposes* a new direction.

It is usually where the external meets the internal that strategy is determined, and it is this point that a strategy of internationalisation is decided upon.

Most internationalisation processes are essentially incremental. Firms begin with agents and distributors and gradually progress to channels requiring greater investment, such as overseas manufacturing plants, as the importance of their exports increases. The tendency is to start with geographically or culturally (psychologically) close markets, and progress outward, perhaps at the same time increasing the number of markets. (12)

The above push and pull factors and internationalisation processes seem to apply to all three groups of international SMEs, albeit in different degrees, depending on the nature of the activities as discussed below.

- **The High Tech Firm**

Among SMEs, high tech or R&D intensive firms are renowned to be the most internationally-oriented, many from the outset of their activities. Such firms know their markets and monitor usually closely developments internationally as their businesses operate in a very dynamic world. Managers are likely to be scientists who have grouped together either as a spin off from a large firm or from the university, and are thus less bound by family relations and local conditions.

	Number	**%**
Threat from multinational firms	16	20
Domestic market saturated	20	24
Insufficient domestic market volume to support competitive R&D	42	51
Inquiry from foreign potential buyer	23	28
Rapid technology development	17	21
Internationalisation of computers	11	13
Global market opportunities	53	65
Lack of domestic know-how and resources	3	4

Table 3: Factors Contributing to the Internationalisation of High-tech Firms

Source: Lindell and Karagozoglou, p.97

A recent study (Table 3, page 46) by Lindell and Karagozoglou of 82 Swedish, Finnish and US high-tech firms with less than 500 employees (mean number 191) has provided some interesting insight into their global strategies and management practices. (13) High-tech or R&D intensive firms, as they call them in the study, are defined as those spending an average of eight percent or more of sales on R&D. They include computer, data communication and electronic/electric equipment firms.

Most of them had a very high degree of internationalisation, the mean share of exports to total sales being 43 percent. However, overseas production was small, on average only nine percent of total. The factors which have contributed to their international expansion clearly included push and pull elements, as shown in Table 3, page 46.

The main conclusion of the study was that these firms were proactive and saw international markets as essential for growth and even survival. In this context, one of major challenges is to engineer an international network of collaborative arrangements to cope with their most common problems. Among these were the need to monitor technology change on a global basis and to keep abreast of it in terms of product and service development. The strongest impediment to internationalisation was, therefore, their shortfall in management competence and experience and their lack of resources.

In analysing the measures taken to meet internal competition, the study concludes that it is necessary:

- *externally*, to develop and intensify relationships, both with customers and suppliers, and to establish alliances (half had established R&D alliances);
- *internally* "to control quality, improvement of management skills and development of technology strategies... organisationally successful R&D-intensive companies respond to international competition by shaping the strategy of the company, improving the competence of managers and devising total quality programmes... Education for managers is more important than increased financial resources". (14)

The study noted that significant differences were observed in the strategies used by Scandinavian and US firms.

➢ *The Business Services SMEs*

SMEs have faced more difficulties in reaching foreign markets in services than in goods, because the former usually requires a physical presence in the foreign country. Although customisation and client supplier interaction may be *important* to goods, they are *inherent* in service transactions. In recent years, however, the international presence of SMEs in business services has grown, especially where supported by improved telecommunications, personnel mobility and the growth of partnerships.

A study by O'Farrell *et al.* provides a unique glimpse into this area, which is largely ignored by the literature. (15) Their paper explored how business service SMEs in the UK had developed their foreign markets over 20 years. The sample covered 400 firms with less than 200 employees (83 percent less than 100) in engineering consultancy, management consultancy, market research, computer software and product design. All had high levels of international business, but in different degrees, ranging from 51 percent for product design and management consultancy to 35 percent for engineering consultancies. According to the authors, "these different degrees of internationalisation reflected, in part, the age distribution of firms, the inherent tradability of specific industries, and the ease with which foreign customers can be served".

The study demonstrated the strategic complexity of the process of internationalisation by business service SMEs and the diversity of its outcomes. Foreign market entry appears to be a relatively casual process for business service firms, as compared with the manner typically adopted by manufacturers. This often occurs when a contract is obtained from a public organisation or multinational abroad, or from an established domestic client who is internationalising. Business service firms are able to enter into a greater number of foreign markets more easily than manufacturers as part of a learning process.

Conversely, the transition from initial presence to subsequent development is probably more difficult for business service companies than for manufacturers There are significant resourcing difficulties in establishing the necessary infrastructure while sustaining a home market presence. The time-cost of supporting overseas business is greater than at home and the level of overseas activity may depend upon domestic demand. Developments in home and overseas markets, therefore, are interdependent Many firms strive to maintain this balance between domestic and foreign business for strategic reasons, continuing to carry out assignments abroad, even if not especially profitable, because it enhances their reputation among domestic clients.

O'Farrell *et al.* conclude that "foreign market entry and development thus requires complex calculations and among the most important elements of this complexity are:

- its dynamic nature, with market decisions under constant review and subject to change, influenced by the prior and ongoing experience of companies in both regional, domestic and overseas markets;

- wider corporate restructuring process by companies themselves in their home markets, or their operations in other foreign countries; and
- inter-firm corporate relationships, including especially between service firms and their clients." (16)

➢ *The Industrial Mid-size Globalisers*

It is only recently that recognition is being given to the role played by a distinct type of SME, which, in fact, has been an international, and even global, player for many years. Such a company entered the international arena once their local markets became too small for their highly specialised products. They are referred to as mid-size giants because they usually have a high share of world markets, even though they are often smallish.

These firms frequently operate in what are widely called "industrial clusters", some of which, like the German Mittelstand, are justifiably famous. These clusters refer to groupings of SMEs in particular geographical locations which have created, enduring international *centres of excellence* in particular industries through a network of vertical and horizontal relationships. Several authors have studied them, but no-one more thoroughly than Michael Porter, who undertook ten years ago a major research project in ten countries in an attempt to discern the reasons underlying the origin and evolution of these industrial clusters. (17)

His findings, which have received much support, were that firms gain competitive advantage where their home base allows and supports the most rapid accumulation of specialised assets and skills. Four broad attributes (referred to by Porter as the *diamond*) create the dynamic and highly competitive environment in which firms build up their competence bases. They are: factor conditions, demand conditions, the support provided by related and supporting industries and the nature of domestic rivalry, especially the intensity of local competition.

In his view, regions will tend to promote industrial clusters where the management practices and modes of organisation are well suited to the industries' sources of competitive advantage. Many Italian firms, for example, are among the most renowned cases of successful world-class industrial product manufacturers. Nearly all are SMEs, but nevertheless world leaders in a range of fragmented industries (eg, lighting, furniture, footwear, woollen fabrics, and packaging machines) in which economies of scale are either modest or can be overcome through co-operation among loosely affiliated companies. They most often compete by employing focus strategies, avoiding standardised products and operating in small niches with their own particular style or customised product variety. Often dominated by a single individual, these firms rapidly develop new products and can adapt to market changes with high flexibility.

In Germany, by contrast, the engineering and technical background of many senior executives, produces a strong inclination toward methodical product and process improvement. Intangible bases of competitive advantage are rarely pursued. These characteristics lead to the greatest success in industries with a high technical or engineering content (for example, optics, chemicals, complicated machinery), especially where intricate and complex products demand precision manufacturing, a careful development process, after-sale service, and, hence, a highly-disciplined management structure. (18)

These German mid-size companies (*Mittelstand Unternehmen)* have probably received the most attention largely because of they are considered to be the powerhouse behind Germany's post-war economic success in the manufacturing sector. This sector included in 1995 about 2.5 million companies, accounting for 80 percent of the employment in the private sector, two thirds of the GNP and relied on exports for 40 percent of sales of Germany.(19)

We can take a close look at their international management model, thanks to a seminal book published in 1995 by Herman Simon *The Hidden Champions*.(20) This major research project, which covered a sample of 500 firms across all sectors from 1989 to 1994, tried to discover what these market leaders were doing differently from the larger firms. The title of the book underlines the extent to which the activities of these firms are relatively unknown in international business circles. Simon adopted a generous definition of mid-size, namely that of occupying a leading international position in a niche market, with sales not exceeding one billion dollars.

The strength of these firms lies in their focused business approach. They specialise in very narrow market segments where they often attain dominant positions. Many of them enjoy world market shares in their particular niche of 70 to 90 percent, the mean market share being 30 percent of the world and 37 percent of Europe.

One reason for the fact that they have managed to escape the attention of the many business researchers is that usually their products or services are inconspicuous. They are used as inputs in manufacturing processes (machinery and equipment) or parts and components of end products (metal filters, sunroofs for cars, bookbinding textiles or labels for beverage bottles). As Table 4, page 51, suggests, they are never seen by the consumer.

Another reason for their low profile is that they actually often relish their obscurity. Being mostly family businesses, they do not publish annual reports and they shy away from publicity. Secrecy becomes a credo. Their corporate culture favours continuity, a steady rather than explosive growth and a *kaizen* philosophy of constantly achieving improvements with vigilant attention to detail.

TETRA: its share in the world market of tropical fish food is more than 50 percent.
HILLEBRAND: the largest wine shipper in the world with offices in 60 countries.
WEBASTO: world leader in both sunroofs and auxiliary heating systems for cars.
GERRIETS: holds a near monopoly position in the world for large neutral lighting cloths for theatre stages.
HAUNI: literally the only supplier of high-speed cigarette machines, with 90 percent of the world market share. All the filter cigarettes in the world are manufactured with a technology invented by Hauni.

Table 4: Invisible Businesses

The following common practices emerged from the study:

- *Specialisation with geographic diversity*

The hidden champions follow a strategy that combines technical competence with world-wide marketing and sales. They focus on niche markets that require technical expertise and direct all their resources towards maintaining a strong position in that market through relentless innovation. The globalisation of marketing and sales provides sufficient scale to recover R&D expenses and to keep costs within range.

- *Providing customer value*

Many of the executives running the hidden champions have been in management for many years and make an effort to work with the same customers, cultivating their loyalty. When going abroad, they show a strong preference for full control over operations, primarily to not delegate the relationship with the customer. In order to offer the same high standard of service as at home, they tend to create strong service networks wherever they do business.

According to the survey, what customers value most are product quality, closeness to the customer, service, economy, quality of employees, technological leadership, and innovativeness – all aspects where "the hidden champions" rated very high or above average when compared with competitors. One area where they excel is training, an increasingly important service as products become more complex. Interactions between technical experts and customers are promoted by emphasising the involvement of their technicians in the commercial activities. While they may under-perform with regard to price, this is compensated for by the other benefits they offer to customers. Moreover, their products tend to be relatively insensitive to price.

➢ *Simplicity*

Simplicity (leanness) is a constant guide, both with respect to organisational processes and structure, in order to avoid building complex organisational models, which would reduce their ability to response to lean changing environments.

➢ *Fierce self-reliance*

The hidden champions are staunchly independent. They trust in their own capabilities to enter new markets and to solve manufacturing and R&D problems. Independence ensures their control over standards and prevents leaks of technical know-how. It reflects their belief in the role of specialisation and concentration and the need to protect their core competencies essential to survival.

Another hallmark has been their tendency to "make" rather than "buy". Less than a quarter said they prefer co-operating with other companies. Only in a few markets such as Japan have they felt the need to seek co-operation with local partners. Their practices illustrate that management concepts such as outsourcing or strategic alliances are viewed as new fashions, which they feel should not influence their thinking too strongly.

➢ *Strong leadership*

The typical hidden champion is located in a small town or village where interdependence is created between employer and employee. Personal ties are established since both the owner-manager and his employees are likely to have been raised in the same town.

Successful leadership results from curbing the authoritarianism and intrusiveness that often characterise patriarchs. In fact, the norm is to apply modern management styles that demonstrate trust in employees and to give workers a lot of leeway. Employees are, in turn, loyal to their employers. The organisational processes and structures have usually followed the rule of simplicity. Many hidden champions have never been anything but lean.

Leadership could be summarized as being authoritarian in setting core values and goals and participative in the processes it uses to encourage workforce contributions.

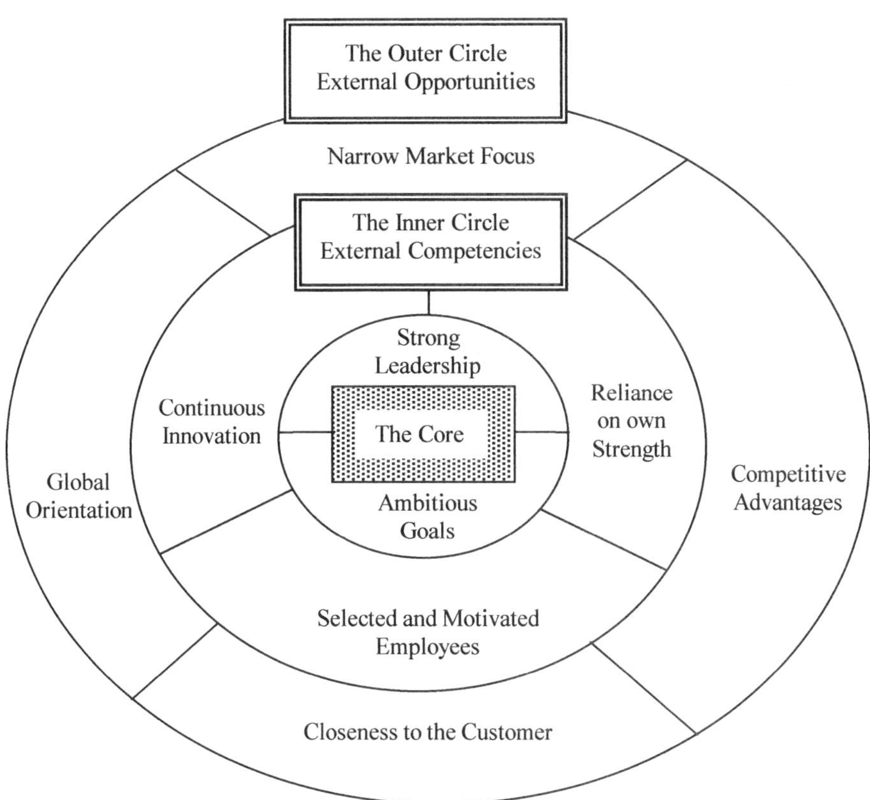

Figure 2: Key SME success factors

Source: Hermann Simon, The Hidden Champions, Harvard Business School Press, 1996, p.125

Figure 2, page 53, integrates all these key lessons. Strategic and operational elements are drawn in three ovals, representing the core values of the firm, the internal distinct capabilities or competences and the market approach. The eight specific lessons embedded in the three ovals are:

1. Set clear and ambitious goals.
2. Define a market narrowly.
3. Combine a narrow market focus with a global orientation.
4. Be close to customers in both performance and interaction.
5. Strive for continuous innovation in both product and process.
6. Create clear-cut competitive advantages in both product and service.
7. Rely on your own strengths.
8. Practice leadership that is both authoritarian in the fundamentals and participative in the details.

The clear message is that, if modest size provides certain advantages that are endangered by increasing size, SMEs should seriously consider remaining small.

Is the hidden champion a purely German phenomenon? This was one of the key issues addressed by Simon. To test the results of his study of German firms, he investigated and visited a number of hidden champions in 16 other developed countries world-wide. He concluded:

> *"Hidden champions are remarkably similar across countries, employing almost identical strategies. They share similar attitudes toward publicity, hold the same core values, and have excellent employee motivation. In my experience hidden champions are more alike from country than they are in relation to large companies within their own countries.* (21)

Once we go beyond western cultures, we can find successful medium-sized firms that are displaying similar features. One outstanding example is the firms owned by overseas Chinese which have a dominant position in the economies and trade of many Southeast Asian markets. Some claim that they are shaping a new form of capitalism based on traditional Chinese family business values. Yet the features described in the study, sound very similar to the family firms discussed above. According to a recent report:

"In Japan it is said that the high growth medium-sized firms use MAGIC! The mnemonic describes ***M***edium size, ***A***gility, ***G***arage-shop (entrepreneurial) ***M***entality, ***I***nnovation and ***C***oncentration (focus)."

It is difficult to draw conclusions, from the above analysis, on what might be the common management practices of successful SMEs in international markets. What is apparent is that they have leaders with a strong vision and commitment, a clear focus and independent spirit, and that their competitive advantage was derived from product design and quality, flexibility and customer closeness spread over many markets. Strategy was not accidental but was *designed*. To sustain their international position, they have had to be very adaptive to the environment in their modes of entry and expansion, the organisational structures and systems they have adopted and the management of networks and partnerships. Management competences and skills appeared to be the most frequently-quoted limiting factor, calling for more education and training and more openness to the hiring of outside professionals. Interestingly, SMEs throughout the developed world use similar internationalisation strategies.

Internationalising SMEs in a unified European market

Which lessons can be drawn from the past to assist newcomers in the international arena? This question is particularly relevant for SMEs operating in Europe. With the advent of the euro, very few firms can afford to continue to play the local game. The creation of the unified monetary market, however, does not mean that SMEs will not face the old non-currency-related barriers to operating in other European markets. The differences in culture and language, in particular, and in legal and regulatory systems, distribution channels, customer relationships, etc, will prevail for a long time.

To promote further involvement of the SMEs in the regional integration process, the European Commission sponsored in 1998 a research project with the remit of preparing a toolkit to help SMEs to internationalise their businesses. The research team, in which the author participated, worked very closely with the managers of SMEs who had recently internationalised in different parts of Europe. (22)

Twelve companies were chosen as case studies in four regions: Saxony (Germany), Emilio Regina (Italy), East Anglia (UK) and Catalonia (Spain). The firms, all recent players in the international scene, operated in very diverse industries ranging from high tech products such as software and motor control systems, to industrial and consumer goods such as medical equipment, garage door mechanisms and fashion clothing.

A similar methodology was used for each case study. For each, questions were asked about the key management issues they faced as they initiated their internationalisation, followed by an analysis of the approaches they adopted in practice. Annex 2, page 64, reproduces the case Fripan of Spain (producer of pre-cooked frozen bread and pastries) as an example of the structure and issues discussed in the cases.

The management queries which were common to virtually all companies related to:

➢ *Commitment and motivation*

How can we make the company culture reflect and support the decision? How do we achieve the critical mass of internal commitment?

➢ *Management structures and resources*

What management structure and administrative systems do we have to put in place?

Do we have the experience and skills to cope with the new venture as well as enough people willing to operate in foreign markets? Can we afford to hire the new people we need? Where is it possible to find the necessary funds without losing our independence and compromising our objectives?

➢ *Identifying markets*

Where do we obtain the relevant information on demand, distribution channels, legal and standards and norms to assess potential markets? We need to avoid the pitfall of choosing the markets which are closest to us from the cultural and language point of view, instead of the markets which are strategically the most advantageous.

➢ *Market entry strategy*

Having identified a pilot market, how do we penetrate it? Do we export directly or work through an agent/distributor; set up a subsidiary by acquiring or opt for a joint venture, become a sub-contractor or license our own technology/know-how? Will we be able to exercise sufficient control in the relationship we will have?

➢ *Product adaptation*

What is the level of uniqueness of our products and to what degree are they suitable for foreign markets? What adaptations will be required and will we have the knowledge and skills to make them? Can we reach the volume of sales we need to justify the development costs? Do we have to register our brand name and how do we protect it?

There were, similarly, many approaches which were common to all SMEs, for example:

- Many companies felt they had attained a high share of their national market in a very narrow niche and had no option but to go international, if they wanted to grow and to counteract the loss in their own markets from foreign competitors. Hence, it was a clear option that usually received the unequivocal support of management and staff.

  It became apparent that the commitment of the head of the firm, often the founder, was essential as internationalisation demands taking risks, opening up the firm's culture and a capacity to learn. When the head lacked international experience and had limited command of languages, firms appeared reluctant to seek foreign markets. The advances occurred shortly after a management change, often a generation change, who had more international exposure and better knowledge of overseas' markets and cultures.

- The markets chosen corresponded with the expected criterion of proximity in geography but also in culture. For example, most Spanish firms chose Portugal, France and/or Italy as initial markets, but also considered Latin-America early in the game. Similarly, a British software company's first international move was to Australia and other English speaking countries around the world.

- Product adaptation was always the norm, given that the strategy was to compete on the basis of developing close relationships with customers by ensuring that each product was tightly specified for a niche market and, therefore, adapted very clearly for the particular task being undertaken. Such firms sell systems and often solutions rather than products, where price is not the key factor. Innovation is a constant to which much effort and resources are devoted.

- Finally, finding initially the right foreign partner, a route chosen by most, proved to be the most critical factor in the entry strategy. The partner, usually an agent, knows the markets and has nurtured customer relationships, which are a difficult to develop for a small newcomer. Above all, they have proven to be the best source of information on client expectations, competitors, distribution channels and norms and standards. Most cases of failure stemmed from a careless choice of local partners. One of the Italian firms producing and designing men's fashion clothes, for example, attained a high share of the German market quickly, largely due to a close working relationship with its German fashion agency. The two agreed on the design and product specifications to ensure that it was a product which benefited from the strong influence of Italian "design flair", but was made of materials and used colours and finishes acceptable to a German client.

The major drawback of using other networks is the lack of direct contact with the customer, essential for firms selling customised products or systems. Hence, as the market develops, the tendency is to set up their own subsidiary for sales, and at times even production, often as a joint venture or through acquisition of a local firm.

From the results obtained in the case studies, consultation with the managers of other SMEs in the four countries and a review of the literature referred to in this chapter, an SME toolkit was prepared. It was intended to help SMEs to "help themselves", based on the notion of being "ready, willing and able". The key recommendations were summarised in a list of "ten tips" shown in Annex 1, page 62.

Facing the Challenges of the Globalised World

It becomes apparent that SMEs are not necessarily at a disadvantage with respect to larger firms when they operate in international markets, nor is this likely to change as the markets continue to globalise. They have a unique and complementary role to play alongside the large multinationals. They form an integral part of the international value chain.

The complexity of the operations, however, is likely to increase. Markets are more sophisticated and competition has intensified. The increased pace of the internationalisation process will further accelerate, putting additional strains on the already limited management resources and skills of the SME. To remain independent will also be more difficult as networking and partnering become more essential as a mode to penetrate simultaneously several markets, especially distant ones.

SMEs that act as suppliers or sub-contractors of large firms will be forced to follow even further the clients who are becoming increasingly multinational themselves and who have become more concentrated as a result of the wave of mergers and acquisitions. The assemblers have shown a marked preference to deal with fewer suppliers with whom they establish deeper relationships worldwide.

For the R&D-intensive SME, the technological revolution in new fields will open new opportunities. But there will be additional pressure to expand to new markets more quickly before its offerings become obsolete, given that product life cycles are now becoming shorter and markets more uniform.

Some may say that the narrowly focused and staunchly independent strategy of the successful medium-sized firms discussed above would seem to be a risky proposition for the next century. Many seem to be facing problems of transition from one family generation to another and have been forced to open the firm to outside finance and professional management. This may make them candidates for a take-over or change the unique nature of their persona. Still, the combination of technical excellence, adaptability and innovativeness is likely to constitute a lasting formula of survival for the future of these "hidden champions" of this world.

The management challenges faced by the newcomers seem to be fundamentally similar to those of SMEs that became world players in the past. They will have the additional advantages of being able to learn from the experience of their forerunners and of being confronted with a more open international community in every respect, politically, socially and legally. Above all, they can benefit from the new information technologies to overcome the frequently mentioned problems in searching for information and in communication. Electronic commerce in particular can help overcome some of the resource limitations in reaching and responding to customers, thus circumventing local intermediaries. Finally, virtual service business is also developing and helps above all small players who have the knowledge but not the financial resources to operate internationally.

References

(1) Bridge, S. *et al. Understanding Enterprise, Entrepreneurship and Small Business*. Palgrave (formerly MacMillan), 1998

(2) As (1)

(3) Kets de Vries, M. The dynamics of family controlled firms: The good and the bad news. *Organisational Dynamics*, 1993

(4) Swords, D. and Turner, I. *Strategy from the Inside Out*. Thomson Business Press, 1997, p.44

(5) As (4), p.45

(6) As (1)

(7) *Family Business Adviser*, July 1998, pp.4 & 5

(8) As (1), p.131

(9) Verhoeven, W. The Export Performance of SMEs in the Netherlands. *International Small Business Journal*, Vol. 6, No.2, 1998

(10) Jenster, P. and Jarillo, J. *Internationalizing the Medium-sized Firm*. Handelshojskolens Forlag, Copenhagen Business School, 1994

(11) Ellis, J. and Williams. *International Business Strategy*. Pitman Publishing, 1995

(12) Holmund, M. and Koch, S. Relationships and the Internationalisation of Finnish Small and Medium-sized Companies. *International Small Business Journal*, Vol.16, No.4, 1998, p.49

(13) Lindell, M. and Karagozoglu, N. Global Strategies of US and Scandinavian, R and D. Intensive Small and Medium Sized Companies. *European Management Journal*, Vol. 15, No.1, 1997

(14) As (13), p.99

(15) O'Farrell, P. *et al.* Internationalisation by Business Service SMEs: An Inter-Industry Analysis. *International Small Business Journal*, Vol. 16, No.2, 1998

(16) As (15), p.31

(17) Porter, M. *The Competitive Advantage of Nations*. The MacMillan Press, 1990

(18) As (17), p.108

(19) *Business Week*, 10/4/95

(20) Simon, H. *The Hidden Champions*. Harvard Business School Press, 1996

(21) As (20), p.259

(22) *The International SME* developed by Cambs Tec & Business Link, Sinnea International, ESADE, Leipzig Chamber of Industry and Commerce, Anglia Polytechnic University, and Managed Learning Ltd., with the support of the European Community, 1999

Bibliography

Davies, E. and Keys, B. Success Factors in Going International. Experiences *from* Small Firms in Southeast US. *European Business Review,* 96, (2), 1996

Jennings, P. and Beaver, G. The Performance and Competitive Advantage of Small Firms: A Management Perspective. *International Small Business Journal,* Vol. 15, No.2, 1997

Murphy, M. *Small Business Management. The Financial Times*/Pitman Publishing, 1996

Reid, P. and Hindley, C. *The Successful Internationalisation of The Small Business.* 23rd European Small Business Seminar, Belfast, 1993

Annex 1: Summary of "Top Ten Tips"

1. *Develop a mission statement*
   Set out a clear agenda for your export activities before you begin.

2. *Get plenty of good advice*
   There are many sources of advice and assistance available. Network as much as possible, through your bank, Export Clubs, Chambers of Commerce, and Trade Associations, etc. Keep up-to-date by reading relevant publications.

3. *Research*
   Do your homework and research continuously. Visit target countries and markets and see what goes on first-hand, even when you're on holiday! Be aware of the competition and their strengths and weaknesses.

4. *Do not over-extend yourself or your company*
   Concentrate on just one or two markets at any one time. Consider spreading risk by establishing a "portfolio" of export activities to maximise potential and minimise exposure.

5. *Build long-term relationships*
   Getting to know and cultivating agents, distributors and end-users should not be a brief one-off affair. Markets take time to build, so work with people you feel comfortable with.

6. *Make sure you can meet the needs of the market*
   Gear up yourself and your company to match demand. Be forward thinking in planning for and recruiting the right people, particularly those with special skills, and be willing to pay them accordingly.

7. *Think through the risks and re-evaluate them*
   Risks are higher in foreign markets than at home. Monitor your progress against your plan; re-assess the risks at regular intervals.

8. *Never forget the need for training*
   As markets change and opportunities present themselves, do not be left behind through lack of training. Plan ahead, and evaluate and review your training needs as a regular discipline.

9. *Think internationally*
   Talk to people in their own language in marketing material and provide language training for staff with customer contact. Understand the cultures and customs of the countries where you are doing business.

10. *Never take short cuts*
   Establish structures and stick to them. It controls costs and risks and minimises wasted effort.

Annex 2: Case Study: Fripan, Spain

By Professor Emilio Herbolzheimer and Xavier Castanyer

THE COMPANY

In 1976, Pere Galles, who had been a baker for twenty years, decided to start a new business to fill what he considered to be a niche within the Spanish market, namely freshly-made artisan bread in clean bakeries with a friendly environment. Mr Galles wanted to return to the small ovens that produced traditional bread, which would be baked just twelve hours before it reached the customer, through bakery shops spread throughout Barcelona. The new bakery shops were called *The Old Windmill (El Moli Vell)* to convey the message of a traditional method adapted to modern habits.

The Old Windmill concept was very successful and it soon spread throughout the rest of Catalonia through a combination of franchises and self-owned shops. By 1986, although annual turnover had reached 2,600 M Pesetas, Mr Galles began to realise the limitations of the business. In order to grow, he needed to develop a new activity with more value added, less dispersed and larger scale production as well as higher productivity. This induced him to expand into the business of deep-frozen, pre-cooked bread and pastries, which had already been sold previously in the *Old Windmill* outlets. In 1988 the decision was taken to invest in their own plant on the outskirts of Barcelona, and Fripan was born.

THE PRODUCT

Now Mr Galles needed to develop a new range of products and processes using his technical skills. He began by searching for information in France where the technology was most advanced and, after much hard work, developed a new concept of pre-cooked bread using traditional ingredients. He also developed natural liquid ferments with the assistance of the University of Barcelona.

At first the production process was very labour-intensive. Twelve men were employed in the production of the mass dough alone. It soon became apparent that new technology was required to increase production capacity, and that the process had to improve in order to guarantee more homogeneous quality, taste and flavour of the product. A Spanish company called AB Asesores invested in Fripan and, with the help of this increase in capital, in 1995 Fripan invested

1,000 M Pesetas in new equipment and buildings, as well as in laboratories. One year later, the last and totally-automated factory was built in Madrid using state-of-the-art technology.

In the new bread factory, all former manual processes were replaced by six highly automated continuous flow lines, with only four people supervising the process. The entire production is now controlled by Oscar, a computer programme which automatically sets up the production chain in accordance with the programmed references and product recipes developed in their own laboratories. This new plant produces more than 70 items, among them puff pastries, apple cakes and different types of croissant (regular, cheese, cream and so on). In 1996 automated refrigeration chambers were built to provide warehousing facilities, previously subcontracted. A software programme (SICAD) calculates the most economic batch sizes to minimise stock costs. There are laboratories with four technicians in support who, in addition to research and development, develop products and make adaptations for new markets. This facility enabled Fripan to unveil 40 new specialities at the 1997 trade fair of the sector.

THE MARKET

At the outset, Fripan's products sold almost exclusively through the *Old Windmill* network in Barcelona and its metropolitan area. Some Spanish retail chains from outside Catalonia also placed orders, but there was neither enough production capacity nor commercial resources for them to be able to respond.

The situation quickly changed when, in 1990, Fripan became the exclusive supplier of a fast-growing and innovative fast-food company, Pans & Company. This chain offered Mediterranean-style sandwiches made of pre-cooked frozen bread, in contrast to the usual hamburgers of other fast-food restaurants. Through aggressive marketing and shrewd strategies, within four years Pans & Company became the leading fast-food chain in Spain. Being the exclusive supplier to Pans & Company demanded a substantial increase in Fripan's production and sales grew from 15 M Pesetas in 1991 to 250 M Pesetas in 1996.

Fripan's expansion in the Spanish market has been concentrated in three areas: the coastal regions (Catalonia and Valencia); Madrid; and Andalucia in the south, with the Catalan region accounting for 60 percent of their Spanish sales. Today Fripan are the market leader in the Spanish frozen dough market with annual sales of 17,201 M Pesetas and a unique position within their market due to their artisan approach.

INTERNATIONALISATION

Despite their strong position in Spain, in 1994 it was felt that there was not much scope left for growth within Spain and a decision was taken to attempt an internationalisation strategy. The starting point was a pilot entry strategy for the Portuguese market. This market was chosen due to its geographical proximity and the similarities between the Spanish and Portuguese markets.

Although Fripan's internationalisation strategy did not always run smoothly, they currently have a well-established market presence in Portugal, France, Germany, and since early 1997, Italy. The company is currently investigating moving outside the European market to Central America, the US and China. Back in 1994 however, Fripan were starting from scratch and faced a number of problems.

THE PROBLEMS

In developing an internationalisation strategy, there were four key problems facing Fripan:

Finance
Fripan wished to become an international player, but did not have sufficient financial resources to engage in the new strategy alone. Where could they find the necessary funds?

Culture
The culture at Fripan could be described as a personalistic culture and, in conjunction with their internationalisation strategy, the management structure required professionalisation. How could they achieve this?

Market Entry Strategy
Having identified a pilot market, how could Fripan attempt to penetrate it?

Product Adaptation
Could Fripan simply sell the same products in the same way in foreign markets, or would they need to adapt their recipes and marketing in accordance with different tastes and cultures?

THE SOLUTIONS

Fripan addressed each of these problems as follows:

Finance
Fripan decided to look for a partner who would be prepared to invest in the company. They sought advice from their friends and business associates and one suggested AB Asesores. This was based on Fripan's past performance rather than the projected international growth potential. AB Asesores accepted an offer of 26 percent of the shares in return for investing 1,000 M Pesetas. Caution led them to limit their commitment to 1999, at which time the position would be reviewed. Although this arrangement provided the necessary funds for the internationalisation strategy, it also brought with it another problem issue. The commitment of AB Asesores was set to last until 1999 only, and they are logically more interested in short term profits then in longer ones, which they cannot capitalise. This is sometimes reflected in intense discussions at board meetings every time investment decisions are dealt with.

Culture
The key issue of the professionalisation of the management structure was dealt with by bringing into the company new people with the desired skills and international experience. The position of chief executive officer was established and staffed by an expert with broad executive experience, including the presidency of the Catalan Railways Corporation. His task was to mediate the usual conflict between the technical and commercial sides of the international strategy. Two individuals with extensive international experience, but without share participation, further strengthened the board. The board of Fripan was doubled in size from five to ten, which included the three new recruits identified above, with two further board members of AB Asesores.

Market Entry Strategy
Fripan decided to look for a Portuguese partner with whom they could create a sales company. They chose a local distributor of food products, especially ice creams. Based on a previous successful formula, they offered the Portuguese company 50 percent of the shares in the new company. Here again, however, an additional problem issue emerged. Having decided on an international strategy, Fripan were very enthusiastic about the prospects for entry into the Portuguese market and

this enthusiasm led to the acceptance of a partner without their usual rigorous search. In other words, their enthusiasm led them to accept the first company that looked about right, rather than waiting until they found a partner which better fitted their requirements. It quickly became apparent that the chosen partner was not really committed and were putting more of their effort into selling ice creams than Fripan's products. Fripan discontinued their relationship after the first year and eventually found a much more experienced and committed choice, which proved to be a great improvement on the first-choice partner.

Fripan learnt this lesson well, and investigated future market entry strategies extensively, often relying on personal contacts and recommendations, before making a choice of partner and the customary 50 percent share offer.

Product Adaptation

In order to penetrate the Portuguese market, Fripan concentrated its efforts on selling bread rather than pastries. Portuguese people have a very sophisticated tradition of pastries. In addition, frozen bread is extremely valued by hotels and restaurants. This strategy of adapting their products and sale strategies to "fit" the target country has been subsequently used to great effect.

In Germany, for example, the market is described as "the chapata market par excellence". While bread consumption is 140 gr. per person per day in Spain, and 180 gr. in France, in Germany it is 300 gr. The attraction of the German market was evident to Fripan's top management, but they waited until they felt they had a good product to penetrate it. It was 1966 before they considered that they could guarantee production with homogeneous quality. A further advantage is the German consumer's preference for natural products, and soon the chapatas produced for that market clearly indicated on the packaging the *traditional* quality of the product.

Once they had the product, Fripan were then able to search for a German partner – of course with the Portuguese experience in that first pilot market entry attempt still fresh in their minds. And thus, a traditional perishable product, such as bread, in principle very local in nature, has been introduced successfully in other markets through sound and cautious strategic thinking.

Chapter 3

BUSINESS ALLIANCES: DRIVING FOR COLLABORATIVE SUCCESS

Janine Stiles

Introduction

Organisations are continuously trying to cope with the turbulence and change which characterises today's international business environment. In many sectors developments in technology and market homogenisation have brought together previously separate industries and markets, offering new opportunities and business potential. In response, the need to incorporate flexibility and change into the company's strategic, structural and operational processes has become increasingly important. Companies are also acknowledging that they can no longer go it alone, and are relying more and more on the development of network relationships and capabilities to help them to operate effectively. This fact is nowhere more evident than in the international airline industry, the basis for our empirical case study examination of these trends.

The use of strategic alliances and collaborative partnerships as a form of business operation has seen steady and rapid growth over the past 30 years in a wide range of industries. Between 1992 and 1996, over 20,000 alliances were formally registered. (1) Naturally, many more informal relationships could be added to this figure. Overall statistics suggest that the move towards alliance partnership has, in fact, been growing annually by 25 percent since the mid-1980s, with no sign of this abating in the foreseeable future.

Enthusiasm for the alliance option has also spread across continents and industry sectors. It has been embraced throughout the developed world from the US, across Europe to the Far East. Major alliance groups are appearing in numerous diverse industries and are continuing to grow. The One World and the Star airline alliances are still developing, bringing together major blocks of players with global scope and influence, networking with both inter- and intra-industry players. The development of such partnerships has prompted further consolidation and reorientation of some industry structures as firms continue to manœuvre for position. This has necessarily raised the competitive stakes for continuing players in this industry.

Strategic alliance management has thus become a vital part of the toolkit for many businesses trying to compete, and is increasingly becoming recognised as the key to achieving competitive success when dealing with today's fast-changing global markets. The benefits of this form of business operation are many-fold. Partnership can provide an entry route into otherwise inaccessible markets, guard against competitive threats and facilitate the development of new ideas and product offerings. It can also bring together sometimes surprising bedfellows, all in the crusade for customer satisfaction and competitive advantage. Given the dynamics and uncertainty in today's business environment, the strategic alliance offers a flexible, responsive and transformational key, allowing the holder the possibility of gaining access to a new world of networks, coalitions and opportunities. (2)

The Challenge

Good alliance management does not, however, happen easily. The history of collaboration is riddled with examples of failed or struggling partnerships where the expected value-added benefits of the relationship have been, instead, replaced by unforeseen costs and difficulties. Even those alliances which appear to plod along, avoiding the major disasters that have befallen others, often fail to achieve the full benefits a good strategic partnership can provide or are commuted by one partner or the other before the true value has been identified or built upon. The statistics consistently reflect a poor picture, regardless of the criteria for evaluation. A survey of the success rate of strategic alliances undertaken by Bleeke and Ernst (3) found that 66 percent of cross border alliances ran into serious managerial problems within the first two years, with a further 19 percent reporting mixed results. On average, over the first four years of the relationship, approximately 50 percent of the alliance population surveyed were recorded as failures. Yet the trend towards alliance management continues to grow undeterred, fuelled by the need to collaborate. The challenge to companies is, therefore, not if, but how, they should seek to manage a strategic partnership.

So why is the failure rate for strategic alliances so high? To begin to answer this it is useful to consider the complex characteristics of the modern-day alliance. Many organisations struggle because they rush into partnerships, often underestimating the complex nature of the beast. They then put too few, or the wrong type of, resources or management into the arrangement. Modern-day strategic alliances tend to be highly dynamic and unpredictable and need to be managed accordingly for any advantage to be gained from the relationship.

Key characteristics are listed in Figure 1, below:

- Frequently central to a firm's strategy
- Greater uncertainty and ambiguity
- Value creation and capture is not pre-ordained
- Evolution of the relationship can be hard to predict
- Emphasis on on-going management of the relationship
- Success relies more on adaptability to change than on the initial agreement
- They increasingly involve multiple partners and aim to develop complex systems and solutions
- Today's ally may be tomorrow's competitor

Figure 1: Characteristics of strategic alliances

Adapted from Doz and Hamel (1998) (4)

Factors impacting the success rate of a collaborative partnership can thus be identified throughout the development and existence of the relationship. However, partner selection and the respective intents of each of the players involved – both at the entry stage and as the relationship develops – are fundamental issues that are often not considered sufficiently prior to operationalisation of the relationship. Yet they can often be rated adversely against many of the criteria noted above and can, therefore, be one of the major causes of partnership breakdown.

This chapter draws on recent research undertaken by the author on strategic alliances in service sector industries. Following on from the discussion above, it considers the key motivational drivers underpinning the objectives of a partner firm entering and operating within an alliance relationship – and the subsequent implications. The research was undertaken in an effort to help understand the management issues, and thus to try to improve the success rate, of this form of business operation.

Underlying forces driving partnerships

The key driving forces for alliance partnerships can be categorised into three areas. They are:

- ***product-focused drivers*** – associated with the need to develop new, or broaden current, product/service offerings and bring them to market ahead of the competition.
- ***market-focused drivers*** – objectives relating to the need to establish, or be part of, a large global presence, to gain market knowledge and size, ensure competitive self-defence and/or to deal with regulatory and political barriers to new market entry, and

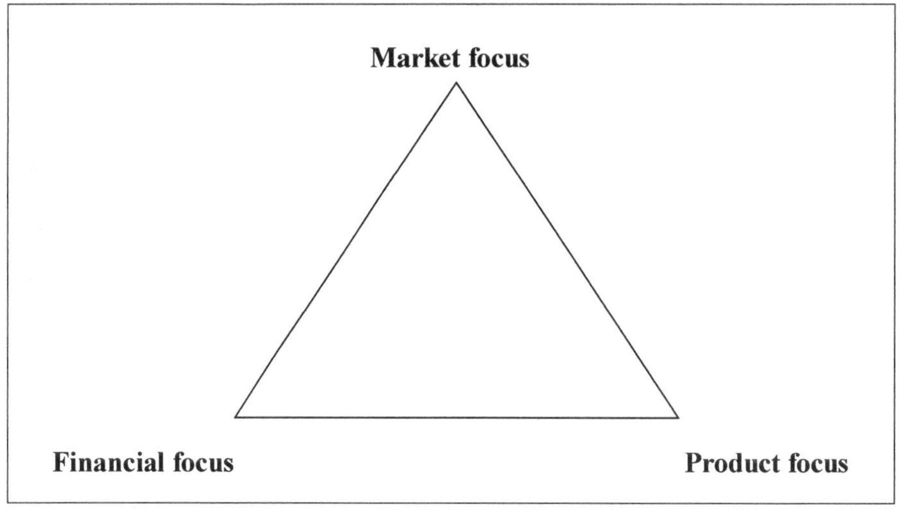

Figure 2: Strategic alliance drivers

- ***financially-focused drivers*** – associated with a means of maintaining, or improving the individual firm's financial position under given competitive circumstances. (See Figure 2, above.)

For many firms, financial benefits may be a key incentive for the pursuance of a collaborative relationship. However, evidence suggests that, at least in the short term, financial gains can be disappointing. The complexity and cost of setting up and operationalising this type of arrangement can take time and effort. All too often potential value-added benefits can be missed because of the need to focus on the day-to-day management problems of the relationship. In the longer term, financial benefits may be realised through such areas as joint purchasing, rationalisation of processes etc, but, all too frequently, the approach is too piece-meal and fails to reap the potential rewards expected at the onset of the partnership.

The overriding aim for many service sector firms entering strategic alliances is, however, the need to gain access to the global market place, to gain market share and to protect their competitive position through entry and operation within one of the growing networks or "blocks" appearing within the respective industries. The more dynamic and competitive the environment, the more emphasis is placed on this aspect.

For some players this can be a reactive response to a threat to their current position, whilst, for others, the alliance strategy can become a more positive and relationship-driven approach to potential opportunities. Once established in a strategic partnership, a company may then benefit from addressing product development possibilities with the partner. Such productive partnerships may not be a driving force for each partner, but can prove highly constructive.

An initial – and it must be said fundamental – consideration, therefore, for any partner considering entry into a strategic alliance is the complementarity of the driving forces between the different players, and their potential influence upon the relationship. The best results are obtained where the two partners share common aims, common reference points and common competences.

The co-operative/competitive dichotomy

As the alliance concept has developed over time, growing in complexity and dimension, partner objectives have developed and become more sophisticated. Traditionally, this form of business operation has been viewed simply as a co-operative arrangement between partners in order to combine resources and share information, thus gaining from the value-added synergies that such ventures can offer.(5) Co-operative drivers are summarised in Figure 3, page 74. (6)

In recent years however, an increasing amount of research has also revealed a more competitive aspect to this form of operation. Some firms will enter alliances to appropriate value from the partner firm, potentially facilitating development of a new set of resources, capabilities or skills for themselves at a relatively more rapid rate. (7) Thus, where co-operation in the past was viewed as the key driver for the relationship, another type of alliance driver – competition – aimed at value appropriation can increasingly be identified. Figure 4, page 74, outlines the key drivers of this approach.

- the pooling of resources or capabilities, and the consequent synergies which can be gained within the partnership and used for mutual strategic advantage;
- a means of upgrading both firms' positions comparatively quickly via, for example, new product development and innovation;
- the reduction of transaction costs, and therefore gaining competitive advantage through increased efficiency; [1]
- the replication of experiential knowledge such as complex;
- organisational routines which may not, otherwise, be transferred;
- easily through the traditional market place.

Figure 3: Co-operative drivers for alliance partnership

Source: synthesised from Berg et al., 1982; Kogut, 1988; Hennart, 1998; Mohr and Nevin, 1990; Grant, 1991; Bleeke and Ernst, 1991; Lorange and Roos, 1992; Mahoney and Pandian, 1992; Mohr and Spekman, 1994 (see references page 84)

- a transfer of skills and capabilities from one partner to another with the intent that one partner gains at the advantage of the other. Ultimately, termination of the partnership can occur in this situation, with a resultant skewing of relative power and position of the now-competing firms;
- induction of a level of dependency in the weaker partner. This can skew influence and control within the relationship and is often a precursor to an aggressive merger or acquisition by the dominant player;
- effective "de-skilling" of competencies or processes crucial to the overall process may be encouraged. This can generate a dependency by one partner upon the other for such things as components, supplies, design, skills and technologies;
- calibration of a partner's strengths and weaknesses, which would otherwise not be possible. As a consequence, the competitive risk in future collisions with that partner may be significantly altered.

Figure 4: Competitive drivers for alliance partnership

Source: synthesised from Devlin and Bleackley, 1988; Hamel, 1990, 1991; Lyons, 1991; Lynch, 1991; Lei and Slocum, 1992; Lorange and Roos, 1992; Lorange, Roos and Bronn, 1992. (see references page 84)

[1] These costs might include both financial and non-financial costs such as the loss of specific knowledge or those associated with uncertainty, or supplier/buyer power.

Thus, it may be seen that both the co-operative and the competitive aspects of the strategic alliance appear to have major implications, both for the individual partners involved and for the future of the alliance relationship. From the co-operative perspective, they can facilitate rapid upgrade of resources and create synergistic benefits associated with economies of scale and efficiency. Competitive drivers will focus, instead, upon skill and competence acquisition, upon control and independent market positioning. They involve the elements listed in Figure 4, page 74.

These intents are not necessarily mutually exclusive, however. Firms entering partnerships are often faced with a complex mix of objectives that may frequently reflect varying combinations of both co-operative and competitive drivers. They must also necessarily recognise the patterns of drivers affecting the way the alliance partner thinks and acts. Nonetheless, all these issues combine to generate the overall complementary thrust of the two partners.

Management issues

Once the potential complementarity of general aims and objectives is established, it is important to consider the other key management issues which can influence the relationship. These include such aspects as culture, balance of power and trust, senior management commitment and communication, the ease of transference of skills and knowledge, and the experience and learning capabilities of the respective partners.

➢ *Culture*

Cultural differences can often make or break an alliance. Language and perception barriers can prevent clear communication and understanding in any relationship, as can preconceived ideas and erroneous opinions of the objectives and operational factors associated with the partnership. Even where language is not perceived as a problem, cultural differences can still influence the relationship and arguably require more, not less, recognition. The alliance between British Airways and USAir faced both corporate and national cultural differences in the way they viewed the operation of the partnership, ultimately contributing to the eventual breakdown of the alliance – they spoke the same words, but not the same language. In comparison the relationship between AirUK and KLM found clear cultural similarities at both levels, encouraging increasing integration over time and resulting in a friendly acquisition by KLM of its smaller partner in the early 1990s.

The need for clear consideration of the choice of partner, prior to the formal partnership agreement is, therefore, essential. A useful approach in addressing this issue is to consider the potential partner profile in relation to the objectives of the relationship. In this respect the need to consider the complementary and contrasting characteristics each player brings to the relationship is important. Bronder and Pritzl have developed a useful cultural evaluation tool (see Figure 5, below) to help consider the different cultural aspects of the relationship needs.

By plotting each of the partner profiles on the web, this can help to provide a clearer picture of the partner contributions and characteristics, and prevent misunderstandings at a later stage in the relationship. Some aspects, such as quality, for example, would require similar profile locations on the web by all partners in order to ensure that the product or service brand offering is not compromised. However, each player also needs to bring something to the table to provide the added-value contribution to the partnership. In this respect certain skills or locational advantage may be expected to be provided by one partner or the other.

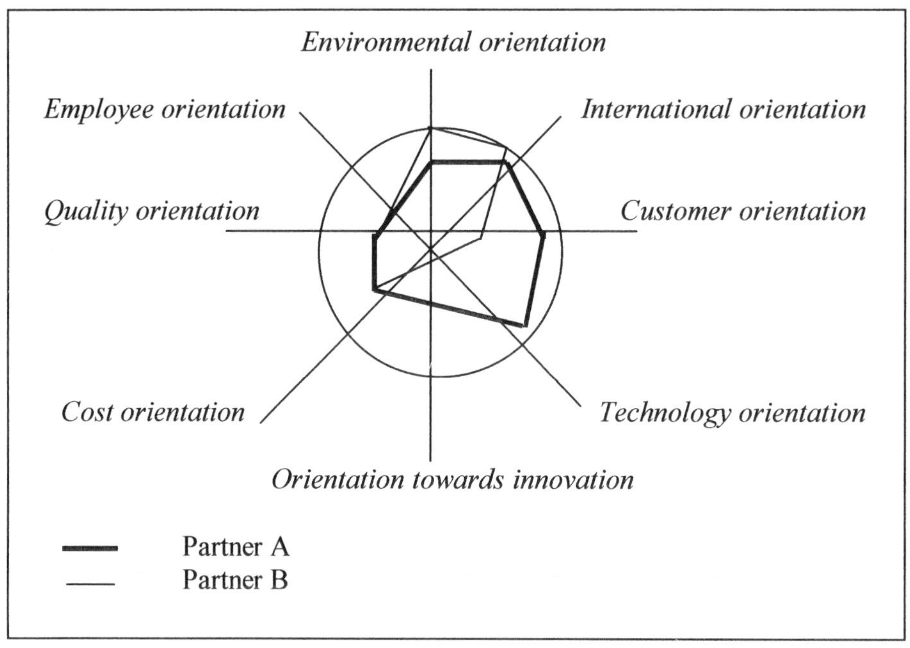

Figure 5: Comparing partners' cultural profiles

Source: adapted from Bronder, C. and Pritzl, R. (1992) (9)

Although this evaluation can assist in identifying a partner with the best cultural profile, in reality the ideal choice may not be available. As a result, there may be a need to work through inter-cultural differences throughout the development and existence of the relationship. The risk in this situation is to allow the differences to reduce the gain from potential value-added benefits. The challenge is to adapt to the cultural mix brought about through the partnership, and to manage this in such a way as to still gain from the benefits both can provide.

➢ *Balance of power and trust*

Establishing a realistic balance of power and trust can prove to be more difficult than it seems. Evidence suggests that many firms, when calibrating the benefits brought to the relationship by each partner, will overestimate the importance of their own contribution – and, therefore, their expected returns – against those of the other players. Where an imbalance of size exists between the players, this can exacerbate the problem. Larger players will often have more advanced systems, processes and infrastructure, and will, therefore, be tempted to assume direction and control of the relationship, sometimes leaving smaller players feeling aggrieved and manipulated. In these circumstances, trust can be reduced and potential benefits from exchange and joint development may be compromised. It is, thus, important in any partnership to recognise and respect the value of the contribution of each of the parties concerned. (In truth, if this is not the case, consideration should be given to whether the relationship is relevant at all!) Where equity can be established, evidence shows that this will encourage a better and more productive working relationship.

For smaller players, where an acceptable balance of power and trust can be established, the resultant partnership can offer a protected market for its service/product offering and allow a specialist provider to work closely with the larger players to tailor products or services as required. Thus, benefits accrue to all parties. Evidence of this was found in the survey of the telecommunications, airlines and the insurance industries. Here, smaller players operated within large network alliances, supplying their service in a particular niche area to members of the network.

A key warning, however, which must be borne in mind is the difference between size and capabilities. A small, but dynamic partner can add significant benefits to a relationship. Equally, a tie-up with a large and competent player can bring advantages. However, where a potential partner is struggling, or is recognised to be a weak player in the industry, it is unlikely that a subsequent partnership with such a player will bring significant competitive advantage to the relationship. On the contrary, it is more likely to bring the stronger partner down to a lower level, if only due to the opportunity cost foregone of alternative partnerships with stronger players in the industry as it continues to consolidate.

Two weak players joining forces will usually create a larger weak operation, with all the added complexities of managing the relationship to deal with. In contrast, two strong players can create a formidable challenge and competitive dynamic within the industry.

- *Senior management commitment and communication*

Although agreement for the strategic alliance is often established at senior executive level, it is at the operational level that the value-added benefits need to realised, and where the relationship will ultimately be made or broken. Many organisations which find partnership a struggle, suffer from poor internal communications and, hence, in many cases, the poor motivation of the employees involved in the day-to-day operationalisation of the relationship. One insurance organisation in the survey allied with another in the same industry admitted struggling for over a year and a half before the relationship finally failed. Those involved in the partnership saw little validity in the alliance and, therefore, had little commitment to making it work.

Employees can also feel highly vulnerable in this situation. Often hived off from the mainstream work of the organisation to work in a complex and possibly-fraught relationship, they may find they lack the key skills required to manage this type of operation. Without support and a clear understanding of the objectives they are striving for from senior management, many can become disillusioned and under-committed to the task in hand. It is, therefore, critical that clear communication of the importance and objectives of the partnership from senior management is ensured, and that on-going support and training for those involved is provided. Figure 6, page 79, highlights the key skills that may be expected from a partnership team when managing this form of operation.

- *The ease of transference of skills and knowledge*

Each partner within an alliance needs to offer something of value in order to ensure its continued existence within the relationship. This raises the issue of openness or transparency between the partners. Access to such things as skills, processes or research and development can provide a valuable glue which links the two partners together and creates the possibility of synergistic benefits being developed for the parties concerned. However, this action can also create potential risks. An aggressive partner may use this opportunity to acquire the other partner's capabilities or market, or use it to calibrate their weaknesses prior to termination of the relationship. The aggressive player may then use these newly acquired abilities and/or knowledge outside the partnership to leap-frog over other players in the industry, or even to acquire the now more vulnerable previous partner.

Thus, the risks and benefits of transparency in an alliance partnership also need to be managed for best advantage. In this respect a clear understanding of the partners' aims and objectives, and the influences acting on them from the external environment will, again, help to balance the perception of the relationship.

Organisational development and change management
negotiation skills
production/service
personnel
finance
procurement
logistics
information systems integration
legal/regulatory issues
public relations
employee communications
organisational behaviour
strategic analysis
cross-cultural understanding
flexibility and co-operation
co-specialisation
learning and internalisation capabilities

Figure 6: Management skill requirements in an alliance team

However, a constant monitoring of this is important as strategic alliances are dynamic entities and motivation and pressures constantly change as the industry and environment develops. This may possibly generate a change in the approach of a partner to the alliance.

➢ *Experience and learning capabilities*

Previous research has suggested that the more experience a firm has in partnering, the higher the success rate of future relationships will be. (10) In this respect, success is defined as the ability of a firm to achieve its given objectives, whether these are restricted to short term acquisitive ones or whether they extend to a longer term co-operative partnership with more synergistic potential. This is logical as increased experience is likely to lead to a better understanding of issues associated with partnering and, consequently, in increased confidence and capability in dealing with them.

However, experience can only be drawn upon if it is well communicated and openly used as a learning tool within the organisation. Often mistakes that are made in one part of the organisation in connection with an alliance may be hidden from other parts in an attempt to disguise the problems they generated. Alternatively, a simple lack of communication, or a poor corporate memory due to high churn rates, will prevent potential future participants from learning of challenges already experienced within the organisation. Consequently, a high level of organisational experience alone does not necessarily indicate a partner with a high level of alliance capability.

As a result, in order to draw effectively on its partnering experience, a firm also needs to have a learning orientation where experiences of partnering and best practice are exchanged through regular meetings or information exchange processes. For many firms, particularly large organisations where, traditionally, communication has been difficult and where size and distance within the organisation can present blocks to communication, this is a highly challenging task. However, without this exchange, experience has little relevance to the partnering equation.

➢ *External factors*

External factors will also have an influence upon a partner relationship. Where the industry is experiencing highly turbulent and unpredictable levels of change, and/or where the market is mature, firms will be more likely to need the security of a partnership. This is particularly the case where networks are already appearing and firms recognise that they will need to remain within a network in order to protect their market positions. These circumstances are more likely to generate greater commitment to a co-operative approach to the relationship by a firm, rather than to a risky approach where the firm runs the risk of losing its position within a larger network by taking a shorter term aggressive stance. Equally, high levels of competition or consolidation within the industry are likely to generate the same response.

As these networks continue to grow, players may, however, take the opportunity to shift from one network to another. A useful example of this is the switch by Finnair during 1998 from Lufthansa's Star alliance to the One World British Airways alliance. This raises the importance of considering the network as the critical business variable, rather than the direct partnership agreement being entered into. The shift to the One World alliance by Finnair increased the weight of that network within the airline industry. Shifts such as these can then stimulate further movements within the industry. It is, therefore, important when entering a strategic partnership to consider the current network and potential shifts that could occur prior to committing to a particular group, particularly as commitment to one group can mean an opportunity cost of exclusion from another.

➢ *Analysing partner positions of intent*

The issues outlined above can influence the form of intent a particular party may pursue within an alliance arrangement. These should be considered together in order to help to determine the potential viability and direction of a partnership, both at the onset of the relationship and through the various phases of its of development.

As Figure 7, below, illustrates, where the factors discussed above engender little co-operative or competitive intent from a partner, the relationship will tend to be disbanded within a short period as little motivation exists to continue pursuance of the partnership (box 1). However, where a high level of co-operative expectation is generated, but little competitive impetus, a partner will be likely to pursue a largely synergistic relationship. This type of approach tends to favour open, longer term relationships with a strong emphasis upon joint value creation and exchange between the players involved (see box 2). In contrast, where influences on a firm encourage a strong competitive, but little co-operative, intent (see box 4) these relationships tend to be shorter term alliances. In this type, once key skills, competencies or resources have been transferred from the other partner, the acquiring firm will either withdraw from that relationship or, in the case of a dominant player, may undertake an aggressive acquisition of the lesser partner.

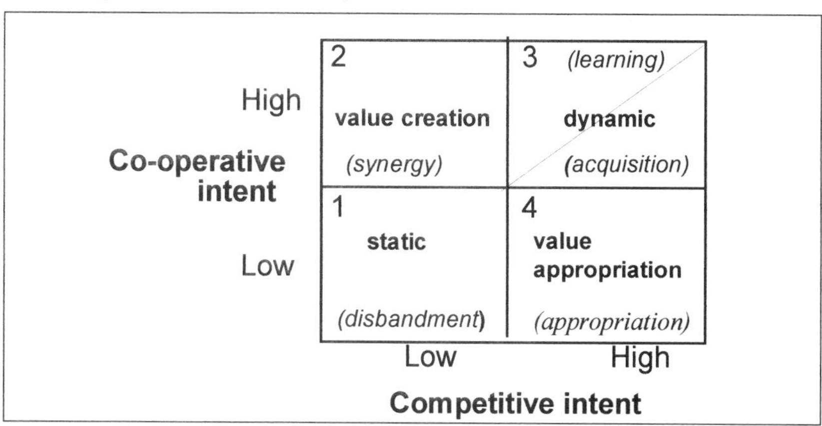

Figure 7: The Co-operative /Competitive matrix

From the research, it was found that neither the solely co-operative, nor the solely competitive player was, however, gaining the maximum value from the alliance. Firms which fell into the co-operative category were generating synergies, but often failed to maximise the potential learning and development that could be gained from the other partner/s. Equally, the purely competitive acquisitive firms were failing to benefit from any potential longer-term synergistic benefits prior to jumping back into the competitive market place. Those firms which did succeed in maximising both benefits fitted into the top right hand box of the matrix (box number 3). These firms were able to use the synergistic benefits of the relationship as the "glue" of the partnership, but were also able to convert the competitive aspect of intent into a positive, learning approach within the organisation.

Consideration of each partner's intent in this way, can enable firms to analyse their own existing and potential position in relation to a partner. Where both partners have similar intents, the relationship can be managed on that basis. However, where partner intent conflicts, or are likely to move in different directions as the relationship and the external environment continues to change and develop, key problems will need to be addressed.

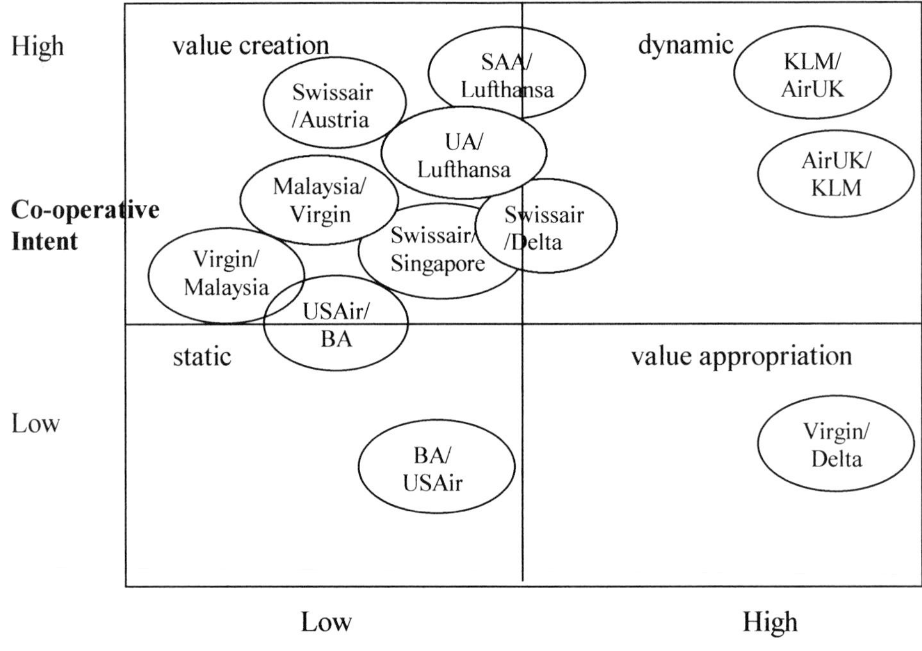

Figure 8: Plotting Organisational Strategic Approaches: Airline Example

The general strategic intent of an organisation in terms of its approach to relationships can also be plotted through this form of analysis. As Figure 8, on page 82, illustrates, the airline alliances that have been plotted on the co-operative/competitive matrix from the research data collected in the survey demonstrate different forms of strategic approach to the relationships by the different companies involved.

Virgin, for example, appears to pursue a highly focused approach to alliance relationships. The company can be seen to target Malaysian Airlines in a very co-operative partnership and Delta Airlines in a more aggressive short term relationship, with specific objectives. In contrast, Swissair's relationships with different partners are consistent and appears to be moving towards a more dynamic approach as they develop a highly co-operative environment. The breakdown in the early 1990s of the British Airways/USAir partnership was predictable, given the lack of co-operative or competitive intent of the company, and the alternative partnership options that were available. However, USAir appeared to have been less aware of the potential vulnerability of the alliance, given their stronger co-operative emphasis to the partnership. KLM and AirUK demonstrated a high level of co-operative and competitive intent, which was transformed into a learning and integrating relationship. This has continued to develop since the research was completed and moved to total integration during the 1990s between the two companies.

Summary and Conclusion

Strategic alliance management offers organisations significant opportunities and potential benefits, providing they can navigate through the maze of pitfalls and complexity that accompanies this form of operation. Partner intent is often ignored or is given insufficient consideration, both prior to entry and often during the existence of the relationship. However, internal and external influences on a firm will combine to dictate the intent with which each partner enters into a relationship, and will continue to do so as the relationship develops. Clear calibration of the intent of all the partners involved in an alliance, the extent of complementarity and areas of uncertainty can, therefore, help to improve the chances of success of the relationship. This is applicable both at the operational level, in terms of on-going management of the direct partnership, and also in tracking the overall strategic approach to alliance building by a particular firm within the industry. This chapter has, therefore, focused upon some of the key factors which research has found to influence partner intent, and which will have a fundamental impact on the successful management of a business partnership.

References

(1) Harbison and Pekar, *A practical guide to alliances: leapfrogging the learning curve*. Booz-Allan & Hamilton, 1993

(2) Doz, Y. and Hamel, G. *Alliance Advantage.* Boston: Harvard Business School Press, 1998

(3) Bleeke, J. and Ernst, D. The Way to Win in Cross-Border Alliances. *Harvard Business Review* November/December, 1991, pp.127-135

(4) As (2)

(5)(a) Berg, S.V., Duncan, J. and Friedman, P. *Joint Venture Strategies and Corporate Innovation.* Cambridge: Oelgeschlager, Gunn and Hain, 1982

(5)(b) Mohr, J. and Spekman, R. Characteristics of Partnership Success: Partnership Attributes, Communication Behaviour, and Conflict Resolution Techniques. *Strategic Management Journal*, Vol. 15, 1994, pp.135-152

(5)(c) As (3)

(6)(a) Grant, R.M. The Resource-Based Theory of Competitive Advantage: Implications for Strategy Formulation. *California Management Review*, Vol. 33, No 3, 1991, pp.114-135

(6)(b) Hennart, J.F. A Transaction Costs Theory of Equity Joint Ventures. *Strategic Management Journal*, Vol. 9, 1988, pp.361-374

(6)(c) Kogut, B. Joint Ventures: Theoretical and Empirical Perspectives, *Strategic Management Journal*, Vol. 9, 1988, pp.319-332

(6)(d) Lorange, P and Roos, J *Strategic Alliances Formation, Implementation and Evolution.* Oxford: Blackwell Publishers, 1992

(6)(e) Mahoney, J.T. and Pandian, J.R. The Resource-Based View Within the Conversation of Strategic Management. *Strategic Management Journal*, Vol. 13, 1992, pp.363-380

(6)(f) Mohr, J. and Nevin, J.R. Communication Strategies in Marketing Channels: A Theoretical Perspective. *Journal of Marketing,* no. 54, 1990, pp.36-51

(6)(g) As (5)(b)

(7)(a) Hamel, G. *Competitive Collaboration: Learning, Power and Dependence in International Strategic Alliances*. Unpublished thesis, 1990

(7)(b) As (6)(c)

(7)(c) Lei, D. and Slocum, J. W. Global Strategy Competence-Building and Strategic Alliances. *California Management Review,* 1992, Vol.35, Fall, pp.81-92

(8)(a) Hamel, G. Competition for Competence and Inter-Partner Learning Within International Strategic Alliances. *Strategic Management Journal*, Vol. 12, 1991, pp.83-103

(8)(b) As (6)(d)

(8)(c) As (7)(c)

(8)(d) Lorange, P., Roos, J. and Bronn, P.S. Building Successful Strategic Alliances. *Long Range Planning*, Vol. 25, no. 6, December 1992, pp.10-18.

(8)(e) Lynch, R.P. Building Alliances to Penetrate European Markets. *Journal Of Business Strategy*, March/April 1990, pp.4-8

(8)(f) Lyons, M.P. Joint-ventures as Strategic Choice: a Literature Review. *Long Range Planning,* Vol. 24, no. 4, 1991, pp.130-144

(8)(g) Devlin, G. and Bleackley, M. Strategic Alliances: Guidelines for Success. *Long Range Planning*, 21 (5), 1988, pp.18-23

(9) Bronder, C. and Pritzl, R. Developing Strategic Alliances: A Conceptual Framework for Successful Co-operation. *European Management Journal,* Vol. 10, issue 4, December 1992, pp.412-421

(10) Pekar, P. and Allio, R. Making Alliances Work: Guidelines for Success. *Long Range Planning*, Vol. 27, no. 4, 1994, pp.54-65

Chapter 4

THE VALUE-BASED APPROACH TO STRATEGY

Scott Lichtenstein

Introduction

What do you really care about? What drives you on? What is your Number 1 priority in life? Is it a lust for money? A craving for adventure? Are you *into* relationships? Are you family-minded? A control freak?

Whatever is important to you – and to all of us as individuals – is a reflection of the values we hold. Our attitudes, opinions and beliefs about what matters to us and to others make up our value system. Key elements in this are, of course, the relative importance of our priorities and, for many people, the level of motivation applied to achieving the goals based on them. Values are of primordial importance to our conduct. And what applies to individuals also applies to companies.

Researchers interested in a *people-focused* approach to strategy, and especially differentiation as a generic strategy, have taken an increasing interest in the role of values as behavioural determinants. In the words of Scott Bedbury, director of Nike's and Starbuck's world-wide advertising programmes, "being different is all about values – your values, your brand's values, and your company's values. Your values are what sets you apart." (1) He sees strategic thinking rooted in *value-based corporate visioning* as an essential springboard to creating something new.

For some firms, such visioning could result in the discovery of sources of intangible competitive advantages, which competitors cannot match, as their value systems are too divergent. For others, value-based visions could result in superior relationships with both internal and external stakeholders, a fact conducive to financial success and longevity, as the firms create a better basis for mutual trust. The more positive values are *embedded* in companies, and the more these values can be *operationalised* through appropriate strategies, the more likely the success.

Academics and practitioners, seeking to understand patterns in individuals' and organisations' decision-making and behaviours, have extensively researched the value-based approach to strategy, as we shall see. In doing so, they have had many different motivations and research angles, organisational effectiveness, strategy formulation and implementation and change programme management, for example. At the heart of all their research thrusts, however, is a purpose that lies at the very heart of all strategic study – the attempt to decipher the real goals of those who lead companies.

This chapter will, therefore, outline the various facets of the strategy-values relationship. The first part will outline a "values as strategy match" perspective and seek to provide a coherent definition of superordinate and subordinate values. Next, we will address the strategic nature of values in the context of organisational identity, purpose and effectiveness. Finally, we will discuss strategic leadership and the relationship between executive values and strategic action.

Strategy as values match: significance and definition

The strategy-as-values-match perspective argues that the strategic analyst's primary concern should be with identifying the purpose, goals and values of an organisation. Secondly, the analyst should be actively focusing on any changes needed in the organisation's value thrust, in order to achieve a better match with the aspirations of employees and expectations of stakeholders and society at large. Those who take this view believe that strategy should be concerned with creatively shaping the future, not merely trying to predicting it. (2)

Managerial research into values and value systems is important because it gives an insight into those beliefs and attitudes, which underpin executive decision-making and ensuing behaviours. There is concurrence amongst researchers like Becker and Connor that values are important as a scientific variable in management research "...primarily because they underline choice behaviour". (3) In strategy terms, choice behaviour includes strategic action, a topic to be discussed more fully in the section on strategic leadership.

Values theorists such as Allport, Maslow, Graves and Rokeach (4) argue that values are central to individual human motivation, beliefs and desires, and that values underpin the actions of groups, in particular organisations and cultures. In fact, they see values as *the* major research variable in the triangular relationship among values, beliefs and behaviour. (5)

In this context, however, a value is not regarded by them as an ethical construct. (6) Ethical issues dealing with moral concerns such as "right" and "wrong" are commonly not the focus of researchers into managerial values, however much we may think otherwise. As Hall asserts, any such confusion between values and ethics is, in fact, linked to the historical tradition of values going back to the Ten Commandments, Socrates and Aristotle when "values" were synonymous with "virtue", a narrowly prescribed set of qualities of human and leadership excellence. (7)

Human values should not, therefore, be confused with moral values. Our concern is with the first and not the second.

Value Type Groupings

In management research, a variety of value categories are used. According to Bourne, these can include personal values, cultural values, social values, institutional values, work values, brand values, consumer values and managerial or executive values. (8) To simplify the numerous types of values found in the literature, we will classify the values with which we are chiefly concerned into two groups. Group 1 contains *personal managerial/executive* values. Group 2 covers *societal/organisational* values.

➢ *Group 1: Personal managerial/executive values*

By definition, these are values which pertain to the individual, as manager or executive. Their nature is trickier to establish, however. According to Becker and Connor, "The most common, and probably most serious, problem encountered in the study of human values is definitional" (9) Nevertheless, Rokeach's lowest-common-denominator definition is one which is widely accepted: "A value" he contends "is an enduring belief that a specific mode of conduct or end-state of existence is personally or socially preferable to an opposite or converse mode of conduct or end-state of existence". (10) Rokeach, perhaps more significantly, differentiates between instrumental values (means to ends) and terminal values (ends in themselves).

But there is a lack of a universal recognition of the importance of the sub-division between instrumental and terminal values (11) and Becker and Conner put the emphasis, instead, on "global beliefs about desirable end-states". (12) Hofstede's definition is similarly bland: "a broad tendency to prefer certain states of affairs over others" (13), as is that of Hambrick and Brandon. They reckon that a value is a "broad and relatively enduring preference for some state of affairs". (14)

VALUE ELEMENT	ATTRIBUTE	LITERATURE
preferences	values are concerned with choices or alternatives	(Jacobs *et al.* 1962)
	with the ordering alternatives according to preferences	(Cyert and March, 1963)
	preferences for courses of action and outcomes	(Beyer, 1981)
endurance	values are enduring beliefs	(Rokeach, 1973)
	or combining with the former dimension, "enduring preferences"	(Hambrick and Brandon, 1988)
guides	values are determined as guides to behaviour or action	(Lewin, 1944; Rokeach, 1968)
	modes of conduct	(Becker and Conner, 1986)
centrality	values are centrally held beliefs	(Rokeach, 1968; Lessig, 1976)
	desired end states	(Rokeach, 1973; Becker and Connor, 1986)
abstractness	values are abstract or ambiguous concepts	(Lessig, 1976; Eden *et al.*, 1979)

Table 1: Value elements

A general agreement among researchers does exist, however, as to the elements which make up values, as summarised by Baker and Jenkins on the basis of the findings of leading scholars. (15) These are given in Table 1, above.

Ultimately, a value is, in short, an internalised personal *action-driver*. Values are deep-seated beliefs about what is desirable, which underpin beliefs and behaviour. Values can result from *a priori* reasoning or can be the product of contextual experience – family, business etc, – or both. They can be strongly or weakly held. Note that personal values always carry a *social* connotation since they affect our relationships with others. They contrast with values which are held by members' of a society at large which are referred to as *societal.*

To the strategy practitioner, the concept of values-as-action-drivers is obviously problematic. It suffers from ambiguity and abstraction. We are on firmer ground when we talk of personal attitudes and beliefs. The former are generally seen as being object-specific (16) or situation-specific. (17) Thus, we could have a positive/negative attitude towards a particular product, person or market-place. The latter – a belief – is the output of our knowledge (or ignorance) base and our reasoning. It is about what we regard, on the basis of what we know or think we know, as fact and fiction; it has to do with what is thought to exist now and in the future (18)*; it is about what is.* Certainly it is a necessary basis for action but, before it becomes an action-driver, it needs to be transformed into a value, just as a value needs to be transformed into purpose and action.

As noted by Kluckholn, values and beliefs reinforce each other but are conceptually distinct. (19) A value is a belief which is so strongly held that it becomes a motivational force.

➢ *Group 2: Societal/organisation values*

Clearly, all societal/organisational values are derived from personal values. Organisations, by definition, are themselves inanimate entities; it is coalitions of people in their various roles as organisation member that give them life. But it is a fact that, firstly, the mere aggregation of human beings and, secondly, their organisation within diverse leadership systems inside organisations makes for manifold differences between the nature of values at the personal and organisational level.

A key question follows from this. Are the values enunciated by the company the result of a co-operative or competitive dynamic between those of important managers and those of the CEO? Are the vision of the leader and his political power within the organisation so strong that his/her value system can be imposed on others? Or are we dealing with a negotiated value concensus around the vision of the leader. Here, the focus of analysis is the interaction between the stated personal values of the individuals and the stated values of the group – be it a team, division, company (or other form of organisation) or even society. (20)

The intriguing feature in this is the possible ambivalence that may lie within the leader's role as a corporate executive (seeking disciplined implementation of agreed strategy) and as politician (seeking value consensus). Given that a key feature of the leader's role is seen, more and more, as harnessing the social forces in the organisation and guiding values, this can pose acute dilemmas. (21)

For example, an analysis of the organisational values of Apple (22) would be nonsensical without reference to Steve Job's vision for the company. What does this mean for the organisational dynamics of Apple? What would happen, one wonders, in a company like Apple to renegade senior executives whose values were at such variance with those of the CEO, as a result of cognitive dissonance, that they were seen as deviant? This is an issue we will return to later.

Corporate and organisational values are, in fact, often used interchangeably in management research. Corporate or "core" values are often seen not as values associated with humans, but as elements of a particular ideology or philosophy. Collins and Porras describe them as, "The organisation's essential and enduring tenets – a small set of guiding principles; not to be confused with specific cultural or operating practices; not to be compromised for financial gain or short term expediency". (23)

Corporate values are part and parcel of organisational identity and their articulation is, in fact, conceived as a function of leadership by Bourne. (24) When core values are strong and a company has a strong sense of what it stands for, the leader embodies the vision and values – and potentially vice versa.

Societal values are based on beliefs that are held by society at large. They amount to group norms that, although they have been internalised by individuals, are held in common by the membership of the group. (25) As such, they represent a societal guide to conduct.

The implications of values for corporate strategy

A key theme in the strategy-as-values-match perspective is the fit between corporate values and the aspirations of employees. It is thought that this "fit" is integral to the establishment of a distinct corporate identity. Such an identity can confer on a company strategy a potential source of competitive advantage that cannot be easily copied and raise commitment to such a strategy. The chance to raise organisational effectiveness through the emotional and logical attachment between employee and company is implicit in congruence between employee and company values, a fact which has major additional implications for the process and implementation of strategy.

➢ *Values and corporate identity*

Collins and Porras conceive of "core values" as part and parcel of organisational identity. (26) Effective leaders embody and communicate the company's core values. For example, Disney's corporate values of No Cynicism; Creativity, Dreams and Imagination; Fanatical Attention To Detail as well as and the promulgation of wholesome American values reflect the original vision of Walt Disney and are what gives the company its unique identity, in part, if not in whole. It is difficult to conceive of a discussion of Disney's strategy without reference to its identity.

These writers argue that the difference between good companies and visionary companies is that the latter have a strong (or stronger) sense of their core values (see Figure 1, page 93). Core values, along with the corporate purpose informed by them, are, as they see it, are the central ideology of a company. Visionary companies such as Sony, Disney, Merck, IBM to name a few, have value-based ideologies as their core.

In strategy terms, Collins and Pore's core ideology and vision represent the "why" of the business. Why do we exist as a business? What is our purpose? If corporate values are central to the "why" of organisations, strategy, obviously, is the "what". What must we do to carry out our value-based vision? Visionary companies are those where the "why" and "what" are in lock-step.

Figure 1: The Vision-Ideology Linkage
Adapted from Built to Last, *Collins and Porass (1997)*

Arie de Geus, in his book *The Living Company*, identified a further connection – between values, identity and corporate longevity. (27) Shell, where he was a strategic planner, became interested in the question "What happens after the oil runs dry?" It commissioned research which found that the average life expectancy of a Fortune 500 company or its equivalent could be, on the basis of past data, 40 to 50 years. It also learned that, from 1970 to 1983, one third of the Fortune 500 companies had either been acquired, merged, or broken into pieces. (28) To find the secrets of success, Shell decided to study companies which not only were older than itself, having weathered fundamental change in the business environment around them, but which had also retained their corporate identity.

In studying these long-lived companies, the Shell researchers found that one of the key success factors was that these companies were cohesive and had a strong sense of their own identity. The corporate identity was not, however, the mission statement or the business definition. In fact, the Shell study found that companies changed their business definition throughout the life of the organisation. What the corporate survivors seemed to focus on predominantly when they made changes was what would bind together the members of the work community. As a result, de Geus states, "only a sense of common identity – a feeling of belonging to a social system with strong definition of self could have surmounted the metamorphosis of the original businesses that the profiled companies went through". (29)

The study revealed "a very suggestive link" between long-lived companies and a strong sense of values. In exploring the boundaries of corporate identity, *introception*, according to de Geus, is key: the awareness of the values of the company co-exist with the values of the individuals within the corporation – and every member is aware of this coexistence. He argues further that:

"A company has a collective sense of the answer to the definitive question about corporate identity: who belongs? Who is considered part of 'us'? Conversely, who does not belong and thus, is part of the surrounding world? There is no ambiguity about who belongs and who does not. At the level of introception, the company's members know who is prepared to live with the company's set of values. Whoever cannot live with those values, cannot or should not be a member."(30)

Common values linking the individual and the organisation, it is argued, establishes common ground as a basis of the relationship between the individual and the organisation. If so, there would be no possibility of political infighting within the company on the basis of cognitive dissonance. In de Geus's view value consonance is a sine qua non – "Members must share the set of institutional values that rest at the core of a company's persona". (31)

➢ *The values-purpose link*

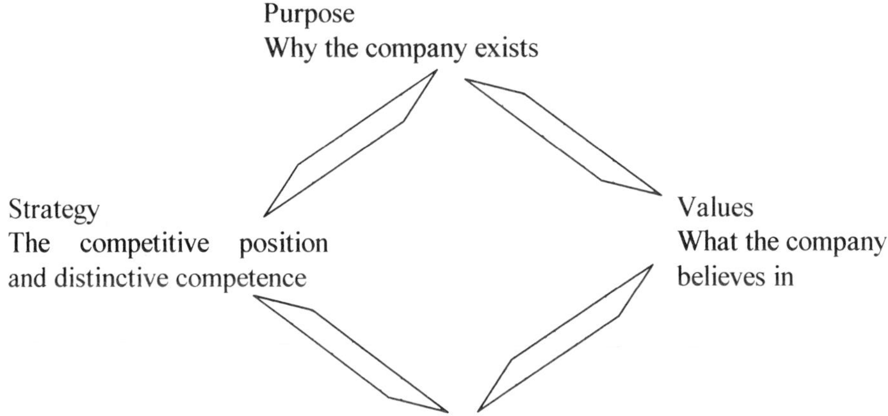

Figure 2: The Ashridge Mission Model
Source: Campbell, Devine and Young, 1990, p.26

Another theme in the strategy-as-values match is the examination of a company's purpose. One of the first group of authors to popularise purpose in the strategy literature was Lynch and Kordis. In their *Strategy of the Dolphin*, they coined the Americanism *on-purpose* to describe companies which were *in synch* with the values of their consumers. (32)

Some business theorists view values as intrinsic to the strategy formulation process through the manner in which a company's Mission is based on its value-driven vision. Based on a research project of 53 companies, Campbell, Devine and Young investigated organisations with a strong sense of purpose, or strong culture, or both. (33) Figure 2, page 94 illustrates the key themes that emerged from their research.

This model argues that a strong sense of corporate purpose exists when these four elements of mission are tightly woven and reinforce each other. Values inform the policies and behaviours to give purpose. Purpose is achieved through the strategy. The authors argue that their model reflects the left and right brain of companies with a mission.

One example of the workings of the model given in Figure 2, page 94 is that of British Airways' "Putting People First" Campaign. There is a commercial logic in this, but also a human element, in that the organisation is a better place to work if people care for each other. Another is the Hewlett Packard approach to management – The HP Way, Managing by Walking Around (MBWA) – not only makes good business sense, it's also "the right way to behave". (34)

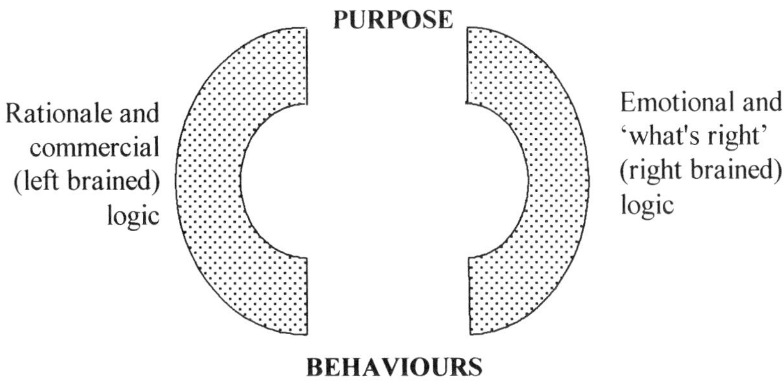

Figure 3: Left brain-Right brain

Source: Campbell et al. (1990), p.32

The conclusion is that, when the management philosophy and value system fit the strategy, the company has a strong sense of mission. When the behaviour standard reinforces the strategy and philosophy, an organisation has integrity. When a company's values, behaviour and strategy is not aligned, what a company does and says are two different things.

Organisational Effectiveness

Peters and Waterman's *In Search of Excellence* (35) and the *McKinsey's 7S* consultancy model (36) both underline the implications for a company of value-behaviour-strategy congruence. Indeed, the McKinsey model (Figure 4, below) points out that organisations are most *effective* when the 7 factors or elements fit together, and especially when strategy fits the values and when all other factors re-enforce the strategy and values.

The McKinsey model is widely used as a tool for calibrating the effectiveness of an organisation and helping to manage change. The lessons that come from this model are that there are hard elements (strategy, structure and systems) as well as soft elements. Companies must consider whether all their S's are *in synch* – especially the manner and speed with which societal values are changing. Companies must assess whether their organisational values – reflecting the personal values of leading executives – are relevant in the context of the changing business environment and in step with the changing values in society.

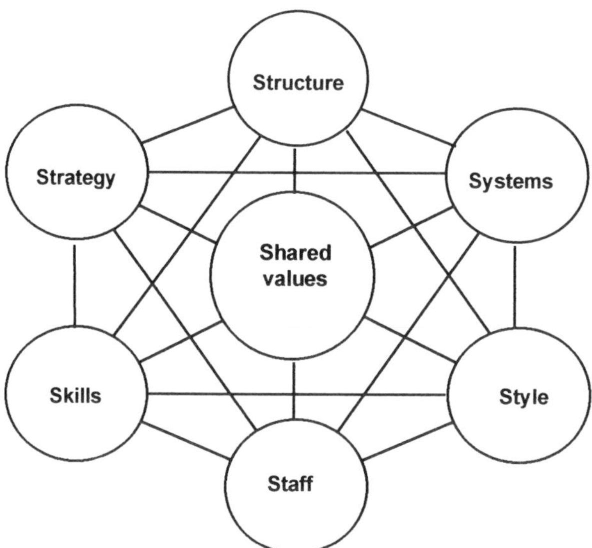

Figure 4: McKinsey 7-S framework

There are several linkages within the 7-S model that bear re-enforcing. Firstly, the match or conflict between the personal values of the employees and company's organisational values. Research by Posner, Kouzes and Schmidt (37) underlined yet again the assertion that shared values – value congruence – amongst companies and employees lead to higher levels of employee commitment. By contrast, managers who experienced "contention" (lack of clarity) about their own and the organisation's values, tended to have low commitment and were the most alienated from their work, having, not surprisingly, unfavourable work attitudes.

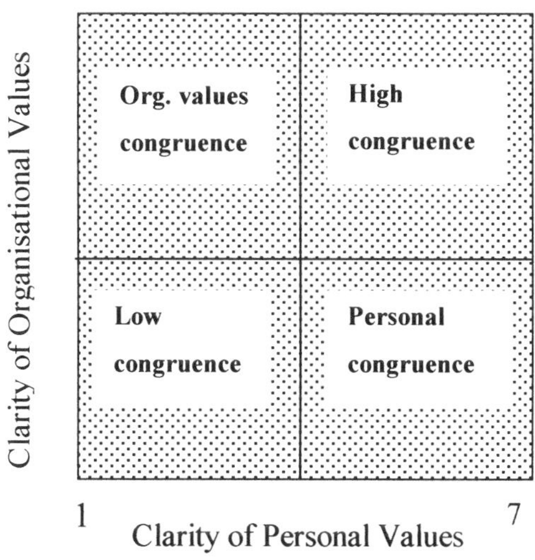

Figure 5: Person-Organisation Value Congruence

Source: Posner, B. Z., Kouzes, J.M. and Schmidt, W.H. 1993, p.174

Other studies have demonstrated empirically how values impact on personal and organisational effectiveness. Person-organisation shared values have shown a direct relationship to positive work attitudes. (38) The person-organisational fit has been shown to predict job satisfaction and organisational turnover a year later, and actual turnover after two years. (39) Operating unit performance has been linked to value congruence. (40) Indeed, Robert Haas, Levi Strauss Co. Chairman and CEO. argued that the alignment between organisational and personal values was the key driver of corporate success in his company. (41)

Recent publications such as Collins and Porras' *Built to Last* and De Geus' *The Living Company* have contributed to the strategy-as-values-match approach. But, whilst values can be a key source of organisational strength and capability, and therefore strategic thrust and competitive advantage, unless organisational values can give some prescriptive advice, its value as an approach is limited.

➢ *Strategic Leadership: The leadership-strategy match*

We now revert to the fundamental building block of values analysis: the individual. As previously discussed, the key individual responsible for embodying the core values of the organisation is the leader. Espousing, enunciating and implementing core values is the business of leadership.

"It's not the strongest that will survive, nor the most intelligent. It is the one most adaptable to change," wrote Charles Darwin in his Origin of Species. (42) Adaptability, in today's turbulent world, is a key leadership value – or should be.

How is it that someone like Al 'Chainsaw' Dunlop, ex-CEO of Sunbeam, can run a company into the ground whilst Richard Branson nimbly navigates various companies that make up the Virgin Group? This question gets to the heart of strategic leadership and allows us to recognise why the values-strategy debate is so important.

Ingrained values can act as filters which influence the perception of decision-makers and affect the strategic decisions of executives – for better or for worse. They can enhance creativity or block innovation. Everything depends on the match between leadership values and the objective market-place realities on which the company's success ultimately depends. And that means keeping value systems up-to-date.

➢ *The process of managerial influence*

Hambrick and Mason provide a pertinent framework for understanding the role of the top managers in influencing organisations. In their "Upper Echelon" theory, they argue that strategic action is a reflection of the values and cognitive bases and styles of top management. Confronted with ambiguity and ill-defined options which characterise strategic decisions, no two managers or management teams will necessarily choose – or even identify – the same solution. (43) Managers will make different decisions based on individual experiences and values. If we want to understand why managers differ in their strategic decision-making, we need to understand the managers themselves. Their model illustrates the process of strategic choice as a series of steps:

"First, a manager or even entire team of managers cannot scan every aspect of the organisation and its environment. The manager's field of vision – those areas to

which attention is directed – is restricted, posing a sharp limitation on eventual perceptions. Second, the manager's perception is further limited because one selectively perceives only some of the phenomena included in the field of vision. Finally, the bits of information selected for perception is interpreted through a filter woven by one's cognitive base and values. The manager's eventual perception of the situation combines with his or her values to form the basis of strategic choice." (44)

Three empirical studies have proven the strong link between the values-based perceptual filters of individual managers and the nature of the decisions they take:

- Prahalad and Bettis argue that managers have schemas or a "world-view" based on their experience which becomes the "dominant logic" prescribing the conceptualisation of a business and the administrative decisions taken. Different managers will make different decisions based on their individual experiences. (45)
- Miles and Snow examined the link between top management beliefs and strategy, structure, and process of companies in a variety of different industries. They found that firms led by managers who focused on effectiveness competed on the basis of innovation, whilst firms led by managers who focus on efficiency competed on the basis of cost control. (46)
- Kotey and Meredith analysed the strategies of owner-managers and found, predictably, that managers who espouse conservative values chose conservative strategies, and managers espousing entrepreneurial values pursued entrepreneurial strategies. (47)

Thomas and Ramaswamy sum up the research in this field by stating that "efforts that examine the impact of top managers on firm performance implicitly assume that the characteristics, biases or values of these managers are reflected in the resource allocation priorities". (48)

The strategic leadership literature does not only suggest that managerial perceptions play a significant role in shaping organisational direction, however. A significant focus is on examination of whether there are leaders with special characteristics suited to organisations pursuing particular strategies.

➢ *Matching managers to strategy*

The study of matching managers to strategy goes back to Chandler. (49) He linked different management styles and thinking by identifying "empire builders" such as Durant of General Motors and Richard Sears of Sears Roebuck, and "organisational builders" such as Alfred Sloan at GM and Robert Wood at Sears. Durant and Sears emphasised new products, markets and acquisitions, whilst their respective successors, Sloan and Wood, focused on administrative reform to seek to make their organisations more efficient and cost effective.

John Scully's *Odyssey: Pepsi to Apple* (50) colourfully describes the importance of the leader-strategy match. In the beginning, Apple embodied its leader, Steve Jobs, and his informal, innovative and creative style. As the company grew, a new style was required and John Scully, an excellent marketer from an eastern US "establishment", Pepsi, was brought in to boost the company's expansion overseas and guide its growth. When price competition became critical Michael Spindler, the conservative Chief Operating Officer, replaced Scully.

Be it Lee Iaccoca and Chrysler, Hewlett and Packard of Hewlett-Packard, or Cohen and Greenfield of Ben and Jerry's, anecdotal, theoretical and empirical evidence supports the need to align organisational priorities and executive profiles. Success seems to come when top executives chart the course of *organisational destiny* which is determined by their own personal characteristics, backgrounds and experiences. (51)

Matching managers to strategy in strategic management theory: The Miles and Snow Typology

In strategic management theory, managerial influence is reflected in typologies of strategic orientation. Typologies enable us to classify organisations in a framework which enables us to develop theoretical perspectives. (52) Typologies are useful because they highlight the essential features of separate, specific strategies, thus capturing their major commonalties and facilitating the study of general strategic patterns. (53) For example, an "expansion strategy" would best be administered by a "conqueror" type of manager. (54)

One of the best-known and widely-validated typologies is that of Miles and Snow. (55) It provides a description of strategy, structure and process identified in objective, observable and measurable terms. In particular, in their *strategic choice* view, they emphasise that:

".... organisational behaviour is only partially preordained by environmental conditions and that the choices which top managers make are the critical determinants of organisational structure and process." (56)

Reflecting on the roles of top management, Miles and Snow have developed a model of three strategic actor types which display an internally-consistent set of attributes relating to the entrepreneurial, engineering and administrative dimensions of the organisation's work. Each of the types works to a different but coherent set of values:

- *Defenders* deliberately maintain an environment for which a stable form of organisation is appropriate by a "creation of a narrow stable domain.... through a limited mix of products and customers, and aggressive efforts to 'protect' the domain from competitors." (57) Strict control of the organisation to ensure efficiency is achieved through "mechanistic structural and process mechanisms". Formal work cultures and centralised structures help control operating costs. Technology choices favour inflexible but cost-efficient methods. Most of their research and development relates to process improvements rather than product innovation.
- In contrast, *Prospectors* emphasise innovation as the source of competitive advantage. Finding and exploiting new product and market opportunities, "...maintaining a reputation as an innovator in product and market development may be as important as, perhaps even more important, than high profitability." (58) Offering a large array of state-of-the-art products, they target a variety of market segments. An "organic" structure-process mechanism accomplishes facilitation rather than control. Flexibility permits rapid responds to changes in the marketplace that reflects the top management group, which is dominated by marketing and research and development (R&D) experts.
- Defenders and Prospectors are at opposite ends of a continuum of "adjustment strategies"; *Analysers* are in the middle. Analysers pursue hybrid strategies that exhibit some features of the Prospector and Defender types. They minimise risk while maximising the opportunity for profit by combining the strengths of the Prospectors and Defenders. The Analysers take a "balanced" approach to strategic adaptation, operating like Prospectors in rapidly evolving domains while in the stable segments using a Defender approach. Intensive planning between the functions of marketing and production, applied research and product managers for the development of new products, centralised control mechanisms in functional divisions and decentralised control techniques in the product groups.

Thomas and Ramaswamy tested empirically the executive characteristics (referred to as the "administration" dimension) of the Miles and Snow typologies (59) and have concluded that:

- organisations pursuing distinctly dissimilar strategies (Analysers and Prospectors) were led by managers possessing distinctly dissimilar attributes;
- the strategy-manager match had a positive influence on performance, and a greater impact on performance than firm age, size, and industry membership.

They also tested Miles and Snow's contention that Prospectors and Defenders would be led by management teams with different profiles of skills, attributes and values.

To operationalise some of the hypothesised concepts, surrogate variables were used in their tests. Innovativeness and risk-taking was measured by age: younger managers are associated with these characteristics, whilst older managers are associated with risk-averse, conservative organisations. Hence, chronological age was used to measure innovativeness and risk-taking. Similarly, based on previous studies that found better educated executives are more receptive to new ideas (ie, more value adaptability) and associated with innovative organisations, innovative organisations are expected to have more top executives with higher levels of education. The number of years of formal education was used as a measure of open mindedness and creativity. As predicted, Prospector managers were significantly younger, had higher levels of education and shorter tenures than their Defender counterparts.

Thomas and Ramaswamy concluded that "this framework provides a generic set of strategies with internally consistent attributes which includes domain definition, which is well rooted in theory and provides a rational view of the competitive modes that organisations choose". (60)

Executive Values Research

Research into executive values had began in the 1960's and took a variety of forms. One of the most prominent early studies was the Allport-Vernon-Lindsay (A-V-L) Study of Values. (61) Six major values were believed to be held by individuals in varying degrees:

- Theoretical: The dominant interest of the theoretical man is the discovery of truth.
- Economic: The economic man is characteristically interested in what is useful.
- Aesthetic: The aesthetic man sees his highest value in form and harmony.
- Social: The highest value for this type is love of people.

Analogues in Other Value Schemes			
Allport, Vernon Lindzey (1960)	Rokeach (1973)	England (1967)	Hofstede (1980)
Social	Personal vs. Social World at peace National security Equality	Social equality Social welfare Liberalism Equality Compassion Employee welfare	Individualism
	Inner vs. other-directed Obedient Opolite Helpful Clean	Personal loyalty Loyalty Trust Obedience Honor Dignity	
Theoretical	Competence vs. morality Intellectual Logical Capable	Irrational behaviour Conflict Emotions Prejudice	Masculinity
		Entrepreneurialism Change Risk Competition	Uncertainty Avoidance
Economic	Delayed vs. immediate gratification Pleasure A comfortable life An exciting life	Extrinsic rewards Money Property	
Political	Personal Influence Prestige Power Influence	Power distance	

Table 2: A Distilled Set of Significant Executive Value Dimensions

Source: Hambrick and Brandon (1988), p.13 (18)(a)

- Political: The political man is interested in Power.
- Religious: The highest value of the religious man may be called unity.

In 1965 Guth and Taguiri used the A-V-L scheme for their study of business executives, and found that economic values were rated the highest. Social values were rated the lowest. Groups of scientists and research managers were also studied with both groups scoring high on the theoretical and lowest on the Social. (62) But the A-V-L instrument was not without its critics. It was seen to be a dubious predictor of behaviour, a major weaknesses in its use in values research. (63)

A variety of other value schemes attempting to explain and measure executive values have been developed since, such as Stanford Research Institute's Values and Life style Survey (VALS) and Kahle and Kennedy's List of Values (LOV). As Baker and Jenkins observe, however, there is no consensus on the most effective values inventory, although Rokeach's value survey has been operationalised by researchers the most. (64)

One of the most powerful recent models is Hambrick and Brandon's *Executive Value Dimensions*. (65) In producing this model they re-appraised the contents of other models (see Table 2, page 103). Hambrock and Brandon's EDV framework has six dimensions:

- Collectivism: to value the wholeness of humankind and of social systems; regard and respect for all people.
- Duty: to value the integrity of reciprocal relationships; obligation and loyalty.
- Rationality: to value fact-base, emotion-free decisions and actions.
- Novelty: to value change, the new the different.
- Materialism: to value wealth and pleasing possessions.
- Power: to value control of situations and people.

In developing this new values scheme, they hypothesized how these six value dimensions might be associated with specific organisational actions and attributes. (see Table 3, page 106 and 107)

Limitations on Executive Discretion

Hambrick and Brandon's investigation into the link between executive values has raised the important issue of the limits to executive "discretion" in converting values into action. Executives do not always have the freedom of action and it is only to the extent that they have that latitude that their values will influence organisational outcomes. Clearly, the firms' operating environment can also limit discretion. Lieberson and O'Conner found that profitability could be attributed to CEO's in industries with high advertising intensity and growth rates, than in commodity-like or low-growth industries.(66)

The degree to which the organisation allows the executive to formulate and execute actions is another important factor. For example, Miller and Toulouse found that CEO personality was more strongly related to strategy and structure in small firms in dynamic environments than in large firms in stable environments. (67) There is also an implicit assumption that the executive is able to envision different courses of action, which may not always be the case.

An executive who is restrained from exercising his or her own values in organisational choices could become extremely frustrated, particularly if they have strong values, which would lead to organisational "self-selection" – they would experience frustration and depart. They could also utilise their preferences into minor organisational choices, or perhaps into activities outside the organisation. It is unlikely they would neutralise their values to suit the lack of discretion. Although there is no research to indicate whether executives modify their values in the context of limits to action, research into the nature of values suggest that organisations don't change people's values – a reason why change programmes based on this assumption fail. A mismatch between values and discretion is an important area, which has not been adequately researched.

Conclusion

Values are a subject that goes to the very heart of our psychological being. It's no wonder then that strategists interested in gaining insight into executives and organisations should take an interest in this area. Business thinkers finding sources of differentiation and competitive advantage in the "soft", people-focused intangibles have bolstered the strategy-as-values match approach.

Like "quarks" in quantum physics, "black holes" in cosmology and "strange attractors" in systems thinking, values are still not adequately understood. This is not surprising considering values research is still a relatively

	Organisational Actions and Attributes				
Executive value	Strategy	Structure	Information/ Decision processes	Rewards	People
Collectivism	Significant corporate philanthropy; related diversification with many inter-unit flows	Flat structure; many committees	Participative decision processes	Rewards heavily tied to overall firm performance	Promote-from-within policies; lifetime employment
Duty	Long-term vertical relationships (suppliers and customers); little contract litigation against firm		Open, two-way communication channels; well-developed audit and control systems	Executive perquisites/ bonuses tightly tied to market norms	Long tenures; few layoffs
Rationality	Incremental strategies based primarily on "calculable" factors (eg, prices, costs, capacities)	Highly formalised structure	Comprehensive/ analytic processes	Highly formalized pay systems (eg, Hay); emphasis on quantitative performance measures)	Routinised personnel policies (eg, selection, evaluation, advancement); large personnel staffs

Novelty	Prospecting (many product-market initiatives)	Frequent re-organisations; structural ambiguity (matrix, etc.)	Spontaneity; decision-making outside formal channels and processes	Frequent changes in reward system; large incentives for innovation	Heterogeneous management cadre; limited pressure for conformity
Materialism	Portfolio churning (frequent acquisitions and divestitures)	Small staffs; low administrative intensity		Extraordinary executive pay and perks	Opportunistic hiring and firing of key executives
Power		Highly centralised	Tight control of information and resources at top of organization; Top-down decision-making	Subjective criteria for awarding (large) incentives	Pliant, supplicant subordinates

Table 3: Some Hypothesized Links between Executive Values and Actions

Source: D. C. Hambrick and G. L. Brandon (1988), Executive Values, p. 23 (18)

young field. It was only in the 1980's when In Search of Excellence (68) highlighted it as a business issue and Hambrick and Mason's Upper Echelon Theory opened up a research stream in the area of managerial perception and strategic action. (69)

Regarding theory development, work is needed in establishing the link between underlying needs, which drive values and beliefs, and ultimately, behaviour. The exploration of underlying needs as value-drivers has been verified by practitioners but not validated yet by academics. This will allow an understanding of the dynamics underlying organisational values as well as the interaction between individuals, markets and companies in the context of social change. This is much needed.

References

(1) *Fast Company*, issue 22, 1999, p.134

(2) Taylor, B., New Dimensions in Corporate Planning. *Long Range Planning*, December 1976, pp.80-105

(3) Becker, B.W. and Conner, P.E. On the Status and Promise of Values Research. *Management Bibliographies & Reviews*, 12, 2, 1986, pp.3-7

(4)(a) Allport, G.W. *Towards a General Theory of Action*, Part 4. New York: Harper Textbooks, 1951

(4)(b) Graves, C.W. Human Nature Prepares for a Monumentous Leap. *The Futurist*, 8, 1974, pp.72-87

(4)(c) Maslow, A. H. *The Farther Reaches of Human Nature.* New York: Viking Press. 1971

(4)(d) Rokeach, M. *Understanding Human Values: Individual and Societal.* New York: Free Press, 1979

(5) Hall, M.L.W. *Systems Thinking and Human Values: Towards a Practical organisational Intervention Methodology.* Thesis, University of Lincolnshire and Humberside, 1997

(6) As (3)

(7) As (5)

(8) Bourne, H. *Managers, Personal Values and Corporate Values: Towards a Research Agenda.* Working Paper, Cranfield Management College Series, 1999

(9) As (3)

(10) Rokeach, M. *The Nature of Human Values.* New York: The Free Press, 1973

(11)(a) Gutman, J. A Means-Ends Chain Model Based on Consumer Catagorisation Process. *Journal of Marketing*, Spring 1982, pp.60-72

(11)(b) Kitwood, T.M. and Smithers, A.G., Measurement of Human Values: An Appraisal of the Work of Milton Rokeach. *Educational Research*, Vol. 17, 1975, pp.175-9

(12) As (3)

(13) Hofstede, G. *Culture's Consequences: International Differences in Work-related Values.* London: Sage, 1980

(14) Hambrick, D.C. and Mason, P.A. Upper Echelons: The Organisation as a Reflection of its Top managers. *Academy of Management Review*, 9, 1984, pp.193-206

(15) Baker, S. and Jenkins, M. *The Role of Values in the Design and Conduct of Management Research: Perspectives on Managerial and Consumer Cognition.* Working Paper, SWP 4/93, Cranfield School of Management, 1993

(16) As (3)

(17) As (14)

(18)(a)Hambrick, D.C. and Brandon, G. L. Executive Values, *in* Hambrick, D.C. (ed.) *The Executive Effect: Concepts and Methods for Studying Top Managers.* Greenwich, Connecticut: JAI Press, 1988, pp.3-34

(18)(b)Jacob, P.E., Flink, J.J. and Shuchman, H.L. Values and their Function in Decision-Making. *American Behaviour Scientist*, 5, 9, 1962, pp.6-38

(19) Kluckholn, C. et al., Values and Values Orientations in the Theory of Action, *in* Parsons, T. and Shils, E.A. (eds.) *Towards a General Theory of Action.* Cambridge Mass: Harvard University Business Press, 1951

(20) Dade, P. *Various discussions and Training Manual.* Synergy Consulting, 1999

(21) Peters, T. and Waterman, R. *In Search of Excellence.* New York: Harper & Row. 1982

(22) Scully, J. *Odyssey: Pepsi to Apple.* Glasgow: HarperCollins, 1987

(23) Collins and Porras, *Built to Last.* London: Century Business, 1996

(24) As (8)

(25) As (20)

(26) As (23)

(27) de Geus, A. *The Living Company.* London; Nicholas Brealey Publishing, 1997

(28) As (27)

(29) As (27)

(30) As (27)

(31) As (27)

(32) Lynch, D. and Kordis, P. *Strategy of the Dolphin.* London: Hutchinson Business Books, 1988

(33) Campbell, A, Devine, M and Young, D. *A Sense of Mission.* Great Britain: Century Business. 1990

(34) As (33)

(35) As (21)

(36) *McKinsey's 7-S consultancy model, developed by management consultants McKinsey & Co.*

(37) Posner, B. Z., Kouzes, J.M., and Schmidt, W.H. Shared Values Make a Difference: A Empirical Test of Corporate Culture. *Human Resource Management*, 24, 3, 1985, pp.293-310

(38) Balazas, A.L. Values Congruency: The Case of the Socially Responsible Firm. *Journal of Business Research*, Vol. 20, 1990, pp.171-181

(38) As (37)

(39) O'Reilly, C.A., Chatman, J. and Caldwell, D.F. People and Organisational Culture: A Q-sort Approach to Assessing Person-Organisation Fit. *Academy of Management Journal*, Vol. 34, No. 3, 1991, pp.487-516

(40) Enz, C. and Schwenk, C.R., Values Congruency: The case of the Socially Responsible Firm. *Journal of Business Research*, 20, 1989, pp.171-181

(41) Haas, R. and Howard, R. *Values Make the Company: An interview with Robert Haas*. Harvard Business Review, January 1990

(42) Darwin, Charles *On the Origin of Species by Means of Natural Selection, or the Preservation of Favoured Races in the Struggle for Life*. London: John Murray, 1859

(43) As (18)

(44) As (18)

(45) Prahalad, C.K. and Bettis, R.A. The Dominant Logic: A New Linkage between Diversity and Performance. *Strategic Management Journal*, 7, 1986, pp.485-501

(46) Miles, R.E. and Snow. C.C. *Organization Strategy, Structure, Process*. New York: McGraw-Hill, 1978.

(47) Kotey, B. and Meredith, G.G., Relationship Among Owner/Manager Personal Values, Business Strategies, and Enterprise Performance. *Journal of Small Business Management*, Vol. 35, No.2, 1997, pp.37-64

(48) Thomas, A.S. and Ramaswamy, K. Matching Managers to Strategy: Further Tests of the Miles and Snow Typology. *British Journal of Management*, Vol. 7, 1996, pp.247-261

(49) Chandler, A. D. *Strategy and Structure: Chapters in the history of Industrial Enterprise*. Reprint edition, MIT Press, 1990

(50) As (22)

(51)(a)Miller, D. *The Icarus Paradox*. Harper Business, New York. 1990.

(51)(b)As (48)

(52)(a)Pinder, C.C. and Moore, L.C. The Resurrection of the Taxonomy to Aid the Development of Middle Range Theories of Organisational Behaviour. *Administrative Science Quarterly*, 24, 1979, pp.99-118

(52)(b)Doty, H.D., Glick, W.H. and Huber, G.P. Fit, Equifinality and Organisational Effectiveness: A Test of two Configurational Theories. *Academy of Management Journal*, 36, 1994, pp.1196-1250

(53) As (48)

(54) Wissema, J.G., Van Der Pol, H.W. and Messer, H.M. Strategic Management Archetypes. *Strategic Management Journal*, 1, 1980, pp.37-47

(55) As (46)

(56) As (46)

(57) As (46)

(58) As (46)

(59) As (48)

(60) As (48)

(61) As (4)

(62) Guth, W.D. and Taguri, R. Personal Values and Corporate Strategy. *Harvard Business Review* 43, (5), 1965, pp.123-132

(63) As (3)

(64) As (15)

(65) As (18)

(66) Lieberson, S. and O'Conner, J.F. Leadership and Organisational Performance: A Study of Large Corporations. *American Sociological Review*, 37, 1972, pp117-130

(67) Miller, D., Kets de Vries, M.F.R. and. Toulouse, J.M. Top Executive Locus of Control and its relationship to Strategic Marketing, Structure and Environment. *Academy of Management Journal,* 25, 1982, pp.237-235

(68) As (21)

(69) As (18)

Bibliography

Beyer, J.M. Ideologies, Values, and Decision Making in Organisations, *in* Nystrom, P.C. and Starbuck, W. H. (eds.) *Handbook of Organisational Design,* Vol. 2. Oxford: Oxford University Press, 1981, pp.166-202

Cyert, R.M. and March, J.G. *A Behavioural Theory of the Firm.* Englewood Cliffs, N.J.: Prentice-Hall, 1963

Eden, C., Jones, S. and Sims, D. *Thinking in Organisations.* London: MacMillan, 1979

Finkelstein, S. and Hambrick, D. *Strategic Leadership: Top Executives and Their Effects on Organisations.* Minn./St. Paul: West Publishing Company, 1996

Hunt, J. and Laing, B. Leadership: the Role of the Exemplar. *Business Strategy Review,* Volume 8, Number 1, 1997, pp.31-42.

Kiesler, S. and Sproul, L. Managerial Response to Changing Environments: perspectives and problem Sensing from Social Cognition. *Administrative Science Quarterly*, 37, 1982, pp.548-570

Lewin, K. Constructs in Psychology and Psychological Ecology. *University of Iowa Studies in Child Welfare*, 20, 1994, pp.1-29

Lessig, V.P, Measurement of Dependencies Between Values and Other Levels of the Consumer's Belief Space. *Journal of Business Research*, 83, 1976, pp.227-239

McDaniel, S.W. and Kolari. J.W. Marketing Strategy Implications of the Miles and Snow Typology, *Journal of Marketing*, 51, 1987, pp.19-30

Posner, B.Z and Schmidt, W.H. Values Congruence and differences between the interplay of personal and organizational value system. *Journal of Business Ethics*, 12, 1993, pp.341-247

Pettigrew, A. On Studying Managerial Elites. *Strategic Management Journal,* Vol. 13, 1992, pp.163-182

Prahalad, C.K. and Bettis. R.A. The Dominant Logic: A New Linkage Between Diversity and Performance. *Strategic Management Journal*, 7, 1986, pp.485-501

Rokeach, M.J. *Beliefs, Attitudes and Values.* San Francisco: Jossey Bass, 1968

Scully, J. *Odyssey: Pepsi to Apple*. Glasgow: HarperCollins, 1987

Shortell, S.M. and Zajac. E.J. Perceptual and Archival measures of the Miles and Snow's Strategic Types: A comprehensive Assessment of Reliability and Validity. *Academy of Management Journal*, 33, 1990, pp.817-822

Starbuck, W.H. and Milliken. F.J. Executives Perceptual Filters: What They Notice and How They Make Sense. *in* D.C. Hambrick (ed.). *The Executive Effect: Concepts and Methods for Studying Top managers*. JAU Press, Greenwich, CT, 1988

Zahara, S.A. and Pearce, J.A. Research Evidence on the Miles and Snow Typologies. *Journal of Management*, 16, 1990, pp.751-768

Chapter 5

GOVERNANCE AND PERFORMANCE: GOODWILL HUNTING

Keith MacMillan & Steve Downing

Introduction

The debate about corporate governance in the UK has moved on dramatically over the past five years and is still doing so in the New Economy era. Companies now must comply with various codes; the powers and responsibilities of independent directors have become greater; boards have become smaller and more focussed; directors generally feel more accountable in the face of the manifold tensions they face.

Institutional investors are now more active in exerting pressure on boards for ever-better financial performance. This is manifested in both the recent dramatic rise in the capitalisation of key stock markets as well as in the current spate of mergers and takeovers as, in the face of globalisation pressures, industry after industry seeks the safety of consolidation. On top of this, more consumer saving in the developed world means that more funds will enter the West's stock and bond markets and be handled by fewer, bigger financial groups. The certainty is that *shareholder activism* will increase.

Is there such a degree of certainty about how companies will be directed and controlled (to use Cadbury's term) to achieve the results demanded by their owners – the shareholders? If we judge companies' performance by financial indicators, then companies have been doing much better in recent years. (1) But the 1998 OECD report on Corporate Governance sounded a cautionary note on wider issues, particularly those involving the *potential social fall-out from the race for higher performance.* This concern was echoed by one of the leading advocates of shareholder activism, Robert Monks, in his latest book T*he Emperor's Nightingale.* The book has a telling subtitle – "Restoring the

Integrity of the Corporation", implying that the financial focus of narrow-minded shareholders is actually undermining the integrity of the corporate system.

This chapter ranges widely in addressing aspects of this issue. Centrally, it deals with the actual and potential challenge of judging a company's performance on the basis of its two sources of capital – economic and social. The first involves increasing the rewards obtained by shareholders and, thus, creating Shareholder Value (SV) on the basis of the use of all the firm's resources, physical, monetary and human. The second involves building the best type of enduring relationships not just within the firm (its social capital) but between the firm and all its partners – creating Stakeholder Satisfaction. This lays greater accent on the human form of capital.

The argument advanced here is that, if SV is pursued single-mindedly and to the exclusion of the softer values inherent in relationship building, then the firm's ability to create the *goodwill* it needs from its manifold business relationships will be damaged. And the building of goodwill is the very basis of corporate purpose and governance.

The Pressure for Performance

"Corporate Governance tends to gain public attention when performance problems are apparent". (2) Thus the OECD report on Corporate Governance, published in April 1998. Against a background of accumulated data on corporate under-achievement of a variety of forms, this somewhat bland statement reflected what had become a rather tense public debate about the adequacy of corporate governance on both sides of the Atlantic.

In the US, poor performance took the predominant form of a major loss in shareholder value in several of the largest corporations – General Motors, IBM, Amex, Westinghouse. Where this happened, it was followed by speedy retribution. Their CEO's got fired. In the UK, the stimulus to the debate was much more noticeable than mediocre company performance. It was outright company failure and fraud, in companies such as Polly Peck, Mirror Group and BCCI. Nemesis may as a result have been harsher than in the US if only individuals such as Maxwell and Nadir had not, in their different ways, eluded the law.

If a number of prominent directors in such companies had been getting their direction wrong, then it was natural to ask what should they have been doing to get it right? Looking back to that time, we might find it strange that there was, in fact, no generally-accepted, available body of knowledge that indicated what boards and directors should be doing and how they should be doing it. Indeed, the well-publicised shortcomings of major companies showed the *black box* of boardroom practice, supposedly powerful and effective in use, was, surprisingly, empty.

There followed a plethora of committees, creating codes, regulations and rules, in the UK and the US and, later, round the world. All are well documented in the OECD report. (3) Companies have had to comply with these and most have done so. The majority of directors hoped, no doubt, that the lid would then be put back on the now well-stocked black box and they could go back to running their businesses in the way they wished. This was not to be, however, for institutional shareholders, having flexed their muscles and become strengthened in their activism as a result of the governance debate, have found that they like the taste of power.

Such large shareholder groups have pressed home their advantage by insisting privately and publicly that companies they invest in produce ever-better financial performance. Pressure has been further reinforced by, firstly, the large increase in pension and other funds being placed in the stock market in the 1990s and, secondly, their concentration in the hands of a relatively small number of fund managers. In the UK, for example, eleven percent of the market is controlled by three institutions; twenty-five percent by ten institutions. One of the most powerful, MAM, has stakes of between 12 percent and 22 percent in seven of the largest ten FTSE companies. If one takes the 100 largest FTSE companies and looks at stakes greater than ten percent in these, then it will be seen that MAM controls one in four. (4)

It is hardly surprising that the boards of such companies must pay close attention to what fund managers demand: an overriding company focus on maximising shareholder value and resistance to what they see as over-generous pay-outs to directors.

The Social Fall-Out

The OECD report goes further than most other recent reports on corporate governance however, in recognising how the above trends may be detrimental to wider societal interests. It declares that "in the new competitive environment the corporate need to quickly shift activities to new or improved products and technologies may be inconsistent with a company's long-term commitments to certain resource providers". Its conclusion is that "pressures for efficient capital allocation and corporate performance may reduce investments in programmes and enterprises that are perceived as having high social but low economic returns." (5) In short, some of the other "stakeholders" can lose out, especially the workforce.

Unemployment and social strife, the main social fall-out from downsizing and cost cutting in the West and bouts of economic misery in Russia, S. E. Asia and Latin America, strengthens the hands of opponents of democratic capitalism. Critics may indeed quote the supposed greater resilience of countries like China and argue the need for stronger state control of economic activity as a way of combating social ills. Others may point to the Islamic model and assert the importance of religious fundamentalism as a way of mitigating capitalistic forces.

The problem with both these models of socio-political management is that they come with less personal freedom as a by-product and they tend to produce less prosperity overall. The critical issue for all such systems is the extent to which they, simultaneously, create wealth and allow it to be shared equitably. Baking the economic cake cannot be disassociated from cutting it up, but the size of the cake is obviously what matters most to most people. Some disagree. For example, Cuba's Fidel Castro has roused himself to argue that help from the imperialistic IMF is "the kiss of the devil" and asserted that people and the environment in the West have to suffer because of the "blind laws of the market". (6) However, no one can realistically expect the egalitarian nostrums of Fidel Castro and others to be on the agenda of most boards! Their focus has to be on: baking an even bigger economic cake rather than sharing out a smaller cake more equally.

Nor would one expect all the world's problems to be solved by company directors. The fin-de-millennium global situation clearly now requires massive international concerted action, led by the G7 group of nations, to address urgent political and social problems. But corporate governance will necessarily have its part to play – as the World Bank and the OECD have pointed out – as it's the corporate sector that creates the wealth which the world's governments then seek to share out.

Similar tensions can be found in countries and companies in the West, albeit on a smaller scale. The debate on the proper purpose of business – "Shareholder Value" or "Stakeholder Satisfaction" – has been ringing around conference halls and seminar rooms the world over in recent years. The usual attempt at resolving the matter is to say that there is no conflict between the two in the longer term. The problem, however, is that *we live in a series of short runs*, a fact reinforced by the imperative placed on companies to maximise short-term shareholder value. In the most recent times the pressure has come from financial analysts, acting on behalf of institutions who are themselves under pressure to demonstrate superior short-term performance, and from the populist media. It is unremitting.

The "Inclusive" Approach

There have been several recent important attempts at resolving this conundrum in the governance debate. One of the most notable in the UK has been the publication of *Tomorrow's Company,* the outcome of an extensive consultation orchestrated by the Royal Society of Arts. (7) In this, it was argued that directors needed to broaden their perspective to "include" the interests of other stakeholders, such as employees, suppliers and the wider community, alongside the interests of shareholders, in the running of companies. The RSA team has continued to advocate this "inclusive" philosophy as a basis of governance, but it has received a mixed reception, not least by City institutions. While a few companies have embraced such a *Balanced Scorecard* approach, the notion has caught on very widely. This is because the principle of Stakeholder Satisfaction cannot easily be accommodated within the dominant imperative of *maximising* Shareholder Value. The two are, in fact, mutually exclusive.

Unless activist shareholder groups actually forego their expectation of higher and higher short-term financial performance from their investments, therefore, it is unlikely that the "inclusive" philosophy can assert itself. This was acknowledged in Robert Monks' *Emperor's Nightingale*. Indeed, in the preface, he refers to the present corporate system as "a machine like system, increasingly based on non-dynamic, non-living, non-human principles: a profit-seeking missile of unlimited life, size and power, operating under the stealth of human guise... delivering increasingly unacceptable results to the human beings who created it". (8) And all this from a man who is claimed on the book's dust jacket to be "the world's most prominent and feared shareholder activist and one its shrewdest economic and business observers"! He even calls for pension fund managers in particular to become more accountable to the interests of pensioners, concluding that this would ensure that companies were managed for "long-term economic value rooted in the social good", rather than for "short-term profit maximisation".

Following publication of his book, Monks argued at a Henley conference that pensioners are likely to become less docile about the investment policy of the funds from which they derive their pensions. Sir Adrian Cadbury, who shared the platform, agreed with him. Monks also observed that "pensioners are not only interested in receiving an income; they also want to retire to a safe, clean world that is good to live in". (9)

Similar sentiments to these have been voiced by a pressure group called PIRC, based in London, which advises pension funds on their investment policies. It advocates investment in so-called "ethical" and "green" funds, which seek to satisfy investors on the basis of broader, long-term performance criteria. Their impact is as yet small, however, when compared to the size of funds who press for more orthodox, financial performance.

Strategy and Social Capital

The "inclusive" approach nevertheless, has attracted some support from some of the latest ideas in strategic management and marketing. The resource-based school of thought in strategy, for example, is associated with scholars such as Grant, Hamel and Prahalad, Ghoshal and Kay. (10) In a world where products look increasingly similar and where outsourcing, joint-ventures and alliances make it sometimes difficult to discern where one business ends and another begins, the focus of such researchers is on the real and tangible sources of competitive advantage.

The answer to the quest, according to the resource-based school, lies in a company's ability to do things that are difficult to copy. Apart from its intellectual capital, which may be patented, other invisible assets may be found in the "core competences" of key employees and in the business networks of relationships – its "social architecture" or "social capital". Long-term collaborative relationships with key customers and suppliers and cooperative ways of working among key staff are thought to produce distinctive competitive advantages. True, they may not be instantly visible and may often be more implicit than explicit, but they nevertheless still *real.* Some marketers may add together some of these invisible assets together in their brand valuation models, whilst others may label the skills inherent in valuable long-term customer-supplier relationships as "relationship marketing". (11)

The similarity among these current ideas in strategy and marketing about the value of social capital is marked. Yet another way of looking at how value is created from the successful working of relationships is to be found in another business school discipline, that of organisation behaviour. Here, contemporary scholars find the notion of "organisation learning" intriguing. (12) They refer to complex, flexible structures and processes which enable organisations to learn, not only adapting to new stimuli from outside, but also building the capacity to learn within. It is hardly surprising that some of this is now subsumed under the banner of *knowledge management.*

What all of these ideas have in common is, firstly, the view that these competences or capabilities are germane to corporate success. Secondly, they indicate that such success cannot readily be built on opportunistic, coercive or overly-exploitative relationships but demands rather a basis of trust and commitment. The arguments stress that trusting relationships are more likely to endure into the long-term, to encourage collaboration, experimentation and innovation, and to be resilient to short-term shocks or crises. They are, in fact, the very essence of added value creation. Thirdly, they underline the fact businesses have two forms of capital which can be exploited: social and economic. Seeking to maximise SV may cause the company's social capital to be put at risk through over-exploitation.

Performance as Shareholder Value

The problem with arguments of this type is that, if there is a direct link to the *bottom l*ine, that is, to orthodox financial performance, it is not immediately apparent. They rely, by contrast, on *a priori* thinking about the importance of soft values in commercial activity or what amounts to an act of faith, the belief that good relationships with stakeholders will produce profits. But even if the link is accepted in principle, it is difficult in practice to demonstrate it in the annual accounts or to relate it to the short-term interests of active shareholders. So, unless and until this is achieved, such ideas are unlikely to become accepted into mainstream management practice. As has been observed already, the maximisation of shareholder value has become the main purpose of corporate governance in most major companies, at least in the US and the UK.

In continental Europe and Japan there is, however, suspicion about the universal relevance of SV. They have traditions of consensual management in which *jobs for life* and avoidance of antagonistic relationships between, say, management and unions, loom large. In mainland EU governments have adopted the social market economy approach to managing economic and social affairs, an approach which stresses egalitarianism, full employment and participative management.

Some leading companies on the Continent of Europe or in Japan which are exposed to the full force of globalised competition and need to sharpen up their competitiveness are therefore caught up in the stakeholder/shareholder value dilemma. Central to this is the *right* blend of success criteria – effectiveness, efficiency and equity – they should pursue. There are signs however, that the flagging performance of some major companies in these non-Anglo-Saxon cultures and their increasing need to access international capital markets, are prompting some to accent efficiency at the expense of equity. Both the companies and, paradoxically, the governments who collect taxes from them are now under pressure to perform much better than in the past. If they do not soon do better, in today's globalised world they will both very quickly start to do much worse.

But if companies in continental Europe are to embrace shareholder value as the pre-eminent principle of corporate governance, they need to be aware of the fact that it is not a mere philosophical construct beloved of the Anglo-Saxons. There is a lot of mystique surrounding the term, which is reinforced by the many consultancies, (usually attached to major accounting firms), who trade on this opacity. Conceptually it is not too difficult, however. It can be seen as the market capitalisation of the company inclusive of dividends. Anything that contributes to raising the share price creates shareholder value.

Delving behind this, we need to distinguish between cash flow and profits. Shareholders have found out, to their cost, that it is too easy for companies to manipulate the calculation of profit so as to present attractive financial results. Cash, by contrast, is much more visible in company accounts. As *The Economist* newspaper put it recently: "Cash is fact; profit is opinion". (13) And cash flows are basic to calculating future values. One of the leading Finance Directors in the UK recently explained the SV term in this way: "Shareholder Value is essentially DCF writ large. If one imagines a company to be a bundle of projects each of which has a Discounted Cash Flow value, then Shareholder Value is the sum of these". This may be a bit of an oversimplification, but it captures the essence of the idea.

Shareholder Value from Stakeholder Relationships: The Goodwill Question

It is arguable that a focus on cash flow may allow a potential reconciliation between those that support the principle of the stakeholder-driven "inclusive approach" mentioned above and those who follow the practice of Shareholder Value. If such a reconciliation can be achieved, it could also constitute a useful re-interpretation of business performance, which may help resolve the wider social problems of corporate governance noted at the beginning of this chapter.

The argument goes as follows: where does cash flow come from? It will be apparent that it derives form monetary exchanges with stakeholders. In each exchange, cash will flow one way in exchange for goods and services which go the other way. Clearly the cash will flow in different directions depending on the stakeholders; thus it comes in from customers and goes out to employees, suppliers etc. Cash flow is therefore dependent upon the *exchange relationships* the business has with its stakeholders. Every business person knows that the better the relationship one has with a customer or a supplier, the more likely it is that the cash will flow appropriately and securely into the future.

Of course there may be a temptation for a business in the short run, if it has monopoly or other sources of power, to use this in a coercive fashion to maximise cash flow; but, in this increasingly deregulated and competitive world, monopoly power does not endure for long. The behaviour of the customer, supplier or even employee, will eventually change in relation to the firm, leading to termination of the relationship or to different terms of exchange. Cash flow will then be adversely affected. Good business will have changed to bad and the firm's social capital will have been reduced in value.

It was noted that, at the heart of strong and value-creating relationships with stakeholders, is to be found trust and commitment to the firm. Stakeholders will feel that they are getting a good deal from the firm; they will be positively disposed to assist; they will wish the firm well; they will be inclined to acquiesce voluntarily to a firm's wishes. Many of these sentiments in a dictionary are grouped under the definition of the term *goodwill,* alongside the accounting term of the same name.

The argument advanced here is that this is, indeed, no accident, for all these meanings are the same. Goodwill is, in fact, the extra value ascribed to a business that is living and enduring, over what value there would be if the business ceased to exist and if its net assets were sold off. A business is alive only through the value of its relationships with its customers, suppliers, employees and shareholders. Goodwill tends to constitute most of the value of successful businesses, especially today's service and hi-tech businesses. That is where Shareholder Value is really to be found.

It is most evident when businesses are bought and sold. Much of the price paid will be accounted for in goodwill. But it is also claimed here that this is directly derived from the favourable terms upon which cash flows in and out of the business, which in itself is dependent upon the nature of the exchange relationships the business has with its stakeholders.

Corporate Governance Revisited

The implications of the above argument for corporate governance are considerable. It will be recalled that Cadbury's definition of corporate governance was "the system by which companies are directed and controlled". This indicates two aspects of governance: direction and control. Cadbury's definition was amplified by Jonathan Charkham, former advisor to the Governor of the Bank of England, when he stated that a good system of governance provides for "dynamism" (by which he arguably meant leadership and enterprise) and "accountability". This latter is similar to Cadbury's use of the term "control" and Monks' use of the term "integrity". (14)

In corporate governance then, there are two forces: one is the source of creative enterprise, with the energy and dynamism of leadership, signalling future direction; the other force is more constraining, stressing accountability and responsibility for the activities and performance of the business. Performance clearly is relevant to both aspects of governance. If there is a reinterpretation of the meaning of performance, as has been suggested above, there can also be a parallel reinterpretation of leadership and accountability, as enacted in boards of directors.

The purpose of leadership would then become the *generation of goodwill*, and the board would become accountable for the amount of goodwill thus generated. Shareholders clearly benefit, because it has been seen that in many, if not most companies, market valuation will be directly related to goodwill. Other stakeholders are accounted for in so far as goodwill is derived from the value of their relationships with the business, at the core of which is their trust and commitment to the firm. It does not mean, of course, that other useful performance measures become unimportant; rather, that these short-term indicators of performance should be considered alongside an appropriate measure of goodwill or social capital as the main indicator of the overall success or health of the enterprise.

It should be apparent that such a focus can help to reduce many of the risks to today's businesses, especially those risks associated with health, safety, environmental, community and consumer issues. As has already been noted, one of the outcomes should be more loyal stakeholders, thus enabling the business to ride-out short-term crises or setbacks. It is in relation to the leadership of the company that there are the greatest implications, however; for it will be necessary for the independent directors on the board to appoint the sort of CEO's and their teams who can lead the business successfully to achieve this new focus for performance. Independent directors will then need to monitor this performance on a regular basis, and assure themselves that the appropriate checks and balances are in place to ensure that this kind of leadership is properly exercised.

Implications for Business Leadership

Which personal competences will business leaders require to deliver this new interpretation of performance – building goodwill through creating, and managing, successful business relationships with stakeholders? Which skills and abilities will be more likely to generate trust and commitment from stakeholders in their relationships with the business? How can the value in stakeholder relationships be measured and enhanced to gain competitive advantage? How will these competences relate to the current and future strategic contexts of the business? These are some of the key questions that boards will have to answer in considering the appointment or succession of the Chief Executive and the top executive team.

Interestingly, a wave of current research is underway to help them in seeking such answers. For example, the current interest in emotional intelligence (EQ) has clear relevance. (15) The competences comprising EQ are related to transformational leadership, where they need to be deployed to engender and maintain trust and commitment among stakeholders when undergoing strategic changes. The linkage of these competences to business strategy may be found for example in the research which focuses on the skills of CEO's in communicating "Strategy as Story" – the use of language and dramatic skills to gain the emotional support of key stakeholders for the strategy of the business. (16) Placing a value on long-term customer relationships is another important current strand of research in marketing. (17) Research is also taking place to measure the strength of business exchange relationships – a kind of "Stakeholder Value Analysis" which may be used as part of new performance measurement systems in organisations. Help is therefore on its way to boards of directors who wish to encourage a shift to this new kind of leadership. What still remains to be researched is how some of these new measures of social capital link to the more traditional measures of market capitalisation.

Conclusion

As we move into a new millennium, corporate governance is changing and needs to change further. The focus of leadership and accountability required in boards of directors is now subject to intense, external scrutiny, particularly in listed companies; but the changes also impact on other kinds of, and sizes of, organisations in the public and voluntary sectors as well as the private sector. This reflects changes in the expectations society has of business. Yet, the acute pressures of competition and technical change, together with the international fluidity of capital markets, do not allow any let-up in the drive for companies to achieve superior performance. Corporate Governance needs to encompass these changing conditions and expectations. Here, it has been argued that one useful means to accomplish this would be to re-interpret orthodox financial performance and to focus on the generation of goodwill as the key driver of shareholder value. This would require a different emphasis in leadership, one specifically focussed on building the value of long-term stakeholder relationships. This would have the benefit not only of revealing where the added-value of leadership really lies, but also will build stronger, more successful businesses.

References

(1) See a recent article which provides some evidence of how an effective board is associated with higher profits: Millstein, Ira M. and MacAvoy, Paul W, The Active Board of Directors and Performance of the Large Publicly Traded Corporation. *Columbia Law Review*, Vol. 98, 1998

(2) Corporate Governance: Improving Competitiveness and Access to Capital in Global Markets. *OECD*, April 1998, p.13

(3) See also more comprehensive guidance for board effectiveness in *Good Practice for Directors: Standards for the Board*, published by the Institute of Directors in association with Henley Management College, March 1995

(4) Mallin, C. *Corporate Governance: Financial Institutions and their Relations with Corporate Boards*, paper presented at the 1st International Conference of the Centre for Board Effectiveness, Henley Management College: Creating Value through Effective Board Leadership and Strategic Direction, September 1998

(5) As (2),*OECD*, pp.70, 72

(6) *Financial Times*, 19 September 1998

(7) *Tomorrow's Company: The Role of Business in a Changing World.* London: Royal Society of Arts, 1995

(8) Monks, R.A.G. *The Emperor's Nightingale: Restoring the Integrity of the Corporation.* Oxford: Capstone, 1998, p.xxii/xxiii

(9) Monks, R.A.G. in an address to the Henley Centre for Board Effectiveness Conference, September 1998, As (4)

(10) See for example,

Grant, R.M., *Contemporary Strategy Analysis.* Oxford: Blackwell, 1991

Hamel, G. and Prahalad, C.K. *Competing for the Future.* Boston: Harvard Business School Press, 1994

Nahapiet, J. and Ghoshal, S. Social Capital, Intellectual Capital and the Organizational Advantage. *Academy of Management Review*, April 1998

Kay, J. *Foundations of Corporate Success.* Oxford University Press, 1993

(11) See for example,

Special Issues on Relationship Marketing. *Journal of the Academy of Marketing Science*, Vol. 23, No. 4, Fall 1995 and

Journal of Marketing Management, Vol. 13, No. 5, July 1997

(12) See for example,

Senge, P., *The Fifth Discipline: the Art and Practice of the Learning Organization.* London: Century Business, 1990

Weick, K.E., *Sensemaking in Organizations*. London: Sage, 1995

Von Grogh, G. et al., *Knowing in Firms*. London: Sage, 1998

(13) Valuing Companies - A Star to Sail By, *The Economist*, 2 August 1997, p. 62, quoted *in* Mills, R.W., *The Dynamics of Shareholder Value*, Mars Business Assocs., 1998

(14) Charkham, J., *Keeping Good Company: A Study of Corporate Governance in Five Countries*. Oxford: Clarendon Press, 1994

(15) See for example, Dulevicz, S.V. and Higgs, Malcolm, Emotional Intelligence. *Competency*, Vol. 6, No. 1, Autumn 1998

(16)(a) Downing, S.J., *A Narrative Analysis of Competitive Advantage,* paper presented at the 3rd International Conference on Organizational Discourse, King's College, London, 1998

(16)(b) Barry, D. and Elmes, M., Strategy Retold: Towards a Narrative View of Strategic Discourse. *Academy of Management Review*, Vol. 22, No. 2, 1997

(17) See for example, Jackson, D.R., Strategic Applications of Customer Lifetime Value in the Direct Marketing Environment. *Journal of Targeting, Measurement and Analysis for Marketing*, 1995

Note

The use of the term "Goodwill Hunting" in the title is derived from the US motion picture title "Good Will Hunting" released in 1997. It is used in this context to indicate the seeking of goodwill *as the basis of corporate purpose and governance.*

Chapter 6

STRATEGY AS GAMBLING

Terry Garrison, Roger Martin-Fagg and Joseph Tse

Introduction

Why is the study of risk and uncertainty currently somewhat neglected, even in the Brave New World of the so-called *New Economy*, in the field of business strategy?

A review of current literature reveals an intriguing finding: the accent writers place on handling risk, arguably one of the key features of the strategic decision-making process, is relatively slight. Today, most commentators seem to be focussing predominantly on the *can-do* approaches that are required to cope with the changing dynamics of industries in flux and the resultant patterns of direct and co-operative competition that exist in them.

Perhaps this positive thrust derives from the often tense relationship between corporations and their owners, as evidenced in today's relentless quest for shareholder value. What the owners and the stock market do rate above all is certainty – the bankable reassurance that the strategies of the companies they invest in will succeed. Any CEO who is publicly less than enthusiastic about the way forward or who, worse still, hints either at boardroom disagreement or at the possibility that the strategy may not achieve its purposes is courting disaster. The market does not wish to hear the risk-laden words "maybe" and "might" used to describe planned outcomes; it tends to be anxious about messengers who bring not just bad, but unreliable, news, as Exhibit 1, page 130 suggests.

Strategy, in the current literature, seems to be more about the will-power behind the vigorous implementation of a chosen set of moves than it is about their painstaking probabilistic analysis. There is a demonstrable absence of the painful recognition that, in an uncertain world, it is quite possible that a firm's competitors may out-game and out-play it, by accident rather than by design. Pessimism, is, of course, the deadliest of business sins at any time. But, in today's Internet-speed world it is far worse than any over-optimistic pronouncements reflecting the wilful over-exuberance of the CEO of the start-up/IPO company or the indifferent complacency of his counterpart who leads the market dominator. And pessimism is anything that questions the likelihood of success. Thus, we are in danger of institutionalising both the need for boundless optimism and the possible distortion of decision-making that can spring from it.

Hoechst AG of Germany and the French company Rhone-Poulenc SA are merging to create Aventis, to become one of the world's leading life sciences companies. The fusion, which comes into effect in November 1999, will focus attention on biotechnology and drug-making and involves the spin-off of Hoechst's Celanese AG operation which makes industrial chemicals.

The deal for Hoechst shareholders is an attractive one. They receive 53 percent of the Aventis stock and a special dividend plus a likely price hike based on a corporate repurchase of 5 percent of outstanding shares. Lehman Brothers, reckoning that Hoechst will be more profitable as a focussed producer (than a conglomerate, as before), have also raised their evaluations of the stock from "neutral" to "outperform". The stock was trading at 41.7 euros as against the bank's estimate of their worth - 47 euros – in June 1999.

The strategy of concentrating on life science as opposed to industrial chemicals will certainly make Aventis less dependent on the economic cycle and create greater earning stability as a result. But, it may not initially turn out to be an easy alliance, according to David Potts, fund manager at Investic Guinness Flight. He said that the deal was "a marriage made in hell, combining Gallic pride and charm with German efficiency. Given the egos involved, it makes one wonder if they can extract the synergies and value in the company".

Exhibit 1: Good News or Bad?

Based on: A French-German Union, Conrad de Aenlle, International Herald Tribune, 5-6/6/99 (1)

This chapter has, therefore, been designed to draw attention to issues that are currently achieving less attention from scholars and practitioners than, in our view, they warrant. We are not, of course, creating an artificial Aunt Sally to aim at insofar as the technicalities of decision-making are concerned. Much work is being done on this in mathematics and statistics, but more, to be sure, in the financial, than in the strategy, field. Certainly, among the more prominent techniques for risk management that are covered in depth are financial ratio projections and sensitivity analysis, decision matrices and situational modelling of, for example, the Monte Carlo form.

In terms of the areas where risk management is seen as crucial eg, evaluating the economic and political factors of a target market country or assessing the viability of investment in a new project, numerical computation, using such techniques, is standard practice. Risk management is also high on the agenda of governments who are faced with the challenge of coping with speculation in their countries' stock and money markets. It is also a preoccupation of major multinationals in key industries like oil or G.M food production, which are becoming more and more exposed to often un-anticipated challenges. But, again, however, the major focus is that of finance and accounting, as exemplified by Exhibit 2 below. As the dèbâcle from 1999-2001 showed, the hyperbole behind the bubble had been only too real, even if the bubble had not.

Over the year they rose phenomenally, then they fell spectacularly. The subject at issue is US internet stocks and their performance over 1998-9. America On-line shot up over this period from $17 to $175. With a capitalisation of $114 billion it was worth more than the whole of BT. At the end of February 1999 the Standard and Poor's 500 Index was trading at 32 times historic earnings and in March 1999 alone the US Internet Stock index doubled in value. The fall was certainly also precipitous; by the start of June the average stock was 52 percent down from its high. Smaller companies like Ticketmaster and Ivillage were 70 percent off and America On-line itself was down in value by 40 percent. It appeared that investors have been paying for potential reward and almost ignoring risk, so manic was the appeal of www.com. Comments Keith Woolcock, technology analyst at Nomura "The danger with the internet is that it's a bubble. It is totally impossible to value these companies, we all know that. It's a bit like the Oklahoma land rush last century. Investors put huge value on everyone on the basis that one or two might get a huge slice of the cyberspace pie."

Exhibit 2: Numbers come first

Based on: Are internet stocks burnt out?, Jemimah Bailey, Sunday Telegraph, 6/6/99 (2)

The fact remains that less mention of key issues associated with handling risk and uncertainty is made in the strategy area than might have been expected. This chapter thus examines in a very down-to-earth way why this should be so and seeks to redress the coverage balance. It deals therefore with

- managerial definitions of risk and uncertainty and methods for appraising their extent;

- methodologies for risk-handling within the strategic decision-making process;
- the people issue: the extent to which attitudes to risk-taking can vary among executives charged with making strategic decisions and, therefore, can affect the rationality of the process and its outcomes;
- the changing risk/uncertainty environment within which companies are operating today;
- the extent to which strategy and gambling are related.

Ways of looking at Risk and Uncertainty

What is risk? In statistics, risk connotes the forecasted probabilities attaching to each of a range of events which are due to happen in future or of outcomes of an action decision that has been made. A risky decision is one that may turn out well or badly but it is, at all events, one we have attempted to deal with by predicting in advance the spread of likely results. If

- the phenomenon at issue is a familiar one of which we have past evidence (ie, a reliable data base); and
- we feel confident about making predictions of what will occur (using a satisfactory method) to the point of actually forecasting what is likely to happen and trying to act purposefully on our forecast;

then we can be said to be trying to *manage risk.*

The meteorologist, predicting tomorrow's weather, relies on a data base consisting of past weather patterns, current observations and mathematical projections based on both. The quality of the data base allow him or her to quantify the likely pattern. Of course, the forecaster cannot be absolutely certain of the likely pattern and, hence, relies on stating the probabilities or chances that the weather will be good, or bad or somewhere in between. These chances are properly called *risks*. Here of course, the meteorologist is acting on a scientific forecast and not one of his/her personal devising. Nor is there any special commitment – logical or emotional – to either the forecast or to the *event* of the weather that actually results. Whilst the forecast may mean everything to TV viewers, preparing (say) for a family wedding or a cricket match, it is simply a matter of cold professionalism to the presenter.

Note that this issue of perspective is important. Assume that you have just made an important decision today, for example, on trying to get a new job. You have been in your existing post for a considerable length of time and are becoming alienated from it. Because the issue is significant and the outcome is profoundly to be desired, you are likely to have made a formal assessment of the likely *outcome* of a job alternative. The result is a situation in which the more serious the analysis, the more committed the decision-maker to a satisfactory result from the decision. The result is emotional involvement in the entire process and, obviously, a will to win. This can get intense, because success matters. An *event*, by contrast with an *outcome*, is something which we cannot control, especially if we have had no hand in shaping it. We may react emotionally to it but we can't do anything about it. Of course, the outcome from one of our decisions may well turn out to be an event for other people not involved in shaping it in the first place.

Interestingly, there is a problem of language usage lurking here. Although purist statisticians think differently, many of us tend to use the word *risk* in a pejorative sense. We don't speak of the risk of sunny weather but of the risk of rain. A spell of fine sunshine is a matter of luck or chance (a value-neutral term – both can be good or bad) rather than of risk (a value-negative term). This is a matter of great significance, as we shall see later, in the business domain. In fact, in this chapter as you will note, we are going to occasionally overlay the formal definition of risk with the more populist version of risk.

Whenever we make a choice, and human life is all about choice, we face the probability that our choice, when implemented through action, will be successful or that it will not be. In everyday parlance we call the chance of making a decisional mistake a *risk*. If the decision results in success we tend, retrospectively, to regard it as a matter of wise judgement and sound calculation, even in situations where it was perhaps very difficult to work out the a priori chances of success or failure. Only if things have not worked out well do we use expressions like "it was a very risky thing to attempt" or " we took a risk".

So what's *uncertainty*? A simple answer is that, whilst a quantifiable assessment of event or outcome probabilities is possible in risk situations, we have no possibility of doing this in situations of uncertainty. In other words, we lack the data necessary for any computation of the odds of success or failure. This may be because the phenomenon has never happened before and we lack information on it. Or, that it may indeed have occurred before but in circumstances that we have been unable to interpret. Or, yet again, it may be a phenomenon which may or may not take place in a future which is outside our control. As Exhibit 3, page 134 shows, some of us are today living in an age of great uncertainty.

The audition is about to begin. A nervous young man steps into the conference room and starts his presentation. In fact, he wants $10m from a total stranger named Jeff Brody. Brody is a long-time venture capitalist in Silicon Valley who spends his entire week hearing pitches from entrepreneurs seeking money from his firm, Brentwood Venture. The young man wants to launch a firm selling furniture over the internet. As of March 1999, this firm and its fellow financiers were pumping money at the rate of $300m per month into tiny new businesses built around the internet. This amounts to some 30 percent of all venture spending, more than the combined total for biotechnology, electronics and microchips. And yet, as George Anders, Wall Street Journals' staff reporter, points out "No-one feeding this internet frenzy can pinpoint the difference between tomorrow's great enterprises and utter follies". You can't even look for the "traditional hallmarks of great start-up" he says – things like brilliant engineers, unique technology, clear profit potential. In fact, if there is a logic associated with winning, it may have to do more with a memorable brand name than with technological mastery. It's not easy to size up people either. College drop-outs in their early 20s may prove to have better insights than seasoned managers. "As for strategic planning" says Anders "it typically is limited to one word: improvise".

Exhibit 3: Buddy, can you spare $10M?

Based on: You expect Big Losses and Want $10 Million? Sure, We'll Consider It, Wall Street Journal, 17/3/99 (3)

As with risk, the phenomenon may be an event or set of events over which we have no control or could be the outcome of a decision we, or others, have taken. It could even be a situation or web of circumstances that have arisen by chance or through natural forces, like an earthquake or a hurricane. Opening Pandora's Box is an everyday metaphor for uncertainty. No one could forecast the workings of the evil forces that were liberated from it. And yet, the strategist needs to be able to come to terms with uncertainty, whether in the business, political, military or environmental context.

Appraising Risk and Uncertainty: a case in point

In October 1998 DaimlerChrysler unveiled its new Smart car. The slogan said that such a small, fuel-efficient car, just made for city traffic and capable of parking in the smallest of spaces, would revolutionise urban motoring. The company confidently predicted that it would sell 130,000 Smarts in 1999 on the basis of the 20,000 it had sold in the last quarter of 1998 and on the basis of the marketing activity that was planned. Sales in the first quarter of 1999 were, however, substantially down on forecast and only 20,000 were sold. This was a profound embarrassment, as well as a major disappointment, to the company which was said to be beginning a make-or-break final marketing campaign costing £40m in June 1999 to get the Smart really moving.

This case illustrates many aspects of the appraisal of risk and uncertainty. The concept and product were created by a tried-and-tested project team, tasked with launching a new product that was central to DaimlerChrysler strategy. The R & D programme ended with the reasonably successful testing of prototypes. The team completed the programme of marketing research and was confident of the finding that the product would be a winner. Each member of the team was brimming over with confidence and had the same entrepreneurial *Go for It* attitude.

Whatever the emotional thrust, however, the plain fact is that the Smart has not lived up to corporate expectations, even though it could be argued that we would be unwise to make a snap judgement on such limited sales results. But what does Jurgen Schrempp, the DaimlerChrysler chairman do now? Even though it is very soon to react to media stories of potential disaster, the big problem is that the existing information on the likely up-take of the Smart cannot be relied upon.

The standard formula to deal with decisions in risk situations is to construct

- a payoff table;
- to adjust the pay-offs with estimates of risk;
- to work out expected values for alternative strategies;
- to select the most attractive alternative, perhaps using an appropriate decision rule;
- to act on the basis of a choice from among selected success criteria.

The framework for this is shown in Figure 1, page 136

Step 1 <u>Construct a Payoff Table for the decision</u>

Initial demand Level (units)	Pretax Profit for alternative strategies (£000)	
	A	B
10,000	300	(400)
30,000	850	750
50,000	1350	1650

Notes 1: Pretax profit = sales revenue – variable cost-fixed cost
2: Alternative strategies A & B are different ways of launching the same product. The figures used are indicative.

Step 2 <u>Construct an Expected Payoff Table to refine the decision.</u>

Initial demand level (units)	Probability of achieving this level of initial sales	Expected Pretax profit for alternative strategies (£000)			
		A		B	
		Payoff	Payoff X Probability	Payoff	Payoff X Probability
10,000	.2	300	60	(400)	(80)
30,000	.6	850	510	900	540
50,000	.2	1350	270	1800	360
Expected Payoffs			840		820

Step 3 <u>Employ an appropriate decision rule to make your selection. Possibilities are:</u>

a) The Bayes decision rule. This focuses attention in the outcome with the maximum expected payout, ie strategy A with an expected profit of £840,000.

b) The Minimax payoff rule. This is a pessimistic criterion which assumes that you want to achieve a favourable result regardless of the difficulties you face. You therefore select the option that gives you the best result from among the worst outcomes. Here the worst outcomes are a gain of £80,000 and a loss of £56,000 both under conditions of light demand for Strategies A & B, respectively. Clearly A is the strategy of choice. Minimax is about choosing the *minimum* of the maximum losses that may occur.

c) The maximum likelihood criterion. This concentrates on the outcome with the best pay off, assuming that the most *likely* outcome will occur. This is strategy B (£540,000) but note that, on an EV (expected value) basis, it is only a slightly better result than A.
The Maximax payoff criterion. This is the gambler's choice and is one based on wholesale optimism. You simply select the criterion which produces the maximum of the maximum outcomes. Here it is B which will result in a payoff of £360,000 but only if the highest level of sale is achieved. The maximax player assumes the very best of all possible worlds.

Figure 1: Structuring decision-making involving risk.

Here, in the Smart case, it is the reliability of the current database which is the challenge. How could the original forecast have been so wrong? Was it, in fact, an over-optimistic assessment of demand in the continental European car market which the company must now face up to? Or was it a possible shortfall in marketing spending in a highly competitive market that has caused this? Maybe, the forecast did not take account of unanticipated events which have caused public confidence to be affected adversely – like the 10 percent depreciation in the value of the euro since its launch in January 1999.

In practice, the company management need to decide what to do, irrespective of the level of reliability or otherwise of the information possessed. They need to know whether the car can ever succeed in achieving the financial and marketing aims set for it.

And this is where uncertainty comes in. The chance of a negative outcome, a market failure, was not, of course, seen as inherent in the *risk* situation executives thought DaimlerChrysler was facing in October 1998. In fact, the company's prototype and user test results, together with the remainder of its marketing research study, must have indicated that success was just around the corner for the Smart. The company simply would not have bargained on a worst case scenario. Now, with the company's self-confidence under strain, it will be difficult to impute reliable probabilities to the new demand level. The company must manage uncertainty, not risk. Either the product is not as acceptable as it was thought or the market-place does not properly recognise the appeal of the product or the team's estimates of success were over-optimistic or the world has changed shape. Whatever the rationale, action is needed.

Three elements make up this lack of certainty:

- The futurity of the action decisions. All decisions taken today have future effects. Can DaimlerChrysler now take into consideration all aspects of the market-place context for the Smart that could possibly affect its success in the future. Can we, in particular, forecast the likelihood and impact of competitors' launching me-too products, for instance, in the near-, medium- and long-term future? The further out into the future the company reaches, the more its parameters become those of uncertainty and not risk. Whereas the past is certain (as history) and the present is knowable (we are living it), the future cannot be never forecasted in advance with 100 percent accuracy because it is *yet to be*.
- The complexity of the action decision. Even if DaimlerChrysler have what we reckon are absolutely cast-iron methods of calculating what is likely and data which are now said to be not

absolutely reliable but realistic, it would still be faced with the chance that things will never turn out precisely as forecast. The more intricate the decision and, in particular, the greater the interdependence of the decision variables (political, economic, financial, product-market, technological etc), the more difficult it will be to produce a forecast that will correspond to the actual results and results that will live up to the forecasts. What would the level of success be in the US market for the Smart?

- The interplay between all the actors involved in the action decision. The actors can be individuals or groups, involved peripherally or centrally with varying degrees of interest, commitment and power. Given the need to forecast decision outcomes, consumers for our product and our competitors also rank as actors. Each has naturally different concerns and possible different attitudes to the acceptability of success and failure. Hence their criteria for judging plans and the real market place results the plans achieve may differ. In other words what is the attitude to risk and return of each of the members of the DaimlerChrysler board, and, in particular, those who will play a dominant role in deciding the Smart's future?

It is this combination of futurity, complexity and actor interplay that creates the level of chance that all our decisions have to come to terms with. Why *all* our decisions? Because everything we do today in terms of choices and actions is designed to achieve success in future – the choice of our food this evening, the holidays we shall be booking next summer, the new jobs we are applying for, for example. What matters, of course, is the extent to which the decision is critical and scores highly on our three elements.

Utility Function – Views and Vision

The common-sense model of rational decision-making, derived from neoclassical economics, called "expected utility theory" (EUT), attempts to estimate the utility of possible outcomes and then selects the best. Such a proposition, based upon the rational actor model, has been subsequently revised into subjective expected utility model as a basis of discussion of strategy, an attempt to take into account normative elements associated with decision-making. Yet even this approach fails to take into account any distinction between gains and losses from the perspective of the actual decision-making principle, and equally precise increments and decrements in overall wealth can be considered "unrealistic". A more accurate model, namely "prospect theory", does address this by mapping the perceived value of various outcomes as a function of gains and losses (see Table 1, below).

Prospect theory - Kahneman and Tversky presented groups of subjects with a number of problems. One group of subjects was presented with this problem:

1. In addition to whatever you own, you have been given $1,000. You are now asked to choose between:
A. a sure gain of $500
B. a 50 percent chance to gain $1,000 and a 50 percent chance to gain nothing.

Another group of subjects was presented with another problem.

2. In addition to whatever you own, you have been given $2,000. You are now asked to choose between:
A. a sure loss of $500
B. a 50 percent chance to lose $1,000 and a 50 percent chance to lose nothing.

In the first group 84 percent chose **A**. In the second group 69 percent chose **B**. The two problems are identical in terms of net cash to the subject, however the phrasing of the question causes the problems to be interpreted differently.

Table 1: Illustration of Prospect Theory During Simulated Games

Source: Daniel Kahneman and Amos Tversky, "Prospect Theory: An Analysis of Decision Making Under Risk," Econometrica, 1979.

In Tversky and Kahneman's model (1979) (4), this function is non-linear, can accommodate "mixed gamble" scenarios and is characterised as an S-shaped curve, with differences in larger values having less subjective weight which indicates that negative response to a loss outweighs the positive response to an exactly similar gain.

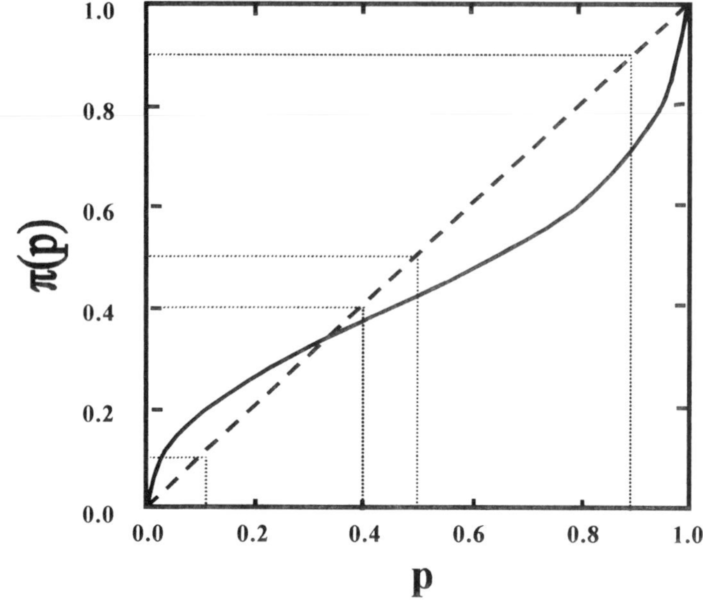

Figure 2: Tversky & Kahneman's Prospect Theory model (1979)

Another feature of prospect theory is the decision weights showing how people interpret (or transform) probabilities. In contrast to EUT, prospect theory shows that the difference between p = .40 and p = .50 is trivial for most people, whereas the difference between p = .90 and p = 1.0 (or between p = .10 and p = 0.0) is powerful ("certainty effect"). As a result, sure gains are much more attractive, and sure losses much more unattractive, than even highly probable gambles. Another surprising result is that the mapping from actual probabilities to the value axis of the previous function is not one-to-one.

The Decision-maker

When an individual or a group *takes a risk* or *faces up to uncertainty,* the implication is that there is an element of daring in the course of action taken, as in the case of our Smart project team. There is also an assumption made widely in business that decision-makers act rationally in an attempt to maximise the pay-offs from the decisions they take. This is a reasonable, but not necessarily correct, assumption to make in all situations, as Exhibit 4, page 141 shows.

On 15th March 1999 the Wall Street Journal reported that "ordinary joes" were moving the Dow Jones Index towards the 10,000 mark. It indicated that the mass of ordinary investors, referred to in the past as "dumb money", was now developing a level of power in investment that was once the prerogative of "smart money". The causes were listed as the billion dollar flow of investment money through mutual funds and the amount and accessibility of stock market data. "Good information", said the paper's What Moves Markets report, "is presented to market-savvy grandmas in small towns in Arkansas first thing in the morning". But were decisions still being made on the basis of indicators such as M-3 Money supply, corporate price-to-book ratios, dividend yields and the trade deficit? No, such measures are regarded as both "arcane" and "quaint". Indeed, one new theory on investment disregards price/earnings ratios and other valuation methods. Called *momentum investing* it means, at its simplest level, buying stocks of companies whose sales or earnings are growing and whose stock price is rising. An advocate of this method is Michael Weiner, a portfolio manager at Banc One Investment Advisors. His in-depth study of the factors which drive stock performance showed that the recent performance of the markets shows that a "return to price momentum" is the deciding factor. The implication? "The only thing you know" asserted Weiner "is that, if you hold the stocks that have done well for a quarter of half a year or a year, those stocks will do well for the next year". Once upon a time, said the report, information whispered over three-martini lunches was what moved markets. Now it's more likely to be "ordinary people double clicking a mouse", perhaps momentum investors.

Exhibit 4: *Ordinary Joes* rule the roost

Based on: New Forces Are Now Powering Surging Stocks, E.S. Browing, Wall Street Journal, 15/3/99 (5)

Consider Table 2, page 142. This table indicates two main types of decisional approach, on the basis of the four parameters which are critical to the exercise of choice. These are:

- the availability of trustworthy information on the decision issue and its context and, in particular, on the outcomes that arise from different choices of what to do and how to do it. This is a matter of great concern to the risk-averse who may go to extreme lengths to try to improve their chances and avoid error. In some situations, however, data is not available, however much one might want it or need it – or accessible only at exorbitant cost;

- the desire on the part of the decision-maker(s) to acquire these data and use them to control the level of chance;
- the extent to which decision-maker(s) are driven by logic or emotion. In the Smart case, one can easily imagine that the project team would try their hardest to ignore the possibility that they could after all be wrong about the car itself. Disgrace, based on a serious error of judgement, would be very hard to live with, especially in such a high visibility industry;
- the use of decision rules or logical frameworks to help think things through. The alternative to this is the use of instinct or gut reaction.

The two types of decisional approach are referred to as ***comprehensive-rational*** and ***uninformed-unstructured.*** In the case of the first approach, the serious decision-taker (or actor) has indeed tried to work out in advance the likely gain/loss outcomes from the choice on the basis of deliberately-gathered information and acted on it. Here the risks are certainly calculated and the decision is made deliberately in the light of their pattern of distribution.

Decisional Approach	Decision Outcome	
	is a success	is a failure
Comprehensive-rational ("CR" approach)	"Clever, well-judged move"	"Was worth a try. Can't win 'em all"
Uniformed-unstructured ("UU" approach)	"Luck of the devil"	"Bound to fail. Flying blind"

Table 2: Decision approaches

Explanation: *Comprehensive-rational* = a tendency to a high level of situational awareness. A carefully-considered decision is based on a comprehensive calculation of likely decision outcomes. Good attempt is made to create a sound data base. *Uninformed-unstructured* = a tendency to a lower level of situational awareness and a possibly unintentional lack of consideration of decision outcomes and their probabilities. Certainly no standardised, thorough decision procedure is used here We may also note a tendency to wilfully ignore adverse risk signs even if there is knowledge of outcomes and their chances of occurrence. Certainly, there is less interest in data gathering per se.

The decision-maker's appraisal may be based on the fact that the course of action is deemed exciting, even if dangerous, or because the prize is worth the amount of daring needed to achieve it or because it is thought success can be relatively easily achieved. All is weighed in the balance.

The uninformed-unstructured style signifies that either the decision-maker is naturally unaware or ignorant of the precise nature of the choice to be made, or the outcomes, to the point of perhaps neglecting to think seriously of what to do. In such a situation it may be quite natural not to spend scarce time and money acquiring information or, indeed, incurring the *paralysis-by-analysis* criticism. Indeed, some decision-makers seem, on occasion, to wilfully to ignore or play down such knowledge as they possess. It may seem peculiar but there are decision-makers who deliberately ignore the probabilities inherent in a significant choice, even if they are aware of them, by refusing to think about them. Motorway madness is one form of this disease. On the other hand, we need to reflect on the facts that that the cost of obtaining *perfect* information may be excessive and that information may have diminishing, as opposed to increasing, marginal utility. Of course, you need adequate information as a basis for sound predictions but that does not mean to suggest that you can value accurately what you mean by adequate. And then, of course, we know from Exhibit 5, below that some people simply do not want to be bothered by facts.

> On 17th March 1999 the American Medical Association Journal ran an alarming report based on a survey of over 3,000 smokers, aged 25-74 from all over the US. Whilst the study was categorical about the risk smokers run of developing lung cancer and heart disease, it found that "many smokers continue to deny their own personal risks". As the report's lead author, Dr John Z. Ayanian, stated "even if they recognise the risks, people don't expect smoking is going to cause problems for them". Why are people in denial about the personal risks they run? Why do they delude themselves? "It's human nature", said Ayanian.

Exhibit 5: Lying to yourself

Based on: Study Finds Smokers In Denial Over Health Risk, Boston Herald, 17/3/99 (6)

Note that we can cross-reference these two approaches to decision-making by observing the risk orientations of the decision-maker(s). These can be categorised along a continuum from *risk-averse* to *risk-seeking,* according to the propensity to take chances that the individual or group reveals. It would be a mistake, however, to assume that the risk-averse player always uses a calculating approach or that, by contrast, the risk-seeker is more carefree.

Indeed, it may be the case that the latter is often more likely to have based the risk-return strategy being pursued on a very careful and hard-headed appreciation of the odds of success, than less. Table 2, page 142 suggests a range of types of decision-maker based on this focus, which contrasts with the Bailard, Biehl & Kaiser Five-Way Model which divides investors into five categories. ***Adventurers*** are risk takers and are particularly difficult to advise. ***Celebrities*** like to be where the action is and make easy prey for fast-talking brokers. ***Individualists*** tend to avoid extreme risk, do their own research, and act rationally. ***Guardians*** are typically older, more careful, and more risk averse. ***Straight Arrows*** fall in between the other four personalities and are typically very balanced.

It might also be a mistake to assume that the rational-comprehensive approach is somehow associated with pessimism and the uninformed-unstructured style with optimism, on the grounds that the more fearful you are of making a mistake the more analysis you do, and vice versa. The approach needs to be understood in terms of the facts that:

- the decision-making approach of the individual or group is possibly both contingent and variable. The contingency arises because of the weight of the decision – private/organisational, monetary/social for instance – and the variability comes from the fact that human beings change their moods over time, if not their opinions and personalities;
- some decisions involve risks that you cannot afford not to take rather than risks you would normally be happy with. This arises where we choose the much disliked option X because we can't live with the risks and returns associated with Y. We decide, therefore, on the basis of opportunity costs;
- the decision-maker(s) have already at their disposal a fall-back position or *Plan B,* as we commonly call it, which softens the risk quotient involved in the most challenging, but attractive decision option considerably.

But is there not an implicit assertion here that the carefree decision approach is, somehow, irrational and that the wily, calculating one is the logical one to go for? Yes, of course. But there is an ever-present danger of labelling decisions and we must always be very careful about imputing rationality or the lack of it to decision-makers. There are many situations where the human being cannot, or simply does not want to, weigh decision outcomes in advance. Perhaps the decision is a trivial one, perhaps it has been made thousands of times before. Perhaps the decision is simply too complex. The individual (or group) making the decision is, indeed, capable of logical analysis of the relationship between means and ends, systematic collection of pertinent data and computation/assessment of the situational probabilities, but the decision defies what we would normally call rational handling. The Chechnya war in 2000 is exactly of such a type.

Risk Orientation	Decisional Approach	
	Comprehensive Rational	Uninformed-unstructured
Risk-seeker	**Navigator**	**Daredevil**
Risk-averse	**Plotter**	**Mole**

Table 3: A typology of decision-makers

© Terry Garrison 2001

Indeed, we can always question our own, and other people's, perceptions of reality and rational choice. What to one person may be a highly reasonable choice to make may, to another, be anathema. (see Table 3 above) Because we are human beings, driven in not inconsiderable part by our emotions, to what extent can we insulate ourselves from the pressure of our feelings when we make important decisions which affect not just customers or shareholders but ourselves? Not only that, it may be quite possible for a decision-maker to wish change his/her posture – Jekyll-and-Hyde like – according to the nature of the situation. In other words to move from being a ***plotter*** in a context where one's personal advancement is at stake to being a ***dare-devil*** so far as the firm's international expansion is concerned. Here, we need to take account not just of the personality dimensions that incline the individual to a certain type of risk-orientation but also the profile of knowledge and skills that the individual possesses. The ***mole*** is someone who should be profoundly out-of-place in the board-room by any standards but is often to be found there – darkly calculating in the least risky fashion, for instance, his/her own self-advancement as opposed to striking out boldly as the ***navigator*** would. This last is the ideal entrepreneur – major challenges are met with innovatory strategies based on sound information and well-considered decisions. Consider, in this regard, the case of Chase Manhattan, illustrated in Exhibit 6, page 146.

The sceptic may also assert, with reason, that people need to be watched very carefully, especially in business decision-making and politics. Sometimes, when a success is achieved by what is in fact a fluke, those enjoying victory have been known to retrospectively argue that the decisions leading to the success were, in fact, well-grounded. The situation is further complicated by the fact that, if decisions turn out to be bad ones since they lead to unsatisfactory outcomes, those involved may seek to disassociate themselves from failure and start to re-write history.

Referring back to the Smart launch example, we can see, of course, that, once the launch decision has been made and the product is actually in the market, the decision framework has changed its focus. Initially, it was about appraisal of the *ex-ante* risk; now the emphasis is on dealing with the *posterior* risk. In other words, the project team began by considering the challenge of launching the product and now we are concerned with what to do to maintain its success.

> Chase Manhattan proved in 1998 to be a bank adept at corralling, at least for the time being, the bogeyman haunting all of Wall Street: risk. While most investment and commercial banks paid lip service to the notion of avoiding financial pratfalls by trying to assess the risks they take, Chase appeared to practise risk management particularly well. "Risk Management" wrote *International Herald Tribune's* Timothy O'Brien, is "as much an art as a science, of course, and Chase benefits from the insulation granted by its sheer size as third largest bank in America". But no risk trading model anticipates every potential catastrophe, as the 1998 collapse of Long Term Capital Management showed. This hedge fund was once operated by some of the "smartest people in the business".

Exhibit 6: A winning machine?

Based on: Assessing Risk Pays Off, Timothy O'Brien, International Herald Tribune, 21/1/99 (7)

A decision tree provides us with a framework for considering these issues. It traces through the chain-linkages that occur in all inter-linked decision sequences. It indicates that the second decision facing us, now or in future, is contingent on the first decision and so on. Hence, the need to make correct choices not only in the immediate present but in terms of maximising our *positive future decision space* as the consequences of our initial decision begin to pan out.

Observe also that every decision leads to an action choice outcome or an event about which we may be able to do little. Indeed, on occasion, inaction may be a better play that action. Either way, decisions and *the will to impose them* sooner or later alter every situation we find ourselves in. This change, in its turn, throws up new threats and opportunities, the result being a set of new choices and decisions to cope with the different level and pattern of risk/uncertainty we now face, and so on ad infinitum. The problem we all face in business is a never-ending, unavoidable chain of inter-linked decisions, each of which has risk/uncertainty connotations. And just as the relationship between the organisation and its environment changes over time, so does the coalition of managers who are called upon to make the big decisions affecting the organisation's future.

The Nature of Gambling

Horse track gambling, however, gives us a good, straight-forward introduction to such issues. Apart from an ability to consider the odds of winning and losing, it teaches some elemental truths such as that it is

- possible to overlook important elements when we are making decisions, however clever you are and however much you think you have covered all the angles;
- possible to win, even if it is a matter of pure chance that you do.

The lessons of the race track also underline for us another two basic truths that we need to underscore at this point: that, whatever the reason, some people simply do use a carefree approach when faced with betting on horses. They become *daredevils.* Of course, those stricken by gambling fever may suffer from permanent distortion of perception and need for the adrenaline that comes only from risk for its own sake. Not so the professional gambler who, almost by definition, needs a scientific approach if he/she is to be successful.

Let us take the three fifteen horse race at Cheltenham as an example. Twelve handicapped runners over the flat. Fine weather. Good racing conditions. Bookmakers shouting the odds – 20 to 1, 5 to 4 on etc. The odds reflect not the probability that the horses will win but the weight of betting on them. So much money is now piling on the favourite that the odds shorten from 5 to 4 on to 6 to 4 on. There is a mixed crowd of on-lookers: naïve, cautious punters who simply want a *flutter,* daredevils who are prepared to back 100-1 outsiders and slow-but-sure professionals. How does this last group go about its work?

The whole purpose of the gambling exercise is to successfully understand, and then minimise, the level of riskiness inherent in the choice of horse in a particular race. If you have insider information, that will help. Of course, it's illegal, but it does ensure that you have more secure data on the performance of individual horses than other people which allows you to make a more informed judgement. It also means that the odds are distorted in your favour. Do not assume, even so, that a win is automatic, however. Racing itself is a hazardous undertaking in which prediction of any sort is fraught. Once the race starts, you have no control over the event on which you are gambling.

We are, in fact, dealing with the interactions among three different types of system:

- a technical system (weather, race track condition, race track parameters such as length, degree of difficulty etc);
- a biological system (the breeding history of the horse, its degree of fitness, its racing record etc); and
- a commercial system (the stable, the chosen jockey, the rules of the gambling sport).

The three systems are integrated in such a way as to create three focuses of risk.

Activity risk concerns the extent to which predicting what will happen in the activity itself is possible. The more data we have on the past pattern of events in racing (eg, race results) and the more we consider that these can be extrapolated into the future, the less the we consider the inherent activity uncertainty to be.

Case or situational risk concerns the particular example of the activity you are deciding about. The three fifteen race at Cheltenham, for instance. What are the precise conditions in which the race will be run, the situation of runners and riders and the ante-post betting as it reflects the popularity of the stables involved. Of course, we should be aware that conflicts can and do exist between principle and practice (the case in point) and that the decision-maker(s) can be sometimes swayed into doing either (a) the most agreeable thing for the wrong reason or (b) doing problematic things for the right reason. Do we act according to our morality and perhaps avoid gambling (principle) or do we bet on a sure-fire certainty because we know it is going to win?

Actor risk is associated with the ability of the punter(s) to acquire and understand pertinent data and to take a balanced, measured decision on the basis of the data. This naturally brings into question the decision-making system which is used by the gambler (or the gambling syndicate) to process the data. While the people involved may have decisional competence (ie, have a history of picking winners), it may be they lack information on the specific horses or the precise state of the track (no form book to hand). Perhaps there is disagreement among the professional gambling experts as to what to do.

Potential strategy of competitor X	Potential strategies of X's other main competitors		
	Price Competition	High Rivalry	Peaceful Co-existence
"No holds barred" price competition	**Market place condition Red**		
High rivalry, but not predominantly on price		**Market place condition Orange**	
Peaceful Co-existence			**Market place condition Green**

Table 4: The theory of strategy types: applying game theory to competition, using a traffic lights analogy

Notes (from the perspective of competitor X):

a) the use of a **red** strategy by any player will provoke fierce competition in the market as it is a major threat to all producers of an equal-quality product and a problem for all the others. In such a context the strongest player may win and force others to leave the market, thus creating better trading conditions later for those that remain. Indeed, such a player may thrive on the advances in productivity the level of competition may force upon the company. The danger, however, lies in the possibility of spoiling tactics from potential losers or the danger of a deflated market. This will arise if all competitors are obliged to reduce their prices. **Red** is a risky strategy which could bring a wide variety of uncontrollable gains and losses to all but the strongest players. Logically, you only play **red** if you're sure of winning or if you are desperate to keep up with rivals.

b) an **orange** strategy is playable in an easier world where risks have more to do with competitiveness as a function of innovation, creativity and marketing capability than with price reductions. It is not a loss-free world, however. You may still be outspent by a rival in R&D or Marketing, for instance. But you don't need to worry that prices will be slashed overnight. Given that cartels (and price fixing) are outlawed, this situation is typically one where the industry leader sets a price context which others accept as being the right sort of *ball park* and stick with.

c) peaceful co-existence tends to occur most in industries which have become oligopolised and where technological advances are few and far between. The stability that arises from the small number of players and their typically large-scale investments makes *price plays* very risky as a central strategy. Much better by far, they think, to *avoid* competition, except at the margin, and share the market-place: hence, one of the key rationales for mergers and takeovers. The strategy that may be indicated here is **green** and amounts to a low risk, control-the-environment approach. It is typical of mature industries.

It is apparent, also, that we need to reconsider the typology of decision makers illustrated in Table 2, page 142. It will be recalled that this allows us to cross-reference the risk profile of the decision-maker(s) against the decisional approach used. The result is the four categories of decision-maker we have met with: ***navigator, plotter, daredevil*** and ***mole.***

What if the decision-maker is, as a result of a personality quirk or particular life experiences, exceptionally optimistic or pessimistic? And not just one or the other, but if the individual or group have a permanently or irrepressibly cheerful or morbid disposition. Most people we meet with in life have moods that change with the circumstances. They move from pleasure to pain, from enthusiastic hope to anxiety or fear depending on the cards that life is dealing them. Some, indeed, are sober realists – much more like the *plotters* in our model than the navigators. But some individuals or groups are driven by dynamics which reflect an abnormal quantity of optimism or pessimism, sufficient to obscure reality and skew the decisional competence to what can be a dangerous extent.

The question is what will happen if we manage our businesses on this basis.

Strategy Matters

It goes without saying that directing a company is vastly different from gambling on horses, dogs or cards. For a start we are dealing with outcomes from our decisions, which we can seek to control after the decision, and not events. Secondly, we have an emotional involvement in a process that is ongoing as opposed to a series of finite engagements. Thirdly, we are likely to have very substantial knowledge of, and insights into, our field of operations. Nevertheless, we are seeking to manage risk or cope with uncertainty in an area where a biological system (management, workforce, company culture and structure) interfaces with a technical system (finance and production processes and resources).

Strategic decisions have a further characteristic that marks them out as a type of *game against nature*, a hazardous form of human occupation. As Ansoff indicated in his theory on decision classes, two types of decision – the administrative and operational – are rooted in a wealth of information, are made by people with substantial expertise and experience and a short-run. If they go wrong they can be put right without overmuch distress. They carry, in other words, little risk since they are decisions which are controllable and which seek to optimise factors internal to the firm.

By contrast strategic decisions are long-term in their consequences just as they are momentous in their content, because they:

- alter the relationship between the organisation and its working environment;
- typically demand new approaches – resources, systems and structures;
- reflect a leadership determination to achieve change; and
- serve as a symbol of the corporation's will to succeed.

The decision to develop and launch the Smart car was a technical one: DaimlerChrysler had (or could acquire) the necessary resources to meet a logical plan for the production and sale of a new car aimed at a valuable market segment. So much for the company ***plotters***. But it was also a decision in which the hopes, pride and reputation of a leading world engineering company – or rather those of its leaders – were involved. Hence, an emotional decision and one where any attempt at abandoning the project means certain loss of corporate face.

Withdrawing the product from the market would mean that critics would evaluate the performance of the decision-makers. Were they ***navigators***, for example, whose approach was highly reasonable and who were the victims of unforeseen circumstances? Or were they ***daredevils*** who sadly over-estimated the chances of success by under-estimating both the technical complexity of the task and the demanding nature of the consumer?

Yet another feature which is of concern in the management of strategy is the extent to which the board of directors, responsible for achieving the long-run success of the enterprise, actually shares a common risk-return profile. Is every single director cast in the same risk-taking mould? In fact, one of the reasons for *boards* of directors, beyond, that is, their ownership stake in the company, is to try to ensure that a balanced view of opportunities is taken. In other words, there is a pooling of the four types of decision-maker in the interests of a measured decision.

This could well be the case with the Smart car. But we shall never know. It may, however, have been otherwise. In other circumstances, it is quite possible for the board to be split on a strategic decision and for the more powerful, better-connected or simply more skilful directors to sway the judgement of the rest. Or to ensure they are out-voted. If this is indeed the case, the strategic decision becomes one not of optimising the match between the organisation and its environment, but of managing risky internal politics. Should there be resignations then the situation becomes one of personal interests and power plays.

Highly uncertain environments are tricky to deal with. True, they encourage high tech companies like Hewlett Packard or Eastman Kodak into making high-risk bets. But many companies lack what it takes to do this – industry position and risk-appetite, for instance – and their executives hedge their bets by making a number of smaller thrusts. Variants of this are maintaining flexibility (to watch evolving markets), waiting-and-seeing (to allow others to get their fingers burned) and making alliances (to pool the risks facing the players).

The problem is not just one of the strategies that are needed to cope but of not over-simplifying the analysis and of making over-hasty strategic responses. The problem arises particularly in firms which have a binary model of uncertainty handling. This model indicates that

- either we under-estimate it by assuming the world to be a certain place and the future to be capable of prediction. This might cause us to neglect danger signals or fail to capture opportunities. We might even focus on internal-optimisation alternatives to strategy,

- or we over-estimate it. This may lead us to the assumption that, as the world is chaotic, we can use gut-feel instead of structured analysis to deal with the vistas that lie ahead, however dangerous might be.

Uncertainty level theory (Courtney, Kirkland and Vignerie) addresses this issue by positing four types: a clear-enough future, alternate futures (ie, two or three scenarios capable of extrapolation), a range of futures (a range of possible outcomes but no natural scenarios) and true ambiguity. It then advocates the use of different tools and techniques to handle the different levels:

- a *clear-enough future* is visible and based on a dependable linear forecast of the likely market-place and competitive line-up. It can be addressed through the use of a traditional strategic tool kit.

• *Alternate Futures* may involve decision analysis based on option valuation models (eg, discounted cash flow) and game theory. Monte Carlo simulations may be used in the financial area to track alternative strategies.

• *Range of futures* connotes the use of scenario planning and technology forecasting. It is the focus of studies in, for example, of emerging markets or innovatory technologies.

• Level 4 uncertainty is what the theory calls *True Ambiguity*. Here we have no basis on which to argue the future environment in which we may be working and depend therefore on using analogical reasoning and non-linear dynamic models.

The notion behind the theory is that the company's strategy should be tailored to deal with the perceived level of uncertainty. Three broad strategic postures are advocated as contingencies, to be used depending on the situation the company is in. These are:

• adapt to the future. The company should systematically aim to recognise and seize opportunities in existing markets;

• shape the future. The company should play a leadership role in establishing how the industry works, by setting standards, for example;

• reserve the right to play. This means investing enough, but not too much, in the likely future pay-off opportunities in the industry.

Each involves a choice from among what the authors refer to as a portfolio of actions ranging from no-regrets moves to big bets, depending on the extent of positive pay-off. The first are decision options which will yield positive payoffs in any scenario whilst the second can have big positive pay-offs in some, but negative results in others.

Exhibit 7: Uncertainty levels theory

Based on: Strategy Under Uncertainty, Hugh Courtney, Jane Kirkland and Patrick Vignerie, Harvard Business Review, Nov-Dec 1997 (8)

If we combine the notion of the risk-uncertainty continuum with an axis representing return (eg, ROCE) then we can construct a basic framework that enables us to categorise strategic decisions in risk-return terms. Each is characterised as a direction and a vector. This is given in Figure 3(a), page 155. Here the company has four strategic choices facing it which, as far as can be ascertained, have different profiles The beta strategy is one where the higher risk is compensated for by the higher return that will hopefully be achieved. The delta strategy, by contrast, represents calmer waters than the company is currently trading in. The returns are lower, certainly, but there is a much higher probability of achieving them. If the CEO wishes to sleep well at night, rather than tossing fitfully over the real success chances of a perfect alpha move, then this is acceptable.

Three of McKinsey's top management consultants have produced a guide to achieving corporate growth. It's called the *Alchemy of Growth* (Telegraph Books, 1999) and it's a compendium of information based on the analysis of some 30 companies. The authors distinguish among three horizons in their review of strategic tasks. Horizon 1 relates to today's business and covers tasks critical to short-term success. Horizon 2 is about increasing revenue and profit flows through major transformation and investment initiatives. Horizon 3 contains the seeds of tomorrow's entreprise – research/pilot projects, alliances and cross holdings. As you move forward along the horizon line, you are meeting with an increasing number of future business-building schemes and as you climb this staircase of growth, so the risk factor rises.

Exhibit 8: Which time horizon are *you* happy with?

Based on: Three horizons on the road to growth, Edmond Jackson, Sunday Telegraph, 21/2/99 (9)

Of course, the strategy of choice would be ***alpha***, since here there is a greater chance of higher returns than are currently being obtained. An eldorado, in fact! By any stretch of the imagination, a strategy which has the gamma profile is to be avoided at all costs. Of course, the problem lies, as the Smart project team have discovered, with the phrase *as far as can be ascertained.* If the decision-makers are faced with information which they cannot trust or which is incomplete in important details, then the positioning of the choice decision moves rapidly rightwards.

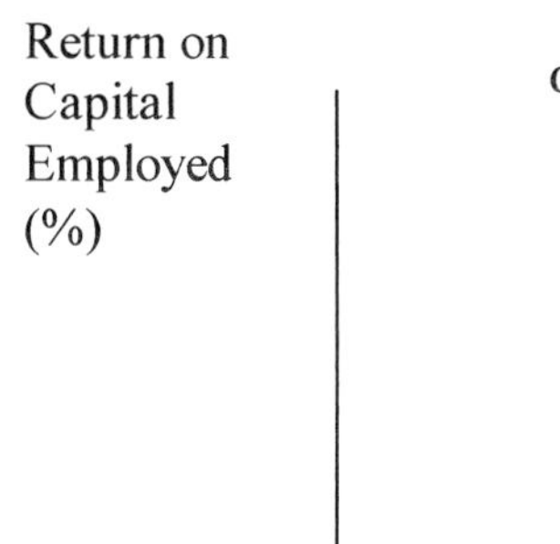

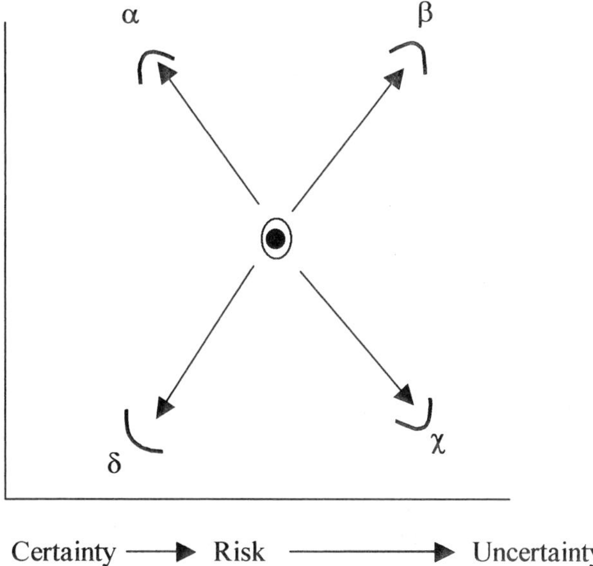

Certainty → Risk → Uncertainty

Figure 3(a) = Risk – Return Trade-off Appraisal

The intriguing feature of this appraisal is that, as Figure 3(b), page 156 shows, the actual expected value of the ***beta*** and ***delta*** strategies is roughly identical. As they lie on the isoquant line, see Figure 3(b), the expected value or anticipated return from a ***beta*** strategy (20 percent ROCE multiplied by a .5 probability = 10 percent) is approximately the same as that for a *delta* strategy (say a 12 percent multiplied by a .8 probability).

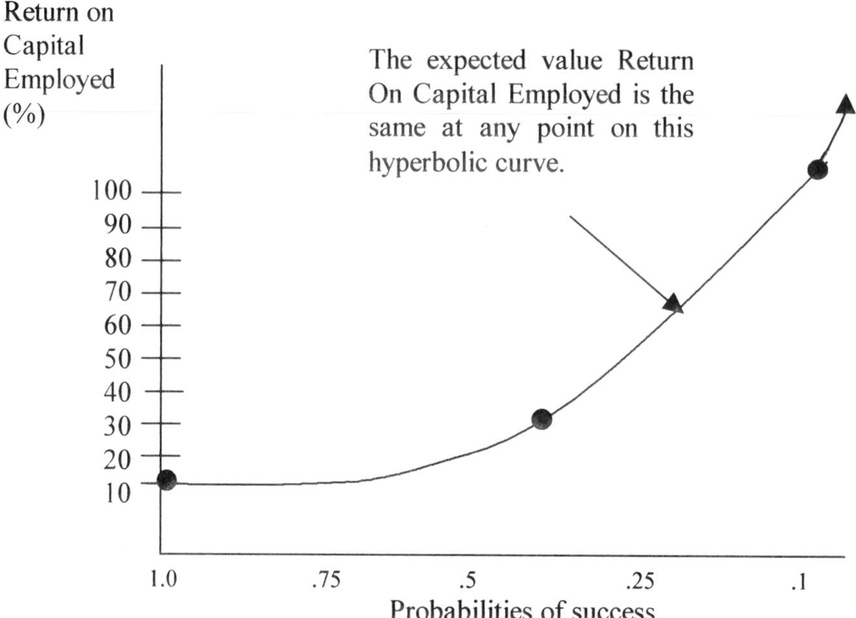

Figure 3(b) = Risk – Return Isoquant Curve

Gambling in the Financial Market

The results of a company's past corporate strategy are manifested, to an extent, in its share price today. This price also discounts the future strategies which the company is known (or thought) to be pursuing. The price multiplied by the number of shares issued gives us the company's market valuation and, naturally, any organisation driven by the principle of *shareholder value* is keen to optimise all the elements that contribute to this end.

Not only the effectiveness of the company's strategy, but also the efficiency of its operations and the vitality of its culture/structure, are at stake here. The ultimate measures of achievement in terms of the financial productivity of the corporation are such things as the price-earnings ratio, the market capitalisation and the market-to-book ratio ie, the market capitalisation divided by the value of the equity on the balance sheet. What happens if the share price falls? The firm's capitalisation and its ability to raise more capital by selling more shares is hit. What happens if the price rises? The ownership stake of directors in the company is increased and the company gains stature – in the market-place and in the stock-market.

But to what extent is the company's share price a function of its own achievements or other factors *over which it has little control*? For instance it could be argued that, at a given point in time, what matters is not the precise achievements of individual companies in an industry, so much as the progress of the industry as a whole.

With the rise of Internet-based competition, David and Goliath battles between "fast flexible entrants" and "dominant incumbents" are becoming commonplace (1). They have tended to use different strategies. The latter typically use a *Sumo* strategy. This is a highly traditional and well-rehearsed approach which reflects their sense of security, being based on a player's strength and weight. The former are *Judo* experts. What matters to them is agility and speed.

The difference in these two strategic approaches has very significant risk-return connotations. The Judo wrestlers typically reduce the risk content by:

- avoiding head-to-head conflicts or unwinnable wars with the incumbents;
- "pioneering" value innovations in pricing and distribution which "settlers" cannot match; (2)
- leveraging speed and incongruity without overdoing it – you cannot manage permanent revolution;
- using equity finance obtained through fast IPO flotations.

The risk challenge facing the incumbent is that they may not recognise the fact that David has changed the *rules of the game.*

Exhibit 9: Changing the rules of the game

Based on

(1) Judo Strategy: The Competitive Dynamics of Internet Time, David Yoffie and Michael A Cusumano, Harvard Business Review, Jan-Feb 1999 (10)

(2) Value Innovation: The Strategic Logic of High Growth, W. Chan Kim and Rene Mauborgne, Harvard Business Review, Jan-Feb 1997 (11)

US stock price movements over the period 1999-2001 are an interesting illustration of this argument.

Of course, the economic situation may play a significant role in setting the level of a nation's stock market in general and at certain times – say, during a boom or a recession. Our conclusion must be, that, at times, the company's performance may be the determining factor and, at other times, the context may exercise substantial influence.

Either way, the valuation placed on a particular company is not absolute, but relative. In theoretical terms, at least, the share price of DaimlerChrysler depends on its performance relative to other companies with which it can be compared in its sector, then on other leading world companies in other sectors and then on other potential investments of whatever type. The reason for this is the existence of share markets – local, regional global – whether of the fixed location or Internet form, where shares are traded. If shareholders have freedom to choose among wealth-creating instruments such as shares, derivatives, bonds, real estate and so on, then *ceteris paribus* they will tend to favour the best payers. By this we mean those producing the best dividend streams, or the best amount of capital appreciation or both.

And this is where gambling enters the strategic equation.

The stock market is one where liquidity is exchanged for shares by not just those who base their trades on the real actual/future value of enterprises but by speculators who, in fact, gamble on actual and likely movements in share prices. They are concerned not with yields (ie, real company performance) but with capital appreciation. The animals to be found in the bourse – *bears* and *bulls* – testify to a human menagerie in which betting is commonplace. The bear sells shares he does not possess in order to buy them back at depressed prices and complete the bargain. He gambles on either the price going down as a result of market movements which are independent of his own action or, if a major player, perhaps as a consequence of his action. The bull buys shares on the grounds that the purchase will drive the price higher and allow him to achieve a profit by selling at that higher price. Given the day trading phenomenon we have discussed, we should not assume that all stock market inventors are comprehensive rational decision-makers.

If we take the perspective of a well-run, highly profitable traditional company, we can also note a further chilling phenomenon which seems to becoming more and more characteristic of the *New Economy*. For such a company's managers, the worst of all possible world prevails when the company, currently highly successful and with what is commonly accepted as a sound strategy for the future, is *put in play* by speculators who are only interested in *making a quick buck*. Or that such a company is ejected from the hallowed rankings of (say) the FTSE Index, on the grounds that its capitalisation is now wholly outranked by a that of an arriviste TMT stock (a company with its base in Technology, Media and Telecommunications).

Of course, in a world where financial instruments are freely traded, it may not be the company that is being buffeted, but the nation. This is a fact of elemental importance since speculation is not limited to the instruments we have listed but also comprises foreign exchange and government bonds. Indeed, some classes of instrument, like futures and derivatives, are by their very nature conducive to gambling, even if their essential purpose is to hedge risks, as the collapse and enforced resuscitation of LCTM has recently shown.

We thus find ourselves with the paradox that is at the heart of our investigation of strategy-as-gambling. On the one hand, strategy purports to be an activity in which, at the optimal level the corporate *navigator* builds the company's strategy on a sound decision-making system and a dependable data base. On the other the company's share price is affected not only by rational evaluation of the financial implications of that strategy but also by the gaming in the market in which companies are treated generically in a not dissimilar way from horses. The more today's speculative *New Economy* thinking about share prices feeds ever-rising or ever-falling prices in the NASDAQ Index, the more dangerous this situation can be.

Whilst it is possible to over-exaggerate this argument, it cannot any longer be baldly asserted that a company's value is predominantly a function of its strategic capability or that shareholder value reflects the real value of the company, as traditionally economically defined. The risks the company seeks to manage, and the uncertainty it tries to come to terms with, in its market–place are, perhaps, the most important part of the challenge facing the firm. But the stock market, with all its speculative features, is another.

Back to Strategy

Our discussion of corporate strategy so far has been deliberately limited to questions which are relatively circumscribed in risk terms. A company's product-market scope moves – productivity, product/market development, diversification – do not, it can be argues, expose the company to a worse category of risk than is currently being dealt with. The argument for this is obvious – the firm would tend to know in detail the environment in which it trades. Even diversification may not take the organisation away from its technical or technological roots.

Once a company begins to examine Porteresque issues of changing the company's generic strategy – moving from *mass* to *class*, for instance – as a result of market-place difficulties or exciting new opportunities, it is moving into different territory. It competitive capability, its resource base and its culture may be inappropriate for the new situation it finds itself in and may have to re-engineer itself, strategically.

By the same token, strategies which have to do with re-positioning the company in its industry's value-added chain (VAC) also take it into a *terra* which is much less *cognita.* Taking over, merging with or even allying with a rival at the same stage in the VAC involve a substantial change in the mechanics of competition. By the same token, integrating forward or backward to hopefully take advantage of scale economies/security in marketing or supply, may also be fraught.

Done within the organisations' home territory; we cannot regard such moves as carrying the highest risk quotient. But if, these strategic moves take place across borders – and, most especially, across trade bloc borders – then the challenge grows. DaimlerChrysler is an example of a corporation whose constituent companies each found themselves confronted with the strategic imperative – for positive or negative reasons – of:

- having to achieve even greater scale economies in production, R&D and marketing;
- having to source world-wide to take full advantage of all positive cost differentials (labour, capital etc) and low value currencies;
- having to sell globally and, particularly, in the most attractive and/or highest growth rate markets.

This imperative is a function of the changing dynamics of competition in key global industries such as telecommunications, financial services, pharmaceuticals and so on. It is a phenomenon which is well recorded in the literature and amounts to the global oligopolisation of strategic industries. Even majors players in these industries are being swept along by the flood of changes – and the so-called *feeding frenzy* involved. There is certainty in such change – even if there is massive uncertainty in how to manage it. Perhaps we are naïve if we find this surprising. Certainly, we shouldn't be, as Exhibit 10 below suggests.

> Giving evidence to the Treasury Select Committee, Lord Lawson, former Chancellor of the Exchequer, said the Bank of England's Monetary Policy Committee relied on complex economic models to create an air of mystique about its decisions. "They have all these complicated equations, all these fan charts, all this juju (West African black magic) they go in for in a big way, which has very little effect on how decisions are taken. *I think this juju is useful for the mystery that is needed for authority".*

Exhibit 10: Getting your data from the JUJU

Source: Lawson blasts Bank for economic juju, Lea Patterson, The Times, 9/6/99 (12)

Where the change pattern is least well understood by traditional strategists, as we have already noted, is in the IT sector, and specifically, that of internet stocks. The fact that there is a lack of dependable data about new market entrants such as *Amazon.com*, because of their typically short lives and even shorter profit histories, does not stop market hyperbole.

Price earnings ratios of some internet stocks currently either discount a wonderful earnings future or a speculative boom – or they point to an over-excessive money supply being fed into the market.

The more the world opens up to global trade, the more technology change will force the re-configuration of competition patterns that have held for a couple of decades. *We will all be forced to talk business with strangers*. In such a context, it is not unnatural to suggest that strategy and power-politics become intertwined. The bigger the cross-border merger, the more *mega* the global take-over, the more likely is it that, under such conditions, companies move willy-nilly and at a fast pace along the risk-uncertainty continuum.

Conclusion

The strategist seeks not to gamble but to manage risk and what the strategist does is never construed in corporate terms as gambling. Investors do not like to think of companies' pursuing strategies, whose risks are not adequately known or which cannot be controlled. What matters to such investors, as opposed to speculators, is guaranteed future performance. Strategists, thus, need to be risk-evaluators par excellence, because the very essence of strategy is about managing future risk in exchange for satisfactory return. What companies, therefore, require to meet market expectations are *navigators* who can achieve what is required.

Yet we are dealing with a context in which the fact of human behaviour creates a gambling aura. This fact is manifested in board room actors who make the strategic decisions and in financial speculators who trade in company shares. The risks that are being run by *all* growth-oriented companies engaged in open global trading, whether working in high technology or commodity products, are increasing daily. Hopefully, your company will not find itself forced to gamble with its future.

References

(1) de Aenlle, Conrad. A French-German Union. *International Herald Tribune*, 5-6/6/1999

(2) Bailey, Jemimah. Are internet stocks burnt out. *Sunday Telegraph*, 6/6/1999

(3) You expect Big Losses and Want $10 Million? Sure, We'll Consider It. *Wall Street Journal,* 17/3/1999

(4) Kahneman, Daniel and Tversky, Amos. Prospect Theory: An Analysis of Decision Making Under Risk. *Econometrica*, 1979.

(5) Browing, E.S. New Forces Are Now Powering Surging Stocks. *Wall Street Journal,* 15/3/1999

(6) Study Finds Smokers In Denial Over Health Risk. *Boston Herald*, 17/3/1999

(7) O'Brien, Timothy. Assessing Risk Pays Off, *International Herald Tribune*, 21/1/1999

(8) Courtney, Hugh; Kirkland, Jane and Vignerie, Patrick. Strategy Under Uncertainty. *Harvard Business Review*, Nov-Dec 1997

(9) Jackson, Edmond. Three horizons on the road to growth. *Sunday Telegraph*, 21/2/1999

(10) Yoffie, David and Cusumano, Michael A, Judo Strategy: The Competitive Dynamics of Internet Time. *Harvard Business Review*, Jan-Feb 1999

(11) Chan Kim, W. and Mauborgne, Rene. Value Innovation: The Strategic Logic of High Growth, *Harvard Business Review*, Jan-Feb 1997

(12) Patterson, Lea. Lawson blasts Bank for economic juju. *Times,* 9/6/1999

Chapter 7

EXPLORING THE STRATEGIC MANAGEMENT-ECONOMICS INTERFACE

Dominic Swords

Introduction

This chapter employs a managerial perspective to explore key aspects of the important, yet often understressed, relationship between economics and strategic management. We will see that economics has had a pervasive influence on the growth and emergence of mainstream models and research in strategic management, but that its influence has at times been implicit rather than explicit. One reason for this is that economics tends to be concerned with broad questions of efficiency and performance at a highly aggregated level of analysis and with questions of public policy.

This means that its macro models cannot always be applied directly to the needs of an individual firm seeking to understand and secure competitive advantage in its market, even though the centrality of economic analysis to all aspects of commercial thinking is unquestioned. However, when its models have been reframed to reflect a commercial orientation or when tangible concepts have been incorporated into strategic management as a part of the framework for research, its influence has become pervasive. (1)

The area of innovation management exemplifies many of these issues and is one where economics has made, and is making, a strong practical contribution. Innovation has received much attention in the practitioner and strategic management literature in recent times. Typically, the key questions addressed are:

- what is the right focus for innovation in specific market circumstances;
- how to create an effective and ongoing process of innovation;

- how to turn the production of innovations into a sustainable source of competitive advantage.

All of these require an explicit understanding of the *process* of innovation itself – how innovation happens in firms – as well as insights into the associated organisational capabilities needed to sustain it. These rank high on the strategic management agenda; in today's globalised world it is not sufficient simply to be good at making new products. Even breakthrough products can be copied and improved on by competitors as never before. Developing an organisation for which innovation, in its widest sense, is a central capability is a much bigger prize to be won. Organisational flexibility and robustness to external competitive changes, for example, may be a critically important source of superior competitive performance and longevity.

This chapter aims, therefore, at using innovation thinking within firms and other features of strategic thinking, such as resource-based strategy, as exemplars of the actual and potential contribution that economics can make.

The Changing Pattern of Strategic Management Thought

Over the period from the start of the 1960s to well into the 1980s, it was the field of industrial economics that made its biggest mark on the development of strategic management thinking. Pre-eminent amongst those that systematically applied economic models to the subject was Michael Porter.(2) His industry competition analysis approach, embodied in the Five Forces model, views the formulation of competitive strategy as a matter of relating a company to its environment. The external environment is an exogenous given, to which the organisation must adapt and fit itself. It is directly derived from mainstream neo-classical theories of the firm.

In the competitive forces approach, five industry-level forces (entry barriers, threat of substitution, bargaining power of buyers and of suppliers and industry rivalry) shape the behaviours of firms by defining the range of strategic options available and ultimately determine the profit potential of the industry. These five forces are a practitioner-friendly description of the functional elements that are used to define an industry structure in economic terms. What Porter did supremely well was to replace articulation of the public policy concern with the need to monitor firms, which might be making excessive, even monopoly, profits, with an analytical methodology showing how a firm could attempt to achieve precisely just such a goal. His framework can be used by a firm to find a position within its industry from which it can attempt to sustain a competitive advantage through taking advantage of competitive forces, protecting itself against them or influencing them to their own benefit. Thus, strategic positioning is key. Clusters of firms that exhibit similar positioning are modelled as strategic groups.

Strategic management has more recently questioned this premise of the deterministic nature of industry structure and its definition of strategic options. Prahalad and Hamel (3) indicate that, from the late 80s, there has been a period of changed thinking, which has challenged the models and concepts previously used in the field. Certainly, the academic, research and also practitioner focus has shifted during that time from a concern with strategic management analysis towards issues of implementation. This reflects the tensions between the need for increasing rates of corporate renewal (issues of change management, innovation, transformation and implementation) and the more static focus of the traditional strategic formation process (concern with industry analysis, strategic positioning and a linear strategy development/execution process).

It also reflects the need for commercial firms to improve their competitive performance in an increasingly hostile and unforgiving commercial world. The pressures on business organisations for more rapid change and innovation can make those who use a structured strategic formation process appear slow and clumsy and raise doubts as to their ability to manage appropriate change.

Lengnick-Hall (4) suggests that macro-environmental pressures of globalisation, greater uncertainty and turbulence, together with increasing rates of technological change, have placed such pressures on established economics-based strategic management models as to render them inappropriate. It is asserted that competitive advantage can be better explained by exploring conditions during periods of prolonged dis-equilibrium rather than by referring to the equilibrium states referred to in standard analysis. In this context, the disillusionment of practitioners and, indeed, members of the academic community like Mintzberg (5), with the traditional strategic management process is easily understood.

Such a re-evaluation of the tools and techniques of strategic management involves assessing the embedded assumptions within traditional strategic models whether they are complete and in resonance with contemporary experience or partial and outdated. This search has become the focus for addressing the need for what Prahalad and Hamel describe as an *alternative paradigm* in strategic management. Clearly, from a corporate perspective, anachronistic economics thinking is no longer tolerable as a major driver in strategic management.

At the same time, similar challenges to the dominance of orthodox theories of the firm have emerged from within the economics discipline itself. Firstly, empirical works by Geroski and Pomroy (6) and Geroski (7) suggest that the line of causality from market structure to performance is two-way. They also indicate that, amongst other factors, there is an inter-dependent and reciprocal relationship between firms' innovation behaviours and patterns of structural change in the industries to which they belong, a relationship determining the pace and need for innovation. This latter challenges the Structure-Conduct-Performance framework implicit in Porter's approach and mirrors the strategic management debate over the relative importance of market conditions compared with company resources as determinants of strategic performance. (8)

Secondly, Barney (9) acknowledges the limitations of neo-classical assumptions of perfect or near perfect knowledge. This recognises the importance of studying the reasons for variances in corporate performance that can persist over time between firms with apparently similar resource endowments. He concludes that tacit knowledge and other "un-observables" are an important determinant of firm performance. They are perhaps not simply minor imperfections in market conditions, but prime drivers of differential performance between competitors.

Resource-Based Strategy

The resource-based approach emerged during the 1990s out of this new thinking about strategic performance The theory suggests that relative performance is best explained and understood through consideration of those distinctive capabilities of a firm that are hard for competitors to imitate. It is a viewpoint which emphasises the qualitative heterogeneity of resource endowments amongst players within an industry.

In the strategic management field, this has been associated with the work of Prahalad and Hamel, who seek to define the resources that are unique to a firm as its *core competencies.* It is on these that its competitiveness is ultimately based. Kay who adds the concept of *strategic architecture,* has developed an alternative perspective. (10) He argues that it is not simply the possession of particular core competencies that is the source of competitiveness. Rather it is the ability to build these competencies into unique and distinctive capabilities that drives superior and sustainable competitiveness for the firm.

In the resource-based approach, the creation and nurturing of firm-specific capabilities is seen as more important to corporate performance and strategy than is competitive positioning and tactical moves in relation to competitors. (11) Resource-based strategic groups are based on the clustering of firms according to their deployment of similar resource bundles, rather than on the congruence of their strategic orientation. (12) This is quite a different perspective from that of Porter and implies quite different strategic actions. Geroski (13) and Kay (14) for example, demonstrate that high-performing, innovative organisations are associated with internal qualities of flexibility and robustness or with specific internal architectures that are valuable sources of superior performance.

Building on the resource-based perspective, Teece, Pisaro and Shuen (15) have proposed an extension of the framework that involves a subtle and important addition to develop a dynamic capabilities framework. They suggest that the resource-based view is somewhat limited in explaining how core competencies are developed in order to achieve competitive advantage and the process by which they may change over time. It is this process, of course, that enables a firm to scan the environment for emerging technological and market trends and innovative appropriately. A dynamic capabilities approach emphasises the pro-active nature of the firm as it consistently seeks to renew competencies so as to achieve congruence with the changing business environment. These writers use the term "capabilities" to refer to the key role of strategic management in appropriately adapting, integrating and reconfiguring internal and external resources and functional competencies to match the requirements of a changing environment.

The Inspiration of Economics

Such developments are widely acknowledged to draw on economics for their inspiration. It is now recognised that the resource-based strategy approach has been influenced by concepts first articulated by the economist Penrose (16) who emphasised the importance of tacit knowledge and the individual differences between firms as an explanation of behaviour. Penrose saw the firm as essentially a pool of resources stretching from physical machines and labour through to licenses and intangibles such as knowledge and experience. She distinguished between objective knowledge and experience-based knowledge. The former is available to all and relates to awareness, for example, of the technical details of how to operate particular production processes. The latter is *the unique and accumulated internal knowledge resource* of a firm that develops over time as a powerful source of superior performance and growth for the firm over its industry competitors. Clear parallels can be seen between this analysis and Prahalad and Hamel's core competencies on the one hand and Kay's distinctive capabilities on the other.

The resource-based view does not ignore the importance of industry factors in influencing corporate performance. It provides a means of exploring variations in performance and in innovation within industries and the importance of internal resources in explaining such variations. The fruit of Penrose's work has significantly shifted the focus away from strategy as simply an externally defined process towards one where firms are more proactively able to determine their own growth performance.

The work of Joseph Schumpeter (17) has also made a striking contribution to strategic management. Indeed Jacobson (18) suggests that Schumpeterian economics has had its most significant impact through its influence on strategic management rather than within his original discipline. In particular, his concept of *creative destruction* has provided us with a framework which seeks to explain the dynamic development of an industry over time.

Tripsas (19), for example, applies the concept of creative destruction to the US typesetter to understand firstly, the overall evolution of business activity in the sector and, secondly, the internal factors that help incumbents to change and adapt to new circumstances or that hinder them from so doing. The typesetting industry was chosen both because of the availability of an unusually long term dataset covering a period of 100 years of the industry and because of the radical technological change that had been experienced over that time. Three waves of creative destruction were classified that had wrought radical changes in the industry. Key to these were the move from traditional hot metal to analogue typesetting and from analogue to electronic digital methods. The point of interest was the list of factors that explained the response of existing players to technological change as compared with that of new entrants. When did incumbents innovate and when were they overwhelmed and overtaken by new players?

The three factors which explained how some existing players successfully innovated in response to each destructive wave were:

- their willingness to invest in the new technology;
- their technical abilities to adopt the new techniques it involved; and
- their ability to appropriate the benefits from the new technology.

The study explains the extent to which previous experience in out-dated technologies actually proved to be a curse and not a blessing in the face of radical industry change. Handicaps of legacy investment, inappropriate skills and established mindsets all hindered early adoption of these new opportunities.

Tripsas suggests that the study confirms the predictive power of a Schumpterian framework for analysis and is an important step forward in our understanding of the dynamic of industry development over time. She points to the need to develop more reliable classifications of degrees of change that impact on an industry and also to the need for more effective ways of discriminating between the resource base of players within the same industry.

Yet another area of economic theory which provides a basis for much developmental work in strategic management thinking and which is distinct from that of Penrose and Schumpeter, is the field *of evolutionary economics,* associated primarily with Nelson and Winter. (20) This is embodied in an approach which views the firm as a bundle of resources that interacts with its environment using a series of search and selection routines to seek out market leading opportunities. It emphasises a dynamic strategic development process and the emergence over time of path-dependent capabilities. That is to say, the initial basis for a firm's competitiveness is its ability to provide a good or service that meets or creates a market need. As markets then change, they cause complementary changes in the capabilities of firms. Thus *strategy becomes an interactive development process over time.*

As Barnett and Burgelman (21) show, this evolutionary perspective on strategy has spawned significant work on the strategic search and selection processes used by firms operating in highly turbulent and uncertain market environments. They suggest that the main benefit of evolutionary techniques is that they track the dynamic process of change as it unfolds in an industry. This avoids a more traditional approach to consider comparative static equilibrium positions. They suggest that the mechanism that moves a market from one equilibrium to another is of more interest in many strategic decisions than a before-and-after snapshot. It crucially enables an understanding of the emergence of new strategic variants. Again traditional approaches are typified as mapping out a given strategic space within which the firm's position is plotted. Finally, a key outcome of the evolutionary approach is that it provides a means of engaging with other disciplinary approaches to understanding strategic process. These, according to Mezias (22), fit very well with organisational learning theory.

The work of Penrose, Schumpeter and Nelson and Winter (23), while primarily associated with the field of economics, has thus made a large-scale contribution to recent developments in strategic management thinking and practice. All three approaches are dynamic and scrupulously avoid taking a static external view of the firm. Penrose predominantly focuses on the unique resource base that a firm has and how this explains its source of competitiveness in the market. Schumpeter and Nelson and Winter tend to focus more on the process by which firms grow and develop over time. Each represents a distinctive, novel and relevant angle on the subject.

Indeed, such developments in the field of economics can well be described as being outside the current framework of the discipline. They are approaches that do not simply stretch or enrich traditional concepts; they require a positional shift. It has even been suggested that this may mark the demise of the dominant paradigm in mainstream economics, with the need to discard traditional assumptions of rationality, perfect competition and partial equilibrium analysis.

Alternatively, we can recognise that these developments are complementary perspectives in our search to understand the process of competition and the growth of firms. (24) While the resource-based view enlarges our understanding of the importance of individual differences between firms in explaining their performance, this is framed within an understanding of an industry's structural constraints. The Schumpeterian and Evolutionary perspectives both provide an insight into market dynamics and also a bridge into behavioural-based theories of organisational behaviour. As such, they are a powerful way in which the subject can develop and maintain a continued contribution to strategic management as an integrated and cross-disciplinary area of enquiry.

Innovation Management – An Inter-Disciplinary Approach

As already seen, economics has featured significantly within recent strategic management thinking generally. We now turn our attention to innovation as a specific topic of interest to decision-makers as they develop and enact their strategies. Innovation appears in a number of guises within the business literature. For some it is concerned with the effective management of technology. For others, the development of new products and processes or the creation of new administrative or organisational innovations. A significant literature, too, addresses the issues of how to develop an appropriate culture within the firm to promote innovativeness. The issue for economics theorists in this emerging field is how to engage effectively with these new themes.

Much established work in economic research on innovation focuses on technical change and its impact on productivity, national competitiveness and economic growth, especially as an input to public policy on R&D activities. (25 and 26) There is a tendency for this type of research to be dominated by R&D based measures of innovation. Griliches (27) notes that the research difficulties of modelling and measuring innovation processes meaningfully at the level of the firm tend to explain this research focus. Moreover, although R&D measures suffer many problems, as an indicator of the total investment in the commitment to innovation resources, it is possibly the best and most reliable measure we have. (28) Thus, an empirical measurement problem, as well as a bias towards a public policy perspective, have driven this high-level approach to measuring innovation performance across countries and industries rather than between firms.

A number of writers have recognised the importance of integrating economics with the findings of other disciplines on this topic. Bowen and Ricketts (29) suggest that effective innovation requires not only a supply of new ideas from research and development, but also the managerial capacity to utilise and develop them effectively and the marketing expertise to ensure that they are embodied in goods and services which consumers want. More recently, Dodgson and Bessant (30) and Tidd *et al.* (31) have articulated this approach as requiring the integration of the management of technological, market and organisational change. This implies not only the need to identify and understand the linkages between the structures and processes which support innovation, but also the opportunity for innovation in specific technological and market environments.

Works such as these are significant and good examples of integrating studies in that they seek to draw together a holistic approach to understanding innovation, which draws on insights from different traditions and research methodologies. What is striking comparing the two approaches is how much the sophistication of the treatment of innovation management has moved on since the publication of the first. Tidd *et al.*, in particular, advance conceptual frameworks for modelling innovation and innovation processes that were absent in the earlier works.

These works highlight a number of issues, which are opportunities for new lines of research in economics, as it contributes to developments in strategic management. These include:

- more effective means of measuring innovative activity – as innovations increasingly stem from non-R&D sources in many sectors – more direct measures of the inputs and the complementary resources needed for innovation are required;
- modelling the dynamic innovation decision making process that occurs within a firm;
- the development of qualitative as well as quantitative means of distinguishing the heterogeneity and tacit qualities of firms and the individual differences that cause variations in innovations performance between firms.

There are clearly ways to build on non-mainstream developments within economics to continue its significant place in the strategic management literature.

Conclusion

This chapter has sought to explore the contribution that economics has made and can continue to make to key developments in strategic management thinking, both in general and also with specific reference to a growing interest in the management of innovation within the business literature. It has argued that, firstly, the initial reliance of strategic management on industrial economics has now shifted with the development of the resource-based school and other recent developments. (32) Secondly, it has been asserted that contemporary models in strategic management are hugely influenced by research and thinking of economists such as Schumpeter, Penrose and Nelson and Winter. (33) Additionally, works such as those by Bowen and Ricketts and Tidd *et al.* are significant and good examples of integrating studies that draw significantly on economics and provide an integrative approach to understanding the effective management of innovation. (34)

That such contributions have not received full acceptance or integration into mainstream economics is widely recognised. They can be categorised as either paradigm-stretching or paradigm-breaking, when benchmarked against the dominant models in neo-classical industrial economics. Such views of economics represent self-imposed limitations on its real world applications – in relation to assumptions of consistency of human and organisational behaviour and rationality in human behaviour. The challenge is to acknowledge these limitations and capitalise on the richness and rigour of economic thought as it continues to the development of strategic management as a multi-disciplinary field of study. Certainly, in this, economics' loss is strategic management's gain.

References

(1) Jacobson, R. The Austrian School of Strategy. *Academy of Management Review*, vol 17, 1992, pp.782-807

(2) Porter, M.E. *Competitive Strategy*. New York: Free Press, 1980

(3) Prahalad, C. K. and Hamel, G. Strategy as a field of Study: Why Search for a New Paradigm? *Strategic Management Journal*, vol. 15, 1994, pp.5-16

(4) Lengnick-Hall, C.A. Innovation and Competitive Advantage: What We Know and What We Need to Learn. *Journal of Management*, vol. 18, 1992, pp.399-429

(5) Mintzberg, H. *The Rise and Fall of Strategic Planning*. New York: Free Press, 1994

(6) Geroski, P.A. and Pomroy, R. Innovation and the Evolution of Market Structure. *The Journal of Industrial Economics*, vol. 38, 1990, pp.299-314

(7) Geroski, P.A. *Market Structure, Corporate Performance and Innovative Activity*. Oxford: Clarendon Press, 1994

(8) Henderson, R. and Mitchell, W. The Interactions of Organisational and Competitive Influences on Strategy and Performance. *Strategic Management Journal,* 1997, vol. 18

(9) Barney, J.B. Firm Resources and Sustained Competitive Advantage. *Journal of Management*, vol. 17, 1991, pp.99-120

(10) Kay, J. *Foundations of Corporate Success: How Business Strategies Add Value*. London: Oxford University Press, 1993

(11) Teece, D.J, Pisano, G. and Shuen, A. Dynamic Capabilities and Strategic Management. *Strategic Management Journal,* vol. 18, 1997 pp.509-33

(12) Mehra, A. Resource and Market Based Determinants of Performance in the US Banking Industry. *Strategic Management Journal*, vol. 17, 1996, pp 307-322

(13) As (7)

(14) As (10)

(15) As (11)

(16) Penrose, E.T. *The Theory of the Growth of the Firm.* Oxford: Basil Blackwell, 1972

(17) Schumpeter, J.A. *The Theory of Economic Development.* Cambridge, Mass.: Harvard University Press, 1934

(18) As (1)

(19) Tripsas, M, Unraveling the Process of Creative Destruction: Complementary Assets and Incumbent Survival in the Typesetter Industry. *Strategic Management Journal*, vol. 18, 1997

(20) Nelson, R.R. and Winter, S.G. *An Evolutionary Theory of Economic Change.* Harvard University Press, 1982

(21) Barnett, W. P. and Burgelman, R. A. Evolutionary Perspectives on Strategy. *Strategic Management Journal*, vol. 17, 1996

(22) Mezias, S.J. and Glynn, M.A. The Three Faces of Corporate Renewal: Institution, Revolution and Evolution. *Strategic Management Journal*, vol. 14, 1993, pp.77-101

(23) As (20)

(24) Gomulka, S. *The Theory of Technological Change and Economic Growth.* London: Routledge, 1990

(25) Griliches, Z. R&D and Productivity: Econometric Results and Measurement Issues', *in* Stoneman. P. (ed.) *Handbook of the Economics of Innovation and Technical Change*, Blackwell, 1993

(26) Van Reenan, J.A. Break for R&D? *New Economy*, vol. 2, Summer 1995, pp.80-84

(27) As (25)

(28) As (26)

(29) Bowen, A. and Ricketts, M. *Stimulating Innovation in Industry*, Kogan Page, 1992

(30) Dodgson, M. and Bessant, J. *Effective Innovation Policy: A New Approach.* International Thompson Business Press, 1996

(31) Tidd, J., Bessant, J. and Pavitt, K. *Managing Innovation: Integrating Technological, Market and Organisational Change.* Wiley, 1997

(32) Rumelt, R.P., Schendel, D.E. and Teece, D.J. (eds) Fundamental Research Issues in Strategy and Economics. *Strategic Management Journal*, Winter Special Issue, 12. 1991

As (2)

As (10)

(33) As (17)

As (16)

(34) As (29)

As (31)

Chapter 8

STRATEGY AND THE VIRTUAL ORGANISATION

Jane McKenzie

Introduction

The dawn of a new millennium is upon us. Turning points in history are good times to reflect back on the forces that have shaped our journey so far, but, perhaps more importantly, they are a vantage point from which to look forward and map out a path to the future. It is a truism that turbulence, uncertainty and rapid change characterize today's business environment. The forces of globalisation, an increasingly knowledge-based economy and the consolidation of communications and computing technology create ripe conditions for the evolution of what we have come to call the *virtual* organisation. Virtual organisations are flexible in form, harness the power of diversity, and depend on continuous learning and effective, high-tech communication. If we define the virtual organisation as "any organisation which is continually evolving, redefining and re-inventing itself for practical business purposes" (1) then clearly there are significant implications for strategy in this new style of business operation.

Sustainable strategies for differentiation arise when leaders bring together and co-ordinate geographically-distributed, varying networks of partners, – customers, suppliers, employees and other independent workers – and enable them to interact and learn together for their mutual benefit. Clearly, there are many uncertainties and risks involved. The challenge is to develop and mould the complex web of organisations and people into a coherent system that handles uncertainty through adaptive strategies that respond to turbulence in the environment.

This chapter starts with a brief review of the powerful converging forces that have been reshaping the face of business operations over the past decade and continue to do so. The impact of these in combination creates massive opportunities for organisations to reconfigure themselves in order to gain competitive advantage; one way that is becoming more attractive to many organisations being the notion of *virtuality.* We then go on to address the benefits and difficulties involved in *going virtual*. The balance of the chapter deals with the potential for organising virtually, and discusses the primary strategic considerations required to move an organization from where it is now, into an advanced state of virtual connection.

Forces Shaping a Shrinking World

Even the quickest scan of contemporary business literature generates an impressive list of the inter-dependent forces affecting organisations. Among this list two drivers are paramount:

- Globalisation, and the geographical dispersion of intelligent resources;(2)
- The advent and potential of the digital form of communication, and the convergence of telecommunications mechanisms. (3)

This background generates greater turbulence, uncertainty and complexity resulting in more intricate business interactions. Of course, the fact that the nature of business transactions is increasingly information-based adds an important extra dimension. (4) It is hardly surprising that knowledge per se has become recognised as a critical business asset in its own right. (5) Clearly, in such a context of accelerating change, the ability to innovate and learn becomes an increasingly important survival skill for both individuals and organisations. (6)

At the beginning of the decade, it was Toffler who re-invigorated the debate into the possibility that knowledge could increasingly supplant money as the primary source of power in our society. (7) Knowledge was known to provide a wholly different sort of power base. For example, in a turbulent world it gave the possibility of greater control over the future than might finance alone. This is because, firstly, unlike money, it can be exploited simultaneously by different people.

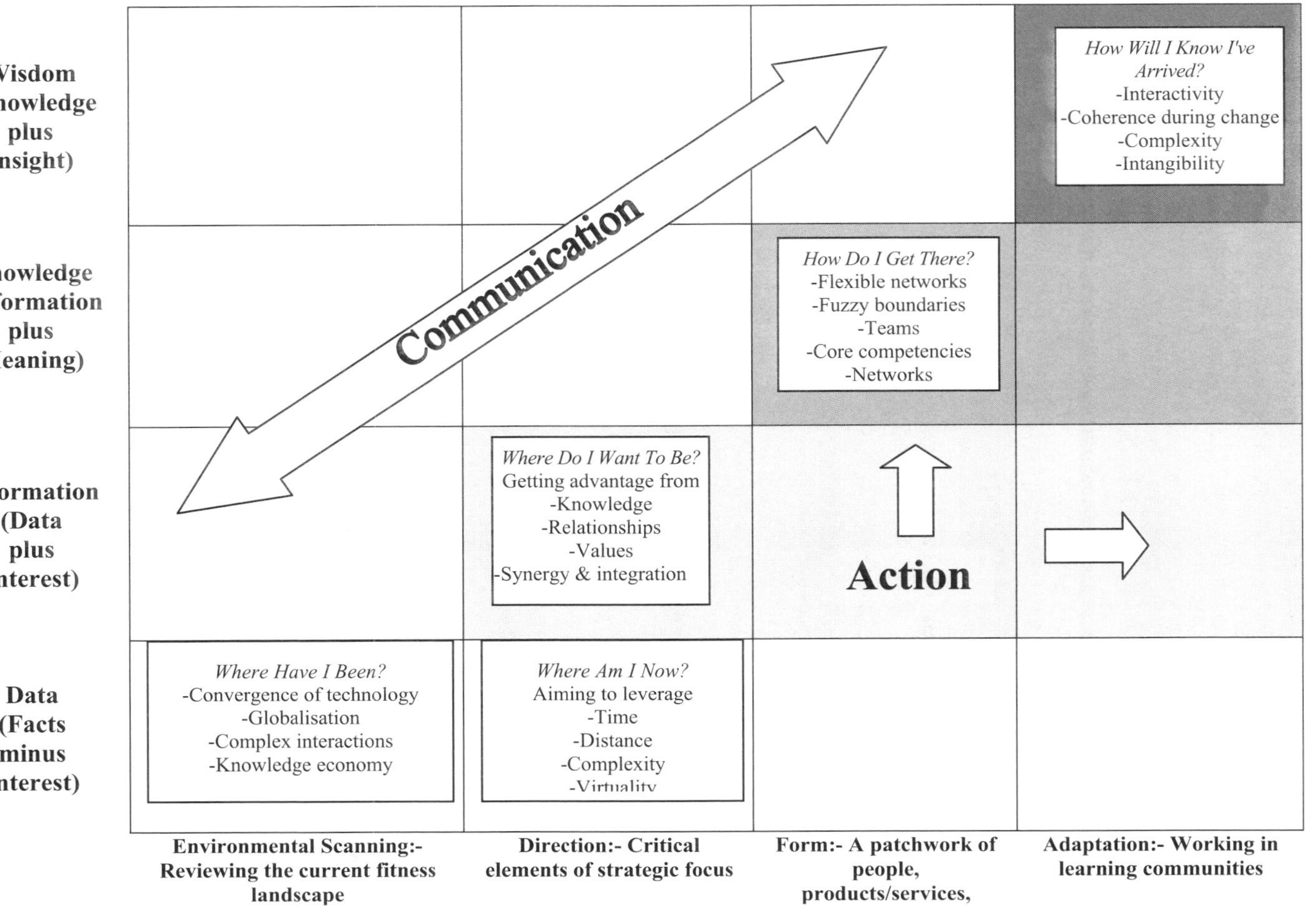

Figure 1: Climbing the Steps of Strategic Learning

Secondly, it is not spent with use. Indeed, the more knowledge is shared, the more it spreads. This means that those with wealth and privilege no longer enjoy the sole prerogative of power and control and, as the knowledge-as-power model gains ground over the money-as-power model, this will increasingly be the case.

Knowledge can, of course, be used to amplify the effects of wealth and physical force, – to persuade, punish or reward. But its key value lies in its predictive nature: it allows those who have it to anticipate events. This allows them to change expected outcomes, transform situations, stimulate creativity as well as improve efficiency. Over the past decade, the effects of what Toffler describes as the "deepest powershift in human history" have started to be played out across a world stage, in business, economies and private lives. The boundaries between the three areas are becoming less clearly defined. Businesses are becoming intricately tied up with a whole range of often-conflicting social, political and economic forces. The distinction between work and private life is becoming blurred and the influence of economic circumstances in the distant macro world can impact heavily on citizens' private lives. This blurring of boundaries is both an opportunity for and a challenge to conventional forms of organisation.

The convergence of communication technologies has created the perfect backdrop for a sweeping knowledge revolution, supporting and driving a panoply of digital scenarios: E-commerce, E-learning, E-business. All these global phenomena have huge sociological and economic implications, because, (for those who embrace them) they transform conventional constraints of time, distance, physicality, simplicity and isolation into new levers for competitive advantage. The more that business actors understand the complexity and interdependency of their diverse and geographically dispersed activities, the more advantage they can take of *speed* as a key success factor, and vice versa. (8) Virtuality is one way to access and leverage this circularity. (9) The key is the manner in which it allows the company to adopt a new and flexible organisational form.

One route to virtuality is laid out in Figure 1, page 177. It involves climbing the steps of strategic learning.

What is a virtual organisation?

Much has been written about the virtual organisation, but, as with all new phenomena, a common understanding of the meaning of the concept is elusive. Handy associates it simply with an alternative work style for the individual. (10) For Davenport & Pearlson the idea of teleworking looms large. (11) Here, a network of individuals may have a range of weak and strong links to organisations that they serve.

Commentators like Boudreau, on the other hand, use the term *virtual* to cover federations of discrete organisations which are linked through a wide variety of mechanisms (eg, partnerships, strategic alliances, joint ventures, outsourcing relationships, franchises, coalitions and consortia). (12) In the widest sense, virtuality can be seen as a system of interacting contributors who seek to meet the strategic objective of a core community, the central features of the system being its knowledge base and its adaptability. It is also clear that its success is a function of contingency – the fact that this form of adaptable organisation framework is adapted to the local conditions in the demanding and fast-moving business environment admirably.

Whether it be an internal or an external federation of knowledge workers, Hale and Whitlam's simple but useful definition, offers a suitably generic guide for the discussion in this chapter:

"A virtual organisation is the name given to any organisation that is continually evolving, redefining and re-inventing itself for practical business purposes". (13)

The strategic management implications of such an innocuous description are vast. But they can be categorized into four main phases of a strategy[1] for virtual organising.

- Direction – How does an organisation continually redefine itself? How does the community establish its strategic objectives? Imagine the people issues, the financial constraints and the uncertainty and ambiguity inherent in constant re-invention.
- Form – How does it co-ordinate the spread of temporal and geographical resources that contribute towards its evolution? Imagine

---

[1] Hale and Whitlam identify the four phases as direction, form, communication and adaptation. Based on the work of Gadman (14), and the arguments of complexity theory, the author has modified the model to introduce environmental scanning as a vital element of the learning cycle, and make communication a central requirement to unify the other stages, as shown in Figure 2, page 181.

the problems of integration, the cultural barriers and the difficulties of managing the interdependencies between countries and national economies.

- Adaptation – What needs to be at the heart of the constantly changing organism in order to allow it to adapt and mutate, yet remain a coherent whole? Imagine how members' desire for more stability may conflict with the rationale for greater change.
- Environmental Scanning – What are the strategic implications of a market place full of interacting and interconnected virtual organisations? Imagine a landscape that is in a constant state of upheaval, unremitting earth tremors, quakes, and rifts. Where is a point of balance? What constitutes fitness to survive in such a landscape?

Communication is the fifth imperative. It is the glue that will unite the community and integrate the four strategic phases into a coherent and flexible strategy, suitably adapted to the external environment, These issues form an interactive learning process, as depicted in Figure 2, page 181. This graphical model of the strategy phases provides a framework to guide our progress up the Figure 1 ladder from data to wisdom about virtual organisation.

Of course, this approach can never be regarded as prescriptive. The intention is to build understanding and, whatever else, the steps involved are neither linear nor sequential. Rather they are part of an iterative process that is constantly shaped by the feedback from the federation of inter-connected community members, and by forces that are affecting the market environment. Successful design and operation are more are a matter of heuristics (learning from experience and adapting accordingly) rather than being based simply on an algorithm (seeking a machine-like success formula and applying it willy-nilly). But there are guidelines in each phase that can help us create the virtual organisation.

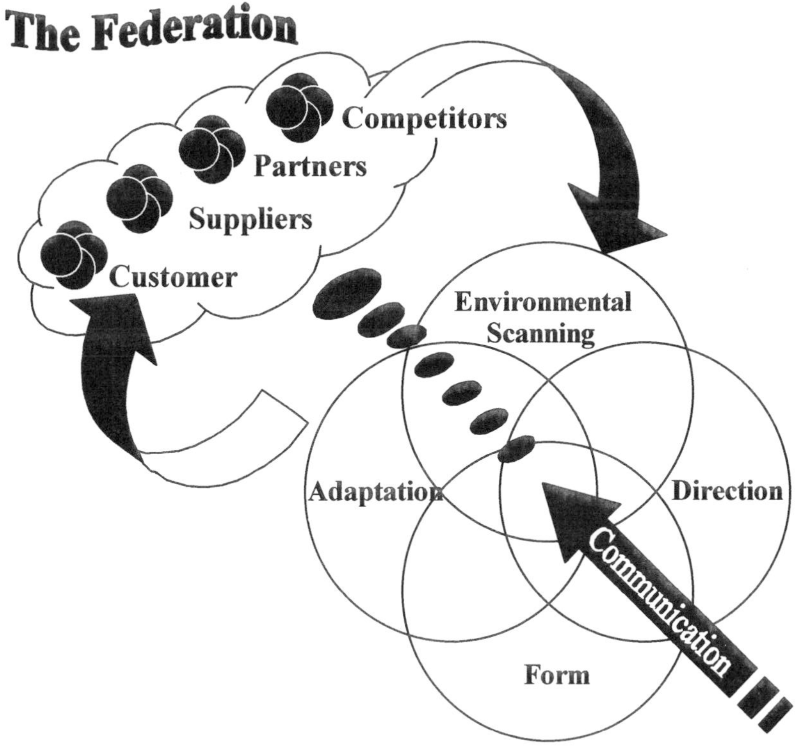

Figure 2: Strategic Phases of Virtual Organising

Direction – Critical elements of strategic focus

A logical place to start would, of course, be to establish a strategic objective and to outline a direction for the organisation to head to, as it starts on the path to continual re-invention. Nowadays, however, this is not the straightforward task that Classical Strategists try to claim it is. According to writers like Ansoff (15) and Porter (16), strategic direction can be defined by:

- collecting data about the various stakeholders in the market place, (eg,. competitors and rivals, potential new entrants, suppliers customers and the possible substitution options,) conducting some rational analysis of the economics of the situation; and
- settling on a master plan that maximizes long term advantage.

Hannan and Freeman and Williamson both challenge this notion of logical rational planning, on the grounds that, in a rapidly changing global market place, environmental uncertainty is too high to allow meaningful anticipation and prediction. (17) They argue for a Darwinian survival-of-the-fittest scenario. Unfortunately in this scenario, fitness can be the somewhat haphazard result of evolutionary market forces' selecting out the weak, rather than the result of strategic choice.

Others such as Mintzberg (18) suggest that strategy is an emergent, bottom-up phenomenon, arising out of the fact that many hands mould the raw materials of business into a shape that may not be optimal, but that still provides reasonable commercial opportunities. This is more in line with the complexity of current business circumstances, but it still implies a tangible end point, a final form rather than a journey of constant re-invention.

In contrast to Mintzberg, there is a school of thought led by Hamel and Prahalad that argues that strategic intent has to be grounded in the social system in which it operates. (19) Profit is not the sole objective. Social interests, class and cultural biases all affect the direction in which an organisation can feasibly develop, and these are in a state of flux at all times. In other words, the actions of one part of the community can not be dissociated from the activities of other organisations, and individuals. (20) They are all elements in a complex interactive system.

As Whittington points out the choice between these four approaches to Strategy shown in Figure 3, page 183, is "quite stark: the four generic approaches differ fundamentally about what people are like and how they got in on the world which surrounds them". (21)

Optimising

Deliberate			**Emergent**
	Classic *Rational, controlled* **Porter** **Ansoff** **Andrews**	**Evolutionary** *Darwinian selection* **Hannan & Freeman** **Williamson**	
	Systemic *A complex pattern of involvement* **Stacey** **McKenzie**	**Processual** *A craft for the people* **Mintzberg**	

Pluralist

Figure 3: Conflicting Strategic Outlooks

Given our review of the interactive forces channelling information and knowledge around the globe, connecting business to business, culture to culture, affecting economies and social infrastructure across national boundaries, it seems reasonable to argue that the systemic approach is the most suitable directional philosophy for virtual organising. But to operationalise it we need a successful guidance model for a complex system. Fortunately we can turn to examples of how natural complex systems resolve the problems of redefinition, form and adaptation, as they organize themselves to thrive and adapt in a changing environment. The new science of complexity offers some relevant insights.

Unfortunately, as Pascale says, the first thing we find is that *"One can not direct a living system, only disturb it"*. (22) Cause and effect are not clearly linked; small interventions can create disturbances of disproportionate proportions. So direction can not be pre-determined, as it can be in a physical system, a fact which suggests that we should always be actively looking for levers that will trigger opportune disturbances, which may carry the organisation in the desired direction.

We also learn that complex systems self-organize and they have ways of maintaining internal coherence, even as they adapt and change. Self-organisation is not a result of a predetermined strategy, rather it emerges out of the complex interaction of certain fundamental mechanisms operating together within the system. So, if we can identify these critical mechanisms in business and uncover what Holland calls *the hidden order* (23) that creates flexible but firm boundaries to sustain the identity of the system without making it rigid, we will have a clue to the critical levers that will trigger the directional disturbances we are after.

Studies of many different complex systems suggest that there are seven common properties and mechanisms, recurring in all systems, which are central to self-organisation and adaptation:

- *Aggregates* – These are linked categories of information/agents, held together by common characteristics and ultimately assembled into a higher level form that is more than the sum of its parts.
- *Diversity* – Mono-technic networks are more vulnerable in unpredictable circumstances, because they can only generate a limited set of responses. Diversity in a community gives the system an option for multiple responses to any given situation. Hence it is an essential, context sensitive insurance mechanism against uncertainty.
- *Tags* – Tags are the selection mechanism that bound appropriate interactions between systems. A tag a sort of docking mechanism, a bit like valency in the periodic table of chemical elements. When the tag of one element in the system matches the tag of another element, the two systems can make a connection. A mismatch means rejection. In natural systems, these connection criteria control co-operation, define the boundaries of interaction, and enable specialisation.
- *Non-Linearity* – Non-linear forces mean that it is hard to see the connection between cause and effect. It means that small inputs to a process can have disproportionate effects. For example, the introduction of a small amount of catalyst into a chemical reaction can increase the output of the reaction many fold. The state of a system at any point in time is the result of a multitude of small disturbances whose effects are cumulatively more than the sum of the parts. The existence of non-linearity is what allows a system to adapt quickly.

- *Building Blocks* – These are aggregates that have been tested for re-usability, and assembled into essential modules that become the basis for complex model building.
- *Flows* – These are energy exchanges between agents in a flexible network, that are delimited by Tags. Energy is any resource that the system needs to survive. Systems need a means of gathering, storing and sharing resources.
- *Internal Models* – The underlying structure, either tacit or overt, that determines an agent behaviour, and provides an essential anticipation mechanism for surviving in a changing world.

The ability to self-organize comes from the "intelligence" embedded in the interacting nodes that form the complex network. Take DNA for example. The helix is the coded intelligence that defines life. For humans, it is the internal model that maintains the coherence of the our bodily system, in the face of constant regeneration and change. (Every cell in your body changes approximately every two years). It works on a simple tagging system that means that only certain elements in the DNA helix can link to each other. Chunks of the whole DNA spiral (aggregates) work together to perform different functions that are the building blocks for life.

Regeneration occurs by splitting the helix model, using resources from an energy exchange to rebuild new cells. Diversity occurs as a result of interaction with other similar complex systems – ie, reproduction. Built into the DNA are elements of redundancy that allow for non linear effects – like cancer, or positive mutations such as higher brain development, or the shrivelling of the appendix as our diet changes. We have only to look at the diversity of human and animal life that has evolved from some very basic shapes to see how the process of reproduction and mutation combined have allowed form to adapt to new environmental conditions.

The question is can we take these principles and translate them into the business context, (a review of the current advice on strategy suggests some obvious relationships between these seven properties and mechanisms) and the critical areas of focus for establishing direction in the virtual organisation:

1. ***Aggregates translate into categories of relationships***. Linked networks of people and organisations (agents) brought together to achieve a super-ordinate objective. For example the development of the B1 bomber which was the work of more than 2000 separate corporations, working in a symbiotic relationship successfully extracted the maximum value from the existing partners assets, with the minimum specific investment. A

virtual organisation needs to concentrate strategic activity upon aggregating and strengthening an appropriate network of relationships that will contribute critical competencies to the corporate vision. Porter (24) identified clusters of related companies and linked industries as a critical factor in effective competition. In this instance co-location is the important contributor to achieving non-linear benefits. A critical mass of organisations like those in Silicon Valley, or the Californian wine region or the Italian leather/fashion cluster generate a whole variety of advantages that together mean that the aggregate is more than the sum of its parts.

2. For the virtual organisation, ***the federation of businesses and people needs to contain an appropriate level of diversity*** in terms of skills and capabilities so that the virtual organisation has the relevant knowledge and expertise to adapt to rapidly changing demands from the environment. As well as a diverse network of partners, suppliers and employees the virtual organisation also needs diversity in

- its product and service range – to satisfy local customer needs, and spread the market risk;
- its geographical location – operationally to take advantage of different economic conditions (eg, cheap labour or special trade benefits), local pockets of excellence in certain skills (eg, India for computer programming expertise), different market anomalies in pricing (eg, the UK for higher prices).

In this way the virtual organisation can buffer against commercial, economic, and resource uncertainty. However, too much diversity becomes unmanageable. So the organisation should seek to balance the trade-off between the value of nodes in its network and the number connections between organisations and people that it has to manage. Clearly, the optimum situation is to have intricate and fairly strong connections with a few core organisations that add most value in providing core competencies and looser connections with a range of other people and/or organisations that flexibly provide the less critical resources without a constant drain on management time.

3. ***Corporate values serve as tags in the virtual organisation***. In Senge's *Fifth Discipline Fieldbook*, Bill O'Brian describes the way Hanover Insurance uses core values as governing constraints to delimit the way the company interacts internally and with outsiders. (25) Clearly defined

values such as openness, honesty, localness and merit provide the tags that guide the flows of information between agents in the corporate network. For example, environmental ethics limit Body Shop's willingness to deal with certain suppliers, and limit the products that can be offered. Care is needed to ensure that values and decisions do not act as blockages to communication and set too narrow boundaries to the scope of activity that a virtual organisation will engage in. By defining a detailed set of corporate values, the virtual organisation can establish flexible yet meaningful boundaries that channel the flow of information appropriately around the business network.

4. ***Catalytic (ie, powerful change agent) mechanisms may be introduced to produce non-linear results*** – Collins describes how companies like Granite Rock, 3M and Kimberley Clark have broken out of standard patterns of logic to adopt radical new ideas that produce desired results in unpredictable ways. (26) Granite Rock produces gravel, concrete, sand and asphalt. They set themselves a daring goal to beat Nordstrom – an up-market American department store – for customer service. Their catalytic mechanism was to implement a policy of "short pay" – if the customer was not totally satisfied, they didn't have to pay. Granite Rock simply deleted the item from the invoice and allowed the customer to keep the goods. Radical indeed, but the small 610-strong company has consistently gained market share against the industry giants, while still charging a premium price. 3M use a different catalyst for innovation. They allow scientists to allocate 15 percent of their time to experimenting and playing in any area of their own choice. That's how they achieve their reputation for being a highly innovative company. The underlying premise of all catalytic mechanisms is, in fact, a paradox. This is that by your giving up deliberate control and reducing predictability, you can actually increase the probability of achieving out-of-the-ordinary results. Usually the catalytic mechanism does not address the obvious cause of a problem – eg, quality control and assurance at Granite Rock, or the innovation process at 3M. Instead it creates a sudden disturbance in the system that has disproportionate knock-on effects.

   In order to make best use of catalytic mechanisms, organisations need to allow for some small degree of slack or redundancy in the system.

5. ***Knowledge is the building block that defines organisational capability***. As Figure 1 page 177 suggests, clusters of data combined in the form of interesting information aggregates, and attributed with context-specific

meaning, provide the building blocks of the system intelligence, which defines the organisation. Strategically, the virtual organisation needs to conduct an audit of the critical elements of knowledge that affect its direction and its ability to thrive in the market place. That knowledge needs to be codified and disseminated as widely as possible across the organisation. But identifying knowledge assets, is only a first step. Knowledge, according to Toffler, has transient value and so it must constantly be replenished. (27) As change ripples across the business landscape, the half-life of knowledge gets shorter and shorter. Hence, putting in place systems and mechanisms for codifying, updating and sharing new knowledge is essential to maintain the value of these building blocks. This is where flows become so important.

6. ***Free-flowing communication is a critical success factor***. The primary energy exchange in a knowledge society is information and know-how, the secondary energy exchange is money. Communication mechanisms are conduits that enable vital flows of energy to pass between members of the corporate network. One core element of any strategic focus should be

- to identify the critical channels of interaction;
- implement systems and mechanisms that smooth the flows along the channels;
- give people, who are likely to be nodes in several networks to tools to manage the volume of information coming through multiple channels, and discriminate as to its value.

7. ***Internal models are similar to visions of the virtual organisation's goals and ambitions and capabilities***. In most firms, a vision statement would typically be a compelling and explicit description of an organisation's model of behaviour crafted to act as motivational benchmark, as well as an unambiguous guide for decision making amongst the various agents in the system. However, it must be open to adaptation, flexible enough to absorb feedback from the external environment but specific enough to provide a clear delineation between what is acceptable and unacceptable behaviour. Implementing this as directional mechanism goes completely against conventional ideas of leadership based on strategy imposed from the top down. But, as Drucker suggests, in a knowledge economy, businesses have to shift away from old fashioned notions of command and control direction, towards a more facilitative style of leadership, based on coaching, influence, encouragement and persuasion. (28) Indeed, Warren Bennis suggests that organisations of the future will not

function adequately with just one leader. A *team* of leaders will be essential to do an adequate job.

It has truly been said that *"a shrinking world in which technological and political complexity increase at an accelerating rate offers fewer and fewer arenas in which individual action suffices. In a global society, in which timely information is the most important commodity, collaboration is not simply desirable, it is inevitable. In all but the rarest cases, one is too small a number to produce greatness".* (29) This suggests that vision should be a product of a diverse range of collaborative inputs, that is representative of the community potential. The qualities required in the leadership team aiming to steer a complex system are outlined in Table 1, below.

Author	Leadership characteristics identified
Gregerson *et al.* (30)	Personal character; Integrity; Emotional connection; Unbridled inquisitiveness; Embracing duality, seeking both and solutions rather than divisive either/or options; Managing uncertainty; The ability to balance tensions; Business and organisational awareness.
Fisher & Fisher (31)	Act as a role model for others; Coach; The ability to unleash energy and enthusiasm; Business analyser – understanding the big picture and translating environmental changes into organisational opportunities; Facilitator; Barrier buster and boundary manager; Customer advocate.
Bennis (32)	Articulate a uniting vision, and create an environment in which individuals have autonomy whilst focused on a collective goal; Willing to make decisions but allow followers to work as they see fit; Understand human beings; Respected by others; pragmatic dreamers; making sure the right information gets to those who need it; Take the sting out of failure; Imbue effort with meaning.
Coleman (33)	Motivation; Self Awareness; Empathy; Self regulation; Social skill.
Koffiman & Senge (34)	Walking ahead; Serving those that follow; Idealist and pragmatist combined.

Table 1: Steering A Complex System: Leadership Qualities Needed

As McKenzie and Swords (35) point out these are primarily supportive, nurturing and empowering qualities. According to Goleman (36) they require emotional intelligence, whilst other researchers stress the need for a *paradoxical* outlook on management, which seeks to integrate and support multiple communities of interest through vision, values and teamwork. (37) There are many more personal than functional competencies on the list and these capabilities are required at all levels within the organisation. Ultimately, strategic direction of the virtual organisation is a community-driven exercise that is the product of putting in place various important mechanisms that enable self-organisation.

Form – A Patchwork of People, Products/services and Processes

The directional principles for virtual organising give rise to some clear principles about the form (or shape) that an organisation can adopt. Primarily the form has to be a fluid knowledge web connecting a diverse community of stakeholders.

This affects three primary categories of business activity – Product, Process and People. Venkatraman and Henderson (38) relate these activities to three vectors of virtual operation.

1. Customer Interaction through virtual encounters with *products* and services;
2. Asset configuration by *processes* associated with sourcing the tangible resources that are the building blocks for organisational operations;
3. Knowledge Leverage by managing the intangible asset of *people's* expertise through virtual communities of interest.

Each vector has three stages – which in complexity terms can be related to aggregates, building blocks and meta-models of virtuality. (See Figure 4, page 191.) Each stage is dependent on the notion of relationships, but the associations demand different degrees of interactive complexity. Aggregates are the virtual information resources that are the raw material of more advance building blocks upon which a virtual organisation can base a meta-model of virtuality that is coherent under change, but responsive to environmental circumstances.

We need first to understand the meaning of each vector in Venkatraman and Henderson's model, so that we can then see how they combine together to create a form that is flexible and adaptable. Form will depend on the way that an organisation answers the big questions (identified in Table 2, pages 193-198) raised in each vector.

It should be noted that the form or shape of the virtual organisation is outlined by the range of relationships and connections, which are created to provide the diversity that enables non-linear results.

Phase

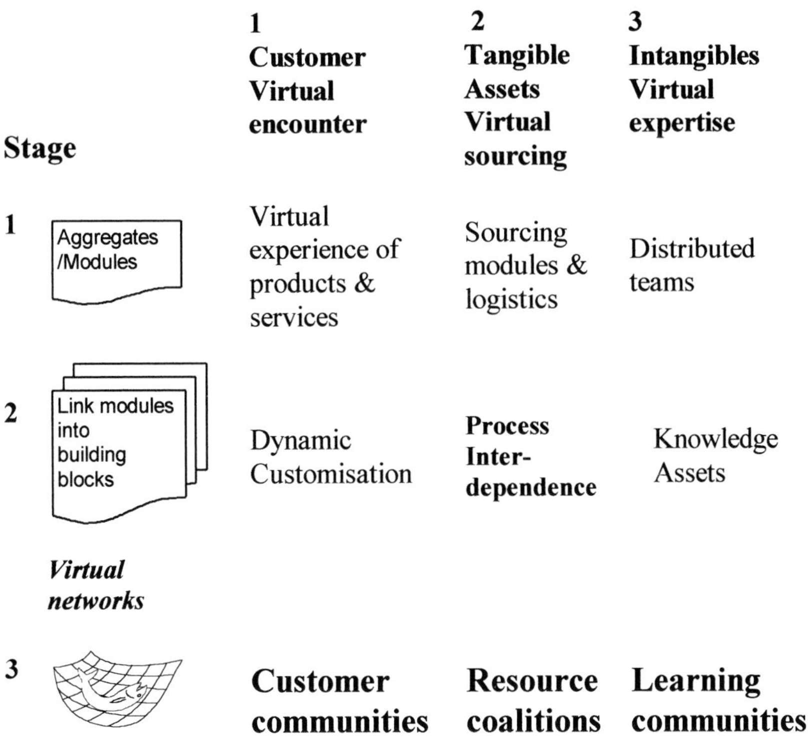

Figure 4: Elements of a Complex Adaptive Model of Virtual Organisation Form

The essential mechanisms that help this to happen are the communication flows around the community and the tags (ie, the criteria that guide the decision of who to include in the community and who to exclude). An integrated network structure is the epitome of form for a complex adaptive system. It supports the vision that will flexibly inform the behaviour of the system in the face of environmental change, whilst offering a self-organising mechanism for anticipating future challenges which the organisation will have to face.

In the following tables we adopt *a three-stage approach* to exploring the strategic relevance of each vector to the virtual organisation's ability to work effectively, and identify the big strategic questions affecting form.

Virtual Encounters with Customers	Virtual Sourcing from Suppliers	Virtual Expertise from communities of interest
VIRTUAL EXPERIENCE	***SOURCING MODULES***	***DISTRIBUTED TEAMS***
The first essential category of information comes from interaction with customers about products and services. This is achieved through a variety of commerce type activities that establish a two-way information link between organisation and customers. For tangible products this involve the obvious routes like sales over the web, via a home shopping TV network, by telephone order from a catalogue. But the virtual encounter is also possible for services too. Schlumberger already reads utility meters remotely. On line diagnostics for cars, lifts and PC's is already a reality for companies like General Motors, Otis Elevators and Sony. Fedex and UPS offer customers the opportunity to monitor their shipments in real time. Nationwide building society's *'Interact'* virtual personal banking experience is a prime example of how redefining the customer interface can be a catalyst that will move a traditional financial services organisation into a new shape and form.	Virtual organisations do not add value through manufacturing components. Their strength is in devising the best product or service architecture. Thus they become expert at sourcing modules, streamlining the procurement process, and reducing inventory in the system. Walmart are perhaps the most renowned example of this but Proctor and Gamble, Nike, Gap and Dell are high on the list of organisations that have modularized for greater efficiency.	Explicit task knowledge and process re-engineering has allowed organisations to re-distribute work around a team to take advantage of different time zones and different locational specialisms. Work units become distributed networks of people linked by collaborative GroupWare. Teams can be formed and reformed according to the specific needs of the task, and knowledge and expertise can be shared and brought to bear as necessary. Hewlett Packard bring together teams from Europe, Asia and America in the design of their new products. Team membership changes depending on where the product is in its lifecycle and what expertise is required.

… **THE BIG QUESTIONS FOR VIRTUAL ORGANISATIONS – in each category**		
How to open up the lines of communication with the customer so as to offer 24h x7 day access to products and services as well as capturing and leveraging knowledge of customer requirements, more effectively than your competitors.	How to select the critical resources that should be kept in house in order to maintain competitive advantage, and which can be obtained from outside. This is a decision that needs constant review. To IBM of the 1980's proprietary hardware was the critical asset, by the 1990's software and chips were the critical market controllers. A wrong decision can be costly if it is adhered to for too long.	How to establish structures and processes that enable you to repetitively assemble the best teams that leverage expertise across the company, Defining the most suitable performance assessment criteria to encourage the desired virtual team work capability? How to manage the cross-cultural differences of perspective, and the conflicts of priority that virtual teams encapsulate?

Table 2: Adaptation – Working in Learning Communities

Stage 1 – Assembling the critical aggregates

Virtual Encounters with Customers	Virtual Sourcing from Suppliers	Virtual Expertise from communities of interest
DYNAMIC CUSTOMISATION Having established the all important intelligence link with the customer, companies can now use this to dynamically customize their product and service offerings to meet individual requirements at minimal cost. This is achieved by modularising the product/ service offering, using the customer intelligence to organized them into optimal configuration for the customer. For example textbook publishers like McGraw Hill's Primis division can provide course books tailored to a specific learning objective, by assembling content modules according to the customer's need.	***PROCESS INTERDEPENDENCE*** Having streamlined the procurement process, then performance will improve if the virtual organisation can establish strongly interdependent linkages at critical points in the value network. This means providing and architecture to support process interdependence, which that smoothes the flow of information and knowledge across organisational boundaries. For example, the service of National Semiconductor, a major chip manufacturer, is interdependently linked with FedEx, who manage all its logistics operations. Kraft foods intertwined their market data collection and analysis process with AC Neilsen to achieve faster response to market trends.	***CORPORATE KNOWLEDGE ASSET*** Having organized around the advantages of distributed virtual teams, the virtual organisation needs to look at ways to identify, capture and leverage the tacit knowledge embedded in the teams across the whole organisation. Knowledge is a corporate asset that should be managed systematically across the organisation. For example, many companies (like Motorola, BP, and GM) are now adopting the Center for Army Lessons Learned (CALL) type strategy to leverage their knowledge assets. Experts in tacit knowledge collection interview soldiers, sit in on after action reviews and read the reports. From this they distill the key lessons, that are used to develop training scenarios for future problems.

… **THE BIG QUESTIONS FOR VIRTUAL ORGANISATIONS – in each category**		
What are the essential product and service modules to support customer needs? How do you organize them in order to satisfy a make to order philosophy? What information do you need to collect in order to do this?	What are the critical processes in the sourcing chain that would benefit from outsourcing? Do your systems allow the creation of interdependent links across organisational boundaries? Does your system respond dynamically to manage a portfolio of inter-organisational relationships?	What IT platform attributes are required to support the collection and use of corporate knowledge assets? How do you use the asset to improve corporate effectiveness? How do you encourage information sharing as a cultural standard?

Table 2: Adaptation – Working in Learning Communities

Stage 2 – Creating the Essential Building Blocks

Virtual Encounters with Customers	Virtual Sourcing from Suppliers	Virtual Expertise from communities of interest
CUSTOMER COMMMUNITIES Using the building block of dynamic customisation the virtual organisation can take full advantage of the phenomenon of customer communities. These are virtual associations of customers united across time and space by a common interest in a product or service. The users may unite around a brand of product or service, – eg, The Harley-Davidson owners group or be company independent, comparing competing offerings – eg, avid readers reviewing books on www.amazon.com or www.photoshopper. com an active community of photographers.	*RESOURCE COALITIONS* Recognising the value of process interdependence, the next stage for the virtual organisation is to integrate itself into a flexible but strong network of capabilities that will allow it to adapt and bend with the changing environment. Imagine a fishing net, in which each company is a knot or node in the lattice. The net changes shape when pulled from various directions, but is strong enough to withstand a vast weight of a whole catch of fish. Just as no one node in the net bears all the strain, so no one company is dominant in a resource net. Nike has gained massive advantage from positioning itself at the heart of a web of resources from ad agencies contracts with athletes, foreign sub contractors and retail outlets. As market forces change, Nike can flex and adapt the loads in its network to meet the increase or decrease in pressure. The net may contain competitors as well as suppliers – eg, Shell and Amoco pool some of their oil fields to improve upstream	***PROFESSIONAL LEARNING COMMUNITIES*** With the building blocks of an accessible corporate knowledge asset, the virtual organisation can take advantage of its place in a wider learning community. By collaborating and sharing its knowledge with other members of the relationship networks (customer's, suppliers, partners, etc) it is possible to leverage knowledge for even greater degrees of competitive advantage. For example, an organisation with an organized knowledge base, can quickly integrate contract workers to absorb much needed expertise quickly whenever it needs to adapt to changing demands – eg, bring in lawyers, financial advisers, trainers etc. Communities of interest might arise in certain industries around new sciences like biotech. Communities of research institutions, biotech product producers and biotech product users increase the rate of

	efficiency, but compete elsewhere. Think also about the variety of different associations between members of the telecommunications industries.	innovation for large pharmaceutical and food companies.

… THE BIG QUESTIONS FOR VIRTUAL ORGANISATIONS – in each category		
When customer communities have the power to make or break a corporate decision or company image, what is the right strategy for involvement? – passive participation or pro-active creation? How and when should the organisation respond to the feedback from these communities to change direction?	How do you balance the interdependencies across the net, so that there are no distortions, or imbalances that will create a disproportionate stress and break the net? For example are coalition resources favouring you over your competitors? How do monitor the strength and flexibility of the net and its suitability for the changing market environment?	What is proprietary information and what is valuable to share? How do you create a seamless but secure platform across corporate boundaries, which will allow knowledge to flow freely when desired, but protect security when necessary? How do you compensate and motivate knowledge workers in a professional community, where loyalties may change, or be to individuals rather than companies?

Table 2: Adaptation – Working in Learning Communities

Stage 3 – Formulating Meta-Models that permit self organized behaviour in the Virtual Organisation

A primary objective of the virtual organisation is to increase its capability to adapt to environmental disturbances in an advantageous way. To achieve this, the organisation needs to embed change as automatic behaviour in its system, by appropriate processes and through the identification of certain core competencies that may be inherent in people and not trainable.

Adaptation is all about change management. Change in complex systems emerges as a result of the seven mechanisms identified in the section on Direction. So far we have established the route to requisite diversity through a form that organizes around knowledge-based aggregates, building blocks, and internal models, the next step is to identify the critical organisational mechanisms which will act as catalysts to virtuality.

This involves the two major complexity mechanisms not yet discussed:

- ***Tags*** – The key strategic question here is what are the value-based mechanisms that facilitate the appropriate flows and connections across the various levels of organisation? Essentially this is about changing the cultural drivers to ensure that, as far as possible, the members of the organisation have individual value systems which are compatible even if they do not share a single homogenous value system.
- ***Flows*** – What communication infrastructure is required to enable the free flow of information and knowledge through the various levels of the system.

An organisation's values should serve as its *tags*, acting as the guiding principle for producing internal compatibilities and smooth-flowing communication. Every organisation will have a set of unique values that underpin its commercial success; these could be anything from an emphasis on customer care to prioritising environmental protection, from being at the forefront of technological innovation to respect for the individual. Compaq, for example, have five guiding beliefs that they see as core to their operation.

- Fostering human dignity, treating people with fairness and respect;
- Building constructive trusting team relationships;
- Fostering individual responsibility;
- Open two way communication;
- Creating a work environment that is fun.

These condition the culture of the business. The organisation will operate harmoniously if all members share these beliefs and express them in their work.

Changing a traditional culture into one that supports virtual organising is quite a challenge. It may seem important to move fast in this process, but it will not be easily achieved unless the change agents are sensitive to the history of the business and the need to encourage, rather than force, change. The virtual organisation needs to build a true sense of partnership between all elements of the network, so that the values that emphasize the importance of partnership are likely to have the most impact. Looking across a range of companies, we can see that this seems to be distilled into four fundamental beliefs for the would-be virtual organisation:

1. Life-long learning;
2. Team working;
3. Trust and integrity;
4. Measure what matters.

1. *Life-long learning is imperative.*

To adapt is to learn. This is where information and knowledge flows become so important. To adapt is to learn. Whilst each individual should take responsibility for their own personal development, the virtual organisation needs a commitment to selecting and developing people so that they understand and fit with the organisational value systems, and have the key competencies that the organisation requires.

The methods and mechanisms to stimulate learning are too many to enumerate here, but what is clear from all the literature is that circumstances and environment have a major influence on the ability to learn. Certain characteristics enable learning, others inhibit the process.

Learning enablers include motivation, action, and experimentation, and feedback and review. The lack of any of these things will inhibit learning, Additional inhibitors are fear and anxiety, lack of resources or a shortfall in capability ie, disempowerment, isolation and disconnection. Table 2, pages 193-198 explores the systems, processes, cultural values and core competencies that promote the enablers and disable the inhibitors to learning.

To promote the enablers and suppress the inhibitors	*Systems and processes*	*Core cultural tenets and required competencies*
Enablers		
Motivation	Reward mechanisms that encourage knowledge sharing, teamwork, and focus on outcomes rather than drivers. As part of BP's efforts to encourage relevant company and community wide learning, they run an annual training fair, at which potential and existing training providers offer taster sessions from things as varied as juggling to career development counseling. Most participants gain some basic learning from the event, but in addition it acts as a motivational force for both employees and suppliers.	Competencies – Communicating a clear vision. Tenacity Cultural attitude – respect for others contribution, fair treatment. A belief that active personal development is more important than specific skills training.
Action and experimentation	Relevant training supporting regular role changes, coaching.	Competencies – Creativity and innovation. Cultural attitude – A sense of urgency and excitement. A no blame environment open to risk.
Feedback and review	GroupWare, Electronic knowledge capture. Mentoring. Benchmarking. Mechanisms that measure output not action.	Competencies – Counselling. Outlining the elements of tacit knowledge. Cultural tenets – no blame approach, matching accountability with authority.

Table 3: System Enablers and Inhibitors

Inhibitors		
Fear and anxiety	Facilitative leadership. GroupWare that provides communication anonymity. Team Based Performance assessment to spread the pressure.	Competencies – Tenacity and perseverance. Cultural attitude - Risk taking is OK, no blame.
Lack of resources	Add some uncontrolled slack into daily routines – for example 3M's 15 percent freedom to explore policy.	Competencies – Initiative, creativity and thinking outside the box. Cultural attitude – redundancy and slack is not a bad thing.
Isolation and Disconnection	IT networks, cyber cafes, training in virtual communication to recapture the socialisation mechanisms that are lost in virtual spaces.	Competencies – integration, managing complex networks. Cultural attitude – people are real and have feelings, even when they are not visible.

Table 3 continued: System Enablers and Inhibitors

2. *Teamwork is the key to success*

Virtual knowledge teamwork permits an organisation to assemble the exact mix of resources quickly and flexibly from anywhere in the world to meet the needs of the moment. However this poses specific challenges for those involved. For example:

- Multiplexing – how to manage the time conflicts and divided loyalties associated with working on several teams at once.
- Cross Cultural working – Many organisations like Hewlett Packard, put together multi-national teams of experts to develop new products. Members need to know how to work across language and cultural barriers, as well as how to bring together and integrate the work of a group of "opinionated" experts across time zones. For example, Price Jamieson, a London based resource consultancy found that achieving results in virtual meetings through desk top based audio conferencing and whiteboard sharing, meant paying more attention to other people's styles. Finnish participants believed that people who talk too much are

disorganized. Italians believe that voluble self-expression is a sign of great involvement and interest. The result was the Italians "press to fill the whiteboard and the audio channels with their verbal flourish, while the Finns become increasingly retiring". Training in cultural sensitivity is also an increasing requirement for the virtual organisation.

Fisher and Fisher (39) suggest that four key integration strategies will resolve many of these issues Table 4, below.

Structure –	**Leadership –**	**Shared values –**	**Rewarded goals –**
Define up front			
The team purpose	Responsibilities of leader and members	What team values	Success
Who the customer is	Accountability	How they will operate to resolve technical and people problems	How to track and measure it
Other stakeholders	Decision making structure	How to prioritise work on multiple teams	How to reward it
A protocol for organising work	Problem solving responsibilities		What customers need
Responsibilities	Boundaries of power		What priorities are
A team name	Sources of help		What the consequences of getting off track are
A communication protocol including timetables and meeting technologies	Mediators in the event of an irresolvable conflict		

Table 4: Integration Strategies

Among the key desiderata are the facts that:

3. *Integrity is paramount and trust is sacrosanct*

Teams achieve high performance, once they reach a high degree of trust and co-operation declares McFadzean (40) whilst, according to Lally and Kostner, "familiarity is what breeds trust and co-operation". (41) Unfortunately, achieving the necessary familiarity is difficult when team members do not meet or interact in traditional ways. In the absence of face to face contact, small breaches of integrity or commitment can have a disproportionately large negative impact on trust. Conflict can arise suddenly and violently from minor miscommunications and reaching consensus and closure on decisions between team members may be more difficult, and time consuming. Building trust in the open-ended environment of a virtual team paradoxically requires more overt discipline and concerted action than less. The following are *inviolable* rules for all virtual teams:

- Appoint a coach who is responsible for facilitating team dynamics. The coach's task is to ensure that the team makes time for socialising and exchanging personal information about each other. There will be discussion of how the team is operating against a background in which the operating dynamics and interpersonal relationships issues are made explicit.
- Train virtual workers in managing conflict, particularly when they can not read body language, voice tone, or achieve eye contact in their communications. NCR and IBM encourage virtual workers to seek out a team-mate or coach as a mediator.
- Prevent feelings of isolation by having everyone commit to prompt responses to all electronic communication, and put in place regular newsletters to ensure everyone keeps up to date with essential team activities.
- Plan activities and allocate clear responsibilities for action.
- Set standards for relevance of communications to avoid information overload.
- Vet all actions and communications against an agreed moral code that everyone has bought into. Implement the agreed means of censure for members' non-conformity to that code.

4. *Detailed measurement of outputs is inherent in every process*

It may seem rather open-ended to allow teams to set their own evaluation criteria for project success against objectives of time saved and change achieved, but research suggests that often teams are harder on themselves in terms of setting performance standards, than external authorities would be. With experience, improvements over previous performance may provide a good measure of success, but whatever happens, benchmarking against external standards remains a powerful driver for performance. In addition, there is always the likelihood that a particular output will become redundant, so the virtual organisation also needs a mechanism to allow its members to relate output measures to market demands.

Environmental scanning – Reviewing one's place on the current fitness landscape

We have now come full circle. We started with examining the forces shaping the landscape, and suggested a strategic approach to virtual organising that is based on a dynamic web or federation of people and organisations linked across time and distance by communications technology and common values. This allows it to be a highly complex and adaptive organism. We should now briefly consider how to navigate in, and make sense of, a business environment peopled with such virtual organisations.

All complex organisms exist in an environment, which is often known as a fitness landscape. A fitness landscape is a representation of the impact that the web of participants has on its contained environment. (See Figure 5, below.)

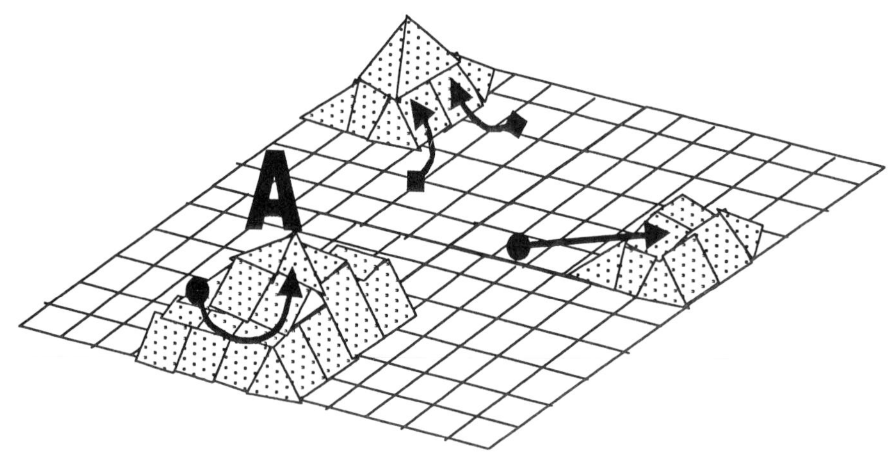

Figure 5: Navigating the Fitness Landscape

The outcomes of community interactions distort the form of the net, to create peaks and troughs. The peaks represent the height of strategic fitness, where profitability is optimal, *given the available resources and environmental conditions in that locality.* The valleys represent weak strategies given the current conditions. But neither the peaks nor troughs remain constant, because competitive forces are bending and buckling the landscape all the time. As a strategist for the virtual organisation the objective is to scale the highest peak, without a reliable map, avoiding being destroyed by an earthquake, and making best use of limited resources in the process. A challenging task indeed!

Fortunately there are some ground rules that have already shown reasonable results for thriving businesses. Beinhocker (42) suggests several ways that organisations can navigate through this heaving landscape, using the principles of success inherent in natural complex adaptive systems.

- **Don't stand still** – Even when you are at the pinnacle of fitness, at the top of a local optimum (Point A in Figure 5, page 204) you can guarantee that the landscape is going to change. Competitors actions change the conditions and reshape the landscape, which means that the criteria defining the local optimum will change. Successful companies like Procter and Gamble, Merck and Hewlett Packard adopt an attitude that is described as "good enough never is". They are constantly scanning the horizon, avoiding the status quo, and integrating new and developing resources into their strategy.
- **Venture out on many fronts** – Parallel searches (see the arrows in Figure 5, page 205) for new resources and new opportunities, increase your chances of success. Innovation and progress are risky, but parallel initiatives spread the risk, and increase the odds of survival, and maintain the essential diversity that keeps the system active. Pharmaceutical companies like Merck apply this sort of philosophy to drug research. The lead-time for drug development is long, and the hit rate is small, but having many products in the pipeline multiplies the possibilities.
- **Take both short steps and long jumps** – When McKinsey and Co. studied the activity of 30 leading growth companies [2], they found that they consistently adopted a balanced portfolio of three types of strategic initiatives:

[2] See Baghai, M.A., Coley, S.C., Farmer, R.H. and Sarrazin, H. 1999. *The Alchemy of Growth. Kick starting and sustaining growth in your company*. London: Orion Business.

- Extend and defend existing business in the short term – fight off invaders climbing up your peak.
- Build on current capabilities to introduce innovation for the medium term – climb higher on the peak you currently live on.
- Invest in long term developments to provide the seed-corn for future growth – look for new areas of the landscape that combine your knowledge and capabilities with new resources arising in different sectors of the landscape.

A portfolio of these initiatives should cover a sufficiently diverse area of the overall fitness landscape for the company to be comfortable that it will always benefit from at least some of the local upheavals. This may sound rather like spreading your resources too thinly, but the process can be managed:

- by selecting a diverse portfolio of strategies;
- exploring them through detailed scenario analysis;
- valuing them according the number of options each creates in terms of future possibilities;
- mapping them against risk, time frame, and connection to current business;
- using selection mechanisms that reflect the market criteria for success of failure in financial terms – Thermo Electron for example funds early stage investments with venture capital floating parts of the business on the stock market through IPO's;
- using performance metrics that are adapted to the different strategic horizons of portfolio investments.

For the virtual organisation the diversity of strategies will be built around the strength and type of connections between members of flexible communities. In some ways this makes it easier to keep on the move, explore in parallel directions, spread the risk through long term and short-term connections. But, in others, it is more difficult because the virtual organisation needs to develop a core competence in multi-cultural, multi-party relationship management. In this way, it can seek to constantly change shape as the landscape moves.

Conclusion – Virtual organising is a journey not an end point

In a turbulent world an organisation must keep varying its direction and form in order to adapt and thrive. Virtual organisation builds flexibility into the business, through the diverse web of partners and resourcing strategies. By putting in place mechanisms to allow smooth communication across boundaries, establishing a flexible core of critical competencies, shared social values, and an IT enabled infrastructure that supports collaboration, knowledge sharing and learning, the virtual organisation can create a coherent core that provides stability during the change. Communities of customers suppliers, competitors and partners create a adaptable but robust network that flexes easily in the face of change. By following some of the key principles governing complex adaptive systems, a virtual organism maximizes its chances of surviving and thriving to the point of creating and maintaining an effective and viable strategy in today's brave new world.

References

(1) Hale, R. and Whitlam, P. *Towards the Virtual Organisation.* London: McGraw Hill, 1997

(2) Venkatraman, N. and Henderson, J.C. Real Strategies for Virtual Organising. *Sloan Management Review Fall,* 1998, pp.33-48

(3a) Tapscott, D. *The digital economy. Promise and peril in the age of networked intelligence.* New York: McGraw Hill, 1996

(3b) Negroponte, N. *Being Digital.* London: Hodder and Staughton, 1995

(4a) Stacey, R. *Strategic Management and Organisational Dynamics.* London: Pitman, 1993

(4b) Handy, C. *The age of paradox.* Boston, MA.: Harvard Business School Press, 1994

See also *The age of unreason.* London: Business Books, 1989

and Trust and the virtual organisation. *Harvard Business Review,* May-June 1995, pp.40-50

(5) Boisot, M. *Knowledge Assets: Securing competitive advantage in an information economy.* Oxford: Oxford University Press, 1998

(6a) Fulmer, R. M., Gibbs P and Keys B. The second generation of learning organisations; new tools for sustaining competitive advantage. *Organizational Dynamics,* Vol. 27, Issue 2, Autumn 1998, pp.6-20

(6b) McGill, M., Slocum, J. and Lei, D. The new learning strategy; anytime anything anywhere. *Organisational dynamics,* 1994, 32 (3) pp.33-47

The Learning organisation in action. A special report from organisational dynamics

(7) Toffler, A. *Powershift. Knowledge, wealth and violence at the edge of the 21st Century.* New York: Bantam Books, 1990

(8a) Stacey, R. D. *Complexity and Creativity in Organisations.* San Francisco: Berrett – Keohler, 1996

(8b) Pascale, R.T. *Managing on the Edge. How the smartest companies use conflict to stay ahead.* New York: Simon and Schuster, 1990

(8c) Pascale, R.T. Surfing the Edge of Chaos. *Sloan Management Review,* 1999, Spring, pp.83- 94

(9a) As (2)

(9b) Davidow, W.H and Malone, M.S. *The Virtual Corporation: Structuring and Revitalising the Corporation for the 21st Century.* New York: Harper Business, 1992

(10) As (4b)

(11) Davenport, T.H and Pearlson, K. Two Cheers for the Virtual Office. *Sloan Management Review,* 1998, Summer, pp.51-65

(12) Boudreau, M.C., Loch, K.D., Detmar Straud, D.R. Going global: Using information technology to advance the competitiveness of the virtual transnational organisation. *Academy of Management Executive,* Vol 12, No 4, November, pp.120-128

(13) As (1)

(14) Gadman, S. *Power Partnering. A strategy for Business Excellence in the 21st Century.* Boston MA: Butterworth Heinemann, 1997

(15) Ansoff, H.I. *Corporate Strategy*. Harmondsworth: Penguin, 1965

(16) Porter, M.E. *Competitive Strategy: Techniques for analysing industries and firms.* New York: Free Press & MacMillan, 1980

See also *Competitive Advantage: Creating and Sustaining Superior Performance.* New York: Free Press, 1985

(17a) Hannan, M.T. and Freeman, J. *Organisational Ecology.* Cambridge MA: Harvard University Press, 1988

(17b) Williamson, O.E. Strategising Economising and Economic Organisation. *Strategic Management Journal,* 1991, Vol 12, pp.75-94

(18) Mintzberg, H. Crafting Strategy. *Harvard Business Review,* 1987, July August, pp.65-75

(19) Hamel, G, and Prahalad, C.K. Strategic Intent. *Harvard Business Review,* 1989, May June, pp.63-76

(20a) As (4a)

As (8a)

(20b) McKenzie, J. *Paradox, the next strategic dimension.* Maidenhead: McGraw Hill, 1996

(21) Whittington, R, *What is strategy and does it matter?* London: Thomson Learning, 2000

(22) As (8c)

(23) Holland, J.H. *Hidden Order. How adaptation builds complexity.* Reading MA: Addison Wesley, 1995

(24) Porter, M.E. Clusters and the new economics of competition. *Harvard Business Review,* 1998, November, pp.77-87

(25) Senge, P. *The Fifth Discipline Fieldbook: Strategies and Tools for Building a Learning Organisation.* New York: Currency Doubleday, 1994

(26) Collins, J. Turning Goals into Results: The Power of Catalytic Mechanisms. *Harvard Business Review,* 1999, July August, pp.71-82

(27) As (7)

(28) Drucker, P, The Coming of the New Organisation. *Harvard Business Review,* 1988, Vol. 66, Jan-Feb pp.44-53

(29) Bennis, W. *Organising Genius – The Secrets of Creative Collaboration.* London: Nicholas Brearley, 1997

(30) Gregersen. H., Morrison, A., and Steward Black, J. Developing leaders for the global frontier. *Sloan Management Review,* 1998, Fall, p.21-32

(31) Fisher, K. and Fisher, M.D *The Distributed Mind: Achieving high performance through the collective intelligence of knowledge work teams.* New York: Amacom, 1998

(32) As (29)

(33) Coleman, D. What makes a leader? *Harvard Business Review,* 1998, Nov, p93

(34) Koffman, F. and Senge, P. Communities of Commitment. The heart of learning organisations. *Organisational Dynamics,* 1998, p.5-22

(35) McKenzie, J. Swords, D. *Maintaining relevance in business education.* Proceedings of the 5th annual conference on Social Values, Oxford, July, 1999

(36) Goleman, D. *Emotional Intelligence- why it can matter more than IQ.* London: Bloomsbury, 1996

(37a) Pascale Tanner, R, *Managing on the Edge. How the smartest companies use conflict to stay ahead.* New York: Simon and Schuster, 1990

(37b) As (4b)

(37c) Hampden Turner, C. *Charting the Corporate Mind.* Blackwell: Oxford, 1990

(37d) As (20)

(38) As (2)

(39) As (31)

(40) McFadzean, E, *The Attention wheel. How to manage creative teams.* Henley Working Paper series 9823, 1998

(41) Lally, R. and Kostner, J. Learn to be a distance manager, Getting results ...for the Hands on Manager. Vol. 42 7. pp.6-7 Saranac Lake, American Management Association, July 1997

(42) Beinhocker, E.D. Robust Adaptive Strategies. *Sloan Management Review*, 1999, Spring, pp.95-106

Chapter 9

GOVERNANCE AND PERFORMANCE: THE FUTURE FOR THE BOARD

Bernard Taylor, Philip Stiles and Mahen Tampoe

Introduction

This is the age of the *new frontier*. It is a period in which a new competitive landscape has emerged, driven by the growth of technology and the increasing spread of globalisation. (1) The pace and scope of these forces has meant that for businesses to survive, the need for strategic flexibility is paramount. Two crucial elements in determining whether a business can achieve the requisite flexibility are the quality and functioning of its board of directors and the system of corporate governance within which the organisation operates. A major criticism of boards, however, is that their form and structure have remained essentially the same under corporate law for over 100 years and therefore they are ill-suited to come to terms with the new environmental context.

In this chapter, we will firstly examine the extent to which boards are adapting to these changing competitive conditions. Then, through a preliminary analysis of a survey of opinion leaders in the corporate governance field obtained through a Delphi study, we will identify the likely changes that will be made in board practice and structure for the 21st century. Our aim in this chapter is to move beyond the traditional view of the board as a monitoring mechanism, which ensures accountability and acts as a "backstop" to corporate management.

On the basis of the Delphi study results, we advocate a broader view of board endeavour, one that involves adding value to the organisation in terms of its performance. In essence, this chapter is, therefore, an attempt to take the next step beyond the official UK Cadbury and Hampel reports on corporate governance (Appendix 1, page 226) in order to provide a new agenda for British boards of directors. This is a necessary, and desirable, focus of concern for all students of strategy.

The Changing Demands Facing Boards of Directors

> *"The nineteenth century notion of the corporate entity was elegantly simple and superbly successful. For a century and a half it has been the basis of capital formation, business growth and wealth creation - not only in North America and the United Kingdom, but also wherever common law based company legislation has percolated.... But could it be that the very simplicity and success of the original conception contained the seeds of the subsequent malaise? Companies have proliferated, corporate groups have become highly complex and the realities of governance in practice can appear far removed from the original idea".* (2)

The assumption behind the line of reasoning advanced above by Tricker is widespread. (3) It is that the current rhetoric about board work is not matched by the reality within organisations. Indeed, the extent to which a board can actually carry out these duties has been, and remains, a major theoretical and practical question in the corporate governance debate.

Certainly, many researchers into the roles and responsibilities of the board have isolated three activities, which are common to most boards. (4) These are:

- *strategy* – reviewing and amending organisational policies and strategies;
- *service* – enhancing the firm's reputation, developing contacts with external constituencies and giving advice to the CEO and other executives; and
- *control* – monitoring and evaluating the performance of the firm and the CEO.

But there is significant and widespread concern about the extent to which boards can effectively manage all three – simultaneously. So much so that shareholder activist, Robert Monks, was moved to refer to boards of directors in a full page advertisement placed in the Wall Street Journal in 1992 as, in effect, *non-performing assets*. (5)

Doubts about the efficacy of boards surfaced prominently in the 1980s take-over boom, when managers sought to entrench themselves in office by adopting a variety of anti-acquisition devices, such as poison pills, greenmail, and golden parachutes, which certainly did not serve the interests of shareholders. The wave of take-overs also promoted renewed, and hostile, debate on the nature of corporate governance systems. A particular concern, in the face of a highly active market for corporate control, was with the increasing and unremitting pressure on management to produce short-term results. This was seen as discouraging long-term planning and investment. (6)

These concerns were compounded at the turn of the decade in the UK by a series of corporate frauds – Maxwell, Polly Peck, the Bank of Credit and Commerce International, Barlow Clowes – and failures – Ferranti, Coloroll, British and Commonwealth. All these showed dramatically the huge financial consequences of unfettered power. More specifically, they revealed the failure of the boards involved to provide adequate checks to safeguard the interests of investors, employees and customers. In addition, the spate of scandals and failures called into question the role of the auditor in ensuring accountability.

The executive pay bonanza of the 1990s has also shown up the wilder excesses of management, with executive directors awarding themselves huge pay increases, often unrelated to the performance of their organisations, showing for many a lack of restraint which was difficult to justify. In Britain, such "*fat cat*" practices have aroused widespread political interest, especially when followed by privatised utility companies effectively enjoying regional monopolies.

Official Studies of Board Shortcomings

Though corporate governance has attracted widespread interest, the nature of the debate on corporate governance – *the system by which companies are directed and controlled* as defined by the Cadbury report – is still heavily shaped by Berle and Means' 1932 analysis of the large American firm. (7) This study documented the split between ownership and control of such corporations, and the resulting dispersion of shareholdings. As organisations grew, their study found, the number of shareholders increased. This diminished the voice of the individual investor, whose stake would typically become so small, as compared to the total number of shares issued, as to be almost negligible (though the financial value of a small stake could be considerable).

The result was that corporate wealth was held by shareholders as a *passive* instrument, while managers *actively* controlled the organisation. (8) The consequent fragmentation of ownership and the shift of power towards managers and, in particular the CEO, had, of course, many advantages. The growth of a professional management cadre and the commercial efficiency of risk sharing, for instance, were evident plusses. But it also brought with it problems in terms of management accountability. In formal terms, the shareholders elected the board (and the board elected the CEO) to ensure that their interests were safeguarded.

It is a commonplace today to suggest that boards are still controlled by executive management. Indeed, the belief that managers control boards rather than boards controlling management has been, and is, a dominant theme in both academic and practitioner writings. According to this view, the board is the *de jure*, but not the *de facto* governing body of the organisation. The real responsibility for running and controlling the company is assumed to be in the hands of corporate management. (9)

As management is expected to, and does, exercise day-to-day operating control, it obtains an intimate knowledge of the business, putting the board at a disadvantage. In addition to possession of this specialised knowledge, managers in profitable companies are able to finance investments from retained earnings, which means they are less dependent on shareholders for capital, a fact which may allow them to pursue aims other than profit maximisation. A further cause of managerial dominance stems from the procedure for selecting directors. As Pfeffer indicates:

> *"The selection procedure by which board members are chosen guarantees that, in most cases, board members are hand-picked by management. In many practical respects, management is, therefore, in control of the board".* (10)

Another strong argument is that, because executive directors work for the CEO, report to him/her regularly, and are generally dependent upon him/her for career advancement and rewards, it is unreasonable to expect a subordinate director to challenge a chief executive at a board meeting.

Though outside directors do not suffer from this handicap to such an extent, the problem remains. The ineffectiveness of the board in monitoring the performance of management stems, it is claimed, from the lack of independence of its outside directors. Management controls the selection of outside directors and, given the prestige and financial rewards of a seat on the board, this generally means that the outside directors are unlikely to criticise management. They are unlikely to know a great deal about the business and management frequently restricts the information given to them. (11) This leads to the board's adopting merely what Herman called a "rubber-stamping" function, a problem significantly increased by the fact of size. Furthermore, large boards, he found, were "weak" boards (12), since they make in-depth discussion unlikely and increase the likelihood of diversity and fragmentation among board members.

Rising Activism

As a result of these concerns, there has been increasing scrutiny from regulators, investor groups and the business media and probes into how corporations in general and boards of directors, in particular, operate. Policy initiatives have mushroomed. The Cadbury Report (1992) sought to improve standards of corporate (and board) behaviour following widespread concern over financial reporting and auditing, and more generally attempted to prescribe best practice in board structures and composition. The Cadbury Report was augmented by the Greenbury Report (1995) into executive pay, which attempted to link directors' earnings more closely to corporate performance, and the Hampel Report (1998), a successor to Cadbury which emphasised that the board should play a major role in improving the prosperity of their companies.

In the US, the American Law Institute published a set of principles of corporate governance (ALI 1992). The National Association of Corporate Directors (NACD), for its part, commissioned a report into performance standards for their members, whilst the US House of Representatives Sub-Committee on Telecommunications and Finance held hearings on the Role of Independent Directors on Corporate Boards (Conference Board 1996).

Activity in Europe, too, has been vigorous. Notably, the Centre for European Policy Studies (1995) advocated that corporate governance guidelines be drawn up with which all listed companies in the European Union should comply. The publication of the Vienot report (1995) in France examined the underpinnings of corporate governance. It focussed, in particular, on the core holdings of French companies by groups of French shareholders to protect firms from foreign control, and the use of cross holdings to lock in obligations and ensure protection. Interestingly, it recommended the appointment of two independent non-executive directors, nominating and remuneration committees and the formalisation of board responsibilities. In the Netherlands, the Peters Committee on Corporate Governance reported in October 1996 making 40 recommendations for reform. In all, since 1992, 19 countries have published codes of practice for corporate governance. (13)

A second consequence of these pressures is the rise of institutional investor activism. The role of shareholders in exercising good corporate governance has long been recognised and in recent years the concentration of ownership in the hands of a small number of large institutional investors has brought about the potential for greater monitoring of management. The change has been dramatic. Forty years ago, private shareholders owned nearly 70 percent of public companies and the institutions owned less than 20 percent whereas today these proportions are almost exactly reversed. And within the fund management industry, there has been further consolidation and concentration of assets under management.

A number of high profile examples of institutional investors flexing their muscles and removing under-performing managers have surfaced. Westinghouse, Kodak, American Express, Saatchi and Saatchi, and Granada-Forte, have all figured prominently as a result of shareholder intervention. Such actions had a number of causes: the poor strategies and empire building of managers, the furore over executive pay and the weakness of corporate boards, for example.

Dissatisfaction at the performance of portfolio companies can trigger an exit strategy. But as institutional holdings increase, exit becomes problematic. Selling has the effect of depressing the market, making exit costly for any player. Moreover, given ownership concentration, they would be selling mainly to one another. The alternative is for institutions to use their *voice* and seek relationships with portfolio companies to develop their influence. They have every incentive to do so.

As the above discussions imply, much of the recent focus on boards has been concerned with issues of accountability. Though this aspect of board endeavour is crucial, it has tended to overshadow the board's potential for delivering enhanced corporate performance – a key focus of the investor activist. The contribution of the board to the strategy process and its role in giving advice to the CEO and executive directors, affords the board strong leverage in terms of power and influence and brings with it significant opportunities to have a direct impact on value-adding activities within the organisation. There is widespread concern about this.

Now, however, the recommendations of Cadbury are seen as solidly in place (14) and the principles of good governance are gaining increasing acceptance. The agenda has, in a real sense, moved on, and now the central question has become for the investor activists: what can the board do to add value? The traditional view of corporate governance principles as a brake to enterprise was given some credence in the Hampel report (1997). That report's concern to move beyond "box ticking" and to urge board involvement in performance was welcomed by most commentators as an important advance. Exactly what were the challenges for boards to achieve this improvement in the next five years was, therefore, the primary focus of the Delphi study.

The Delphi Study: Focus

This chapter draws on the results of a study on The Future Role of the Board which was carried out by a British working party set up by the

Barcelona-based Centre for Organisation Studies.[1] Comparisons were also made with other surveys carried out in 1998 and 1999 in the UK, continental Europe and the USA. The aim of the working party was to promote a dialogue about the future of corporate governance in general and the changing role of boards of directors, in particular. In so doing, it aimed to contribute to the current agenda for business and public policy.

The specific goals of the study were to identify important trends and events, which may have an important impact on the future development of boards of directors, and to predict how and when these significant changes might occur. As befits a study which seeks to develop such visions of the future to guide practice for today's directors, a Delphi methodology (Appendix 2, page 229) was chosen to focus comments from members of the business and the academic community on the key issues.

An initial review of the literature and interviews with directors, board advisors and academics produced a preliminary list of questions. These questions were then piloted with a number of experts in the field. The subsequent feedback produced a final list of 73 questions, separated into seven categories: membership of the board; reports to shareholders; employment of directors; regulation and litigation; improving board effectiveness; key trends affecting boards; and barriers to reform.

Following this stage, a panel of 39 UK experts was selected and the final questionnaire was sent to them for the first round. It is this feedback that is reported on in later sections of this chapter. The results reported are, thus, based on the responses of respondents, whose views on the future are grounded in a highly specialised knowledge of this field.

The chief topics that were addressed in the study were:

- *Board composition.* Given the rapid changes occurring in all aspects of companies' market-places and their strategic activities, the issue of how to build stronger and more diverse boards to cope effectively with this challenge is paramount.
- *Board Effectiveness.* How to make boards more effective in carrying out their roles.
- *Converging Cultures.* Whether there were indications of convergence of corporate governance – around an international or US model – or not.

---

[1] The Centre for Organisational Studies (COS) based in Barcelona is an international network of academics and practitioners interested in organisational development.

The main findings are given in Table 1 below.

- Directors will not be required to have professional qualifications in direction as a condition of their appointment. However, written guidelines for corporate governance practice will become commonplace and boards of companies will undergo frequent systematic self-assessment. The performance of the CEO and other directors will be evaluated on a regular basis.
- Companies operating with a unitary board system will split the roles of chairman and chief executive, if they have not already done so.
- Institutional investors will be obliged to use their votes at annual general meetings.
- Companies in the UK will not see a large increase in the number of women or foreign nationals on their boards.
- UK companies will follow the US trend and pay non-executive directors partly in shares.

Table 1: Key findings from the Delphi study

Review of the Study's Findings: Board Composition

Board composition has rightly been identified as one of the major influences when shortcomings in board performance have been studied. The central issues are, of course, whether there is the right balance (or ratio) between inside and outside directors and whether the number of outsiders constitutes sufficient weight to balance the views of the CEO and the executive cadre. The Cadbury report highlighted the need for "independent" non-executive directors (NEDS), whose independence rests on not having previously been employed by the company nor having received any other fees except those involved with the role of non-executive director.

The main interest of respondents was not so much the efficacy of non-executive directors but concern over the potential *pool* of non-executives that could be accessed by a company. The respondents thought that there will be increasing pressure on existing executive directors in terms of time, prior non-executive commitments and also an increasing climate of litigation, for them to take on further non-executive directorships but considered, somewhat contrary to popular opinion, that the problem was not immediate.

A second major issue concerning board composition is whether the chairman and chief executive should occupy the same role, (CEO duality). CEO duality has been seen by a number of commentators as creating an unhealthy concentration of power and representing a conflict of interests, given that the chairman of the board has the mandate to monitor and evaluate top management. Agency theorists argue that CEO dominance can lead to opportunistic behaviour, which can reduce shareholder wealth. (15) Effective boards, on this view, should favour the balancing of CEO power, through a splitting of the top roles. In other words, there needs to be someone who stands as a higher court of appeal (16), both for the executives and non-executives. The succession process, too, is helped when the roles are split, since the chairman is responsible for CEO succession. If the roles are combined, there may be a temptation for the CEO to groom a successor in his own image or even subvert the succession process in order to further entrench himself. However, one chief executive who is also the chairman of his company stressed that splitting the roles should not be made mandatory.

However, a number of organisation theorists argue that, for the purposes of strategy formation, organisations should be led by strong CEOs, with clear lines of authority. Miller and Friesen's thesis that firms without strong and unified leadership are unsuccessful has received strong support. (17) Powerful leadership from a CEO may also send positive signals to shareholders that there is a clear sense of direction in the company, which may confer legitimacy on the firm.

In this study, respondents were clear that the split was a positive step in ensuring good governance, not only for large companies but also for small and medium-sized enterprises.

Review of the Study's Findings: Board representation

Much attention has been paid to the issue of board composition, but much less to the related issue of board representation, the extent to which women, ethnic minorities and foreign nationals are found in the boardroom. This is one of the most contentious issues in corporate governance and the presence of women and foreign nationals were two areas, which exercised our respondents to a great extent.

The issue of women in the boardroom has long been a major debate in corporate governance. Table 2, page 220, based on research undertaken by Sundridge Park (1994), shines an illuminating light on the continuing under-representation of women at board level:

Age: over 50	75
Sex: male	96
Born in the UK	90
Attended public school	43
Attended Oxbridge	20
No public sector experience	83
No international experience	74
Holding other directorships	61
Career primarily in one organisation	32

Table 2: Characteristics of UK directors (% of all directors)
Source: Sundridge Park, Corporate Research 1994

Women are under-represented not only at board level but also in senior managerial positions. As Pettigrew writes, "*it is difficult to see greater female representation without increased representation of women in the business community as a whole*". (18) At present, there is only one female CEO of a FTSE 100 company – Marjorie Scardino at Pearson – and figures overall do not look encouraging, as Table 3 below suggests.

Companies with (at least) one woman on the board		
	Average Size of Board	Total Directors
In FTSE 100: 40 companies	12	1,200
In FSE 350: 73 companies	10	3,500
% Females on the board		
	Non-Executives	Executives
FTSE 100 companies	3.1%	0.6%
FTSE 350 companies	2.0%	0.5%
National Health Service Trust Boards		
	Non-Executives	Executives
% Females	27.9%	31.5%

Table 3: Women on UK boards

Source: Martin J Conyon & Chris Mallin, Women in the boardroom: Evidence from large UK companies, Corporate Governance, July, 1997

Table 3 confirms that women who do make it to board level are more likely to do so with backgrounds in the public services or the not-for-profit sector rather than in commercial life. In mainland Europe, the picture is much the same, as Table 4, below indicates.

So far as non-executive directorships are concerned, one survey of 1,800 firms found that only 17 percent of chairmen had actively sought to appoint a woman. The usual (and derogatory) argument for such a move was, in fact that many of their customers were women, or because having a woman on the board was deemed to be socially and politically desirable. According to Burke:

> *"The nomination process is still pretty much the result of the 'old boys' network'. Many qualified women would not be visible to this small but insulated group of men. This it is unlikely that the small percentage of current board members that are women will change appreciably in the short-run."* (19)

Country	Type of Board	% of Women Board Members
UK	Unitary	5%
Germany	Management	1%
	Supervisory	5%
Northern Europe	Management	6%
	Supervisory	5%
France & Belgium	Unitary/Management	5%
	Supervisory	9%

Table 4: Women on European boards

Source: Korn Ferry International, European Boards of Directors Study, London, 1996 (p.14) Survey of Europe's 5,000 largest companies

The results of this survey confirmed that women continue to be under-represented and revealed that respondents were pessimistic about the prospects for improvements in this area in the next five years.

With increasing globalisation, and a growing interconnection of markets and corporations, boards need to have experience of international markets and individual country cultures and contexts. Very little attention has been paid to the role of the board of directors in managing across borders. The major route to increasing the international awareness of boards is to appoint foreign nationals, usually as non-executive directors. A foreign director can bring wide experience of local country conditions and a broad awareness of international issues in general. The Korn Ferry 1996 survey of Europe's largest 5,000 companies showed that 38 percent of UK boards do have a foreign national director, a figure largely consistent with the rest of Europe.

The results from this survey, however, suggest that despite increasing concerns about globalisation, this figure is unlikely to increase.

Review of the Study's Findings: Board Performance

We noted at the outset that the large majority of texts on boards of directors concentrate on the notion of accountability, leaving the performance-enhancing capability of boards relatively uncovered. This study sought to gather opinions on how best boards might increase their own effectiveness and, by implication, the effectiveness of the organisation as a whole. The following issues loomed largest: board self-assessment, director training and increasing the use of electronic information in the boardroom.

- *Self-assessment*

A number of prescriptive texts have highlighted the issue of the board's evaluation of its own performance as a major omission in board scrutiny, arguing that without critical self-analysis, problems can occur in the dynamics and performance of the board. Harvey-Jones (20), for example, urges that:

> *"... the board ought to spend more time, reasonably regularly, discussing among themselves how the board is actually working, in what ways the process can be improved, what the role of the board actually is, and how it can be more effective, but this occurs far too seldom... unless a board continuously criticises the way it is working, is clear as to what it is seeking to achieve, and its members are able to learn from each other, it is extraordinarily difficult for it to improve its performance."*

Companies which do undergo such a process usually admit that they do not employ any "hard" metrics by which to gauge the effectiveness of the board and its processes, but had instead have a number of *informal* checks to measure the health of the board. For example, at one leading UK company, there is annual review of board processes and practices, which is conducted by a leading non-executive, who interviews all board members individually and relatively informally to ask whether there is any area which can be improved. At another, a chairman's advisory committee examines the performance of the board and its committees overall. The clarification of accountabilities and the assessment of directors' contributions enhance the board's evaluation and control role and also allow board norms to be uncovered and examined. It also provides a further opportunity to analyse the skill mix and the size of the board and determine whether any new directors need be selected (or whether any incumbents should be retired). For both individual directors, and the board as a whole, this mechanism was thought to be very important.

- *Training*

The issue of board self-assessment is linked to the issue of director training. A number of studies have documented the low level of take up of director courses in the UK. (21) The reasons given for this state of affairs range from the unattractiveness of the content (or at the least, the framing of the course), the unwillingness of directors to admit to needing training to lack of time for training. Nevertheless, it is surprising, given the recent managerial emphasis on continuous transformation and the learning organisation, that many directors consider themselves exempt from this process. According to a survey by Broadbent, the main training and development opportunities continue to be business school courses, but greater emphasis is now being placed on individual coaching and mentoring of directors as a more effective way of increasing capability. The notion of introducing a formal qualification for directors as a condition for appointment was not well received by respondents in this study.

- *Information*

Another issue was information. Respondents predicted that the increasing use of information technology in the boardroom might help to reduce the information disadvantage suffered by non-executives and speed the flow of knowledge to the whole of the board. The use of IT would also help to improve communications between the board and the shareholders/stakeholders, particularly small shareholders, who could access information about the company relatively cheaply. Greater use of video-conferencing to link up to overseas operations was also considered an important way forward.

Other issues which emerged were for directors to have access to independent advice about research into new technologies and new markets from management consultants, advisory boards of scientists and technologists and international specialists. This requirement to keep abreast of the latest moves in a rapidly changing environment also produced a suggestion from the experts, for boards of large companies to form separate strategy committees, to help weigh strategic proposals.

Review of the Study's Findings: Converging Cultures

One area which has been the subject of keen debate in the literature and which held the attention of respondents, was the notion of the possibility of international convergence. Traditionally, two models of governance have been identified as dominant forms:

- *the US/UK model* which emphasises high liquidity in capital markets and a market for corporate control by take-over bids;
- *the continental model.* This features prominently in Germany and Japan and is characterised by less liquid financial markets and a concentration of shareholder power in banks, families and governments. (22)

These models have been viewed as almost antithetical, but such a view is now under pressure. With increasing globalisation, the development of world-wide capital markets and rapid information flows, there now seems to be the prospect of increasing convergence of corporate governance systems. As Kay states: *"today we see different national models of corporate governance, but firms in a single region operate, in the main, in similar ways. Tomorrow we can expect fewer national differences but more variety in the matching of organisational structure to the requirements of different markets and industries."* (23)

The idea of convergence is being driven by a number of forces. One is the fact that many continental European countries have under-funded pension schemes. Fewer than one in four working people in the European Union is currently covered by a funded pension scheme and as Price Waterhouse argue: "the need to shift the burden of pension liabilities away from the state into the private sector is urgent". (24) In future we could see a greater percentage of funds going into equities, with the result that shareholder value is likely to become a major consideration for European companies. Investors can now operate on a worldwide basis. Their decisions on investments will be affected both by the degree of openness offered by companies and the yield they can expect.

Such concerns would work against companies in Japan and Germany, where the shareholder's voice is, at present, muted and financial disclosure has a mixed track record. At the same time, the short-termism which dogs UK and US systems of governance may be altered by the formation of long-term relationships between investors and companies in the style of Japanese/German governance. Their concern for employees will also be seen to be increasingly significant. Cross-border linkages between US and German companies, such as those between Daimler-Benz and Chrysler and between Deutsche Bank and Bankers Trust, could be important change drivers in this area.

In terms of potential convergence, therefore, the UK is well placed as a result of its relatively high degree of transparency and delivery of shareholder value. There seems little value in trying to impose overarching governance frameworks on different national and cultural structures. Institutional investors, in particular, will have to expand their knowledge of different cultures and systems of governance, and ensure that they continue to secure a dialogue with the key decision-makers within organisations. At a macro-level, governments should be wary of introducing too many governance prescriptions, though this may increase the confidence in the market; too much focus on compliance may make other markets more attractive for listing purposes.

The UK survey respondents were cautious on this issue. The implementation of the EU Fifth Directive encouraging a two-tier structure for boards in the UK was dismissed by the experts, as was the idea of companies gaining a European registration by the European Union to simplify legal and fiscal complexities involved in running international business.

A number of respondents thought, however, that increasing internationalisation, through alliances and partnerships, using joint boards and frequent meetings, would *ipso facto* create a natural, informal move towards greater convergence. This might certainly affect the structure of boards (unitary or two-tier) but it would have greater impact on processes and systems of regulation and reporting standards. Many respondents also expected that companies would report on employee attitudes and employee satisfaction in their annual reports.

Conclusion

The findings of this analysis indicate that though much recent policy work – such as Cadbury and Hampel – in corporate governance has made for better conditions in boardrooms, there is still room for improvement. Much work in this vein has been concerned with prescriptions on improving accountability. In this chapter, we have focused on the relatively neglected area of how boards can add value, casting an eye forward to the future to see what experts believe are the key factors for improving board performance. Two areas stood out – board diversity and increasing board effectiveness – as issues, which particularly exercised our respondents. Other areas, which surfaced, were also revealing. These included the nature of electronic communications for the board, improvements in corporate reporting, and a convergence of international trends.

Boards moving into the 21st century face strong challenges from an increasingly competitive and more global environment. This chapter has gone some way to showing what may change and what may not change in the future.

Appendix 1: Official Reports And Commentaries

American Law Institute. *Principles of corporate governance: Analysis and recommendations*. Philadelphia, PA: The Institute, 1992

Cadbury, Sir Adrian. *The financial aspects of corporate governance. Committee on the Financial Aspects of Corporate Governance*. London: Gee & Co., 1992

Cadbury, Sir Adrian. *Board focus: The governance debate*. Zurich: Egon Zehnder International, 1997

Cadbury, Sir Adrian. Highlights of the proposals of the committee on financial aspects of corporate governance *in* Prentice, D.D. & Holland, P.R.J. (Eds.) *Contemporary issues in corporate governance*. Oxford: Clarendon Press, 1993, pp.45-55

Greenbury, R. *Directors' remuneration: Report of a study group chaired by Sir Richard Greenbury*. London: Gee & Co., 1995

Hampel, Ronnie. *Committee on Corporate Governance Final Report*. London: Gee & Co., 1998

Institutional Shareholders Committee (ISC). *The roles and duties of directors - A statement of best practice*. London: ISC, 1991

Korn/Ferry International. *Board of directors, Annual Studies*. Los Angeles: Korn/Ferry International, 1998

Vienot Report CNPF/AFEP. Paris: Editions Techniques Professionelles, 1995

Whittington, G. Corporate governance and the regulation of financial reporting. *Accounting and Business Research*, 1993, 23, pp.311-320

Appendix 2: A Note On Delphi Studies

A Delphi survey is essentially a poll of expert opinion carried out by direct mail or by computer. The technique was invented by the Rand Corporation and used by the US Department of Defense in the 1960s in an attempt to set priorities for investment in research. It was later used by the Japanese, German and other governments to set priorities for peace-time research. The Delphi method also formed the basis of the UK Technology Foresight Programme which was started in 1994 and has involved 7,000 experts from government, industry and academia assembled in 15 sector networks.

The Delphi survey is one of a battery of techniques which companies and governments use in uncertain situations to explore possible future developments. The researchers assume that there are many possible futures depending on the actions taken today. The Delphi technique has a number of advantages:

1. *Communication*: It can help to create a network of people with a common interest.
2. *Concentration*: It encourages people to think about the longer term, to anticipate problems and opportunities.
3. *Consensus*: There is always the possibility that a clearer picture of one or more futures may emerge.
4. *Commitment*: If the process is extended there is a chance that people will decide to work together to "create a future" which they want to happen.
5. *Co-ordination*: Also, people with very different backgrounds may form partnerships to address particular issues or to launch new policies and programmes.

The technique is particularly helpful where there is insufficient data for trend analysis and where the future is uncertain. The idea is to gather the opinions of a number of experts and to avoid the personality conflicts which can arise in a face-to-face meeting where a few articulate individuals can dominate the discussion.

In essence a Delphi survey is in four phases:

1. *Planning*: Consultation with a small group of specialists
   - to list the topics which need to be covered;

- to design and pilot test the questionnaire; and
- to identify a balanced group of experienced and knowledgeable "experts".

2. *Survey and Analysis*: Distribute the questionnaire and analyse the results by computer.
3. *Feedback Meeting*: Communicate the results to the experts to clarify the reasons for any disagreements and make any necessary amendments to the questionnaire.
4. *Second Survey*: Conduct a second survey to enable members of the group to take account of new ideas and to have second thoughts. The second survey usually produces greater consensus and a clearer picture of alternative futures. The results of this survey usually appear in the published report.

The Delphi questionnaire asks the panel of experts to estimate when, if ever, a particular event might occur, eg, the introduction of a new technology. The output is usually presented in the form of a series of horizontal bars each with a peak. The length of the bar represents the period of time when the event might occur, and the peak shows the median date. It has been found that where the average date of an event is around five years or less the range of estimates is sufficiently bunched to be helpful, after excluding the highest and lowest estimates. For time periods further ahead estimates can diverge widely.

References

(1) Hitt, M.A., Costa, J.E. & Nixon, R.D. The new frontier *in* Hitt, M.A., Costa, J.E. & Nixon, R.D. (eds) *Managing strategically in an interconnected world*, London: Wiley, 1998

(2) Tricker, R.I. Corporate governance: A ripple on the cultural reflection *in* Clegg, S.R., Redding, S.G. & Cartner, M. (eds) *Capitalism in contrasting cultures*. New York: Walter de Gruyter, 1990

(3) Watching the boss: A survey of corporate governance. *The Economist,* 1994 January 29th.

(4) Zahra, S.A. & Pearce, J.A. Boards of directors and corporate financial performance: a review and integrative model. *Journal of Management*, 1989, 15, pp.291-334

See also Goodstein, J., Gautam, K., & Boeker, W. The effects of board size and diversity on strategic change. *Strategic Management Journal*, 1994, 15, pp.241-250

See also Johnson, J.L., Daily, C.M., & Ellstrand, A.E. Boards of directors: a review and research agenda. *Journal of Management,* 1996, 22, pp.409-438

(5) As (3)

(6) Kay, J. Corporate strategy and corporate accountability *in* Dimsdale, N.H. & Prevezer, M. (eds) *Capital Markets and Corporate Governance.* Oxford: Clarendon Press, 1994, pp.50-64

See also Marsh, P. R. *Short-termism on trial.* London: Institutional Fund Managers Association, 1990

See also Paul, A. Corporate governance in the context of takeovers of UK public companies *in* Prentice, D.D. & Holland, P.R.J. (Eds.) *Contemporary Issues in Corporate Governance*. Oxford: Clarendon Press, 1993, pp.135-150

(7) Berle, A. & Means, G.C. *The modern corporation and private property*. New York: Macmillan, 1932

(8) Roe, M.J. *Strong managers, weak owners: The political roots of American corporate finance*. Princeton, NJ: Princeton University Press, 1996

(9) Vance, S.C. *Corporate leadership: boards, directors and strategy*. New York: McGraw-Hill, 1983

See also Kosnik, R. Greenmail: A study of board performance in corporate governance. *Administrative Science Quarterly*, 1987, 32, pp.163-185

See also Mace, M.L. *Directors: Myth and reality*. Boston, MA: Harvard University Graduate School of Business Administration, 1971

(10) Pfeffer, J. Size and composition of corporate boards of directors: the organisation and its environment. *Administrative Science Quarterly*, 1972, 17, pp.218-29

(11) As (9) Mace

(12) Herman, E. *Corporate control, corporate power.* New York: Cambridge University Press, 1981

See also Isaksson, M. & Skog, R. (eds) *Aspects of corporate governance.* Juristforlaget, Stockholm: Corporate Governance Forum, 1994

See also Wymeersch, E. Elements of comparative corporate governance in Western Europe, *in* Isaksson, M. & Skog, R. (eds) *Aspects of corporate governance.* Juristforlaget, Stockholm: Corporate Governance Forum, 1994

(13) Cadbury, Sir Adrian. *Board Focus: the governance debate.* Zurich: Egon Zehnder International, 1997

(14) Conyon, M.J., Gregg, P., & Machin, S. Taking care of business: executive compensation in the United Kingdom. *Economic Journal*, 1995, 105, pp.704-714

See also Conyon, M.J. Institutional arrangements for setting directors' compensation in UK companies *in* Keasey, K., Thompson S. & Wright, M. (eds) *Corporate Governance: Economic, Management and Financial Issues.* Oxford: Oxford University Press, 1997, pp.103-121

(15) Jensen, M. & Meckling, W. Theory of the firm: managerial behaviour, agency costs and ownership structure. *Journal of Financial Economics*, 1976, 3, pp.305-360

(16) Demb, A. & Neubauer, F.F. The corporate board. New York: Oxford University Press, 1992

(17) Finkelstein, S. & D'Aveni, R.A. CEO duality as a double edged sword: how boards balance entrenchment avoidance and unity of command. *Academy of Management Journal*, 1994, 37, pp.1079-1108

See also Miller, D. & Friesen, P.H. *Organisations: a quantum view.* New York: Prentice-Hall, 1984

(18) Pettigrew, M.A. *Boards of directors: a review of recent research.* Working Paper, Centre for Corporate Strategy and Change, University of Warwick, 1992

See also Pettigrew, A.M. On studying managerial élites. *Strategic Management Journal*, 1992, 13, pp.163-182

(19) Bruce, A. & Buck, T. Executive reward and corporate governance *in* Keasey, K., Thompson, S. & Wright, M. (eds) *Corporate Governance: economic, management and financial Issues* Oxford: Oxford University Press, 1997, pp.80-102

(20) Harvey-Jones, Sir John, *Making it happen: reflections on leadership.* London: Collins, 1988

(21) Garratt, B. *The fish rots from the head.* London: Harper Collins, 1996

(22) Price Waterhouse. *Converging Cultures: trends in European corporate governance.* Price Waterhouse, 1997

(23) Kay J. *Foundations of Corporate Success.* Oxford: Oxford University Press, 1993

See also Kay, J. & Silberston, A. Corporate governance. *National Institute Economic Review*, 1995, 84, pp.84-97

(24) As (22)

INDEX

D

K

L

M

N